GUIDE

ORD

Discovery CHANNEL

ABOUT THIS BOOK

Editorial

Editor
Sarah Hudson
Managing Editor
Tony Halliday
Editorial Director
Brian Bell

Distribution

UK & Ireland
GeoCenter International Ltd
The Viables Centre, Harrow Way
Basingstoke, Hants RG22 4BJ
Fax: (44) 1256-817988

United States
Langenscheidt Publishers, Inc.
46–35 54th Road, Maspeth, NY 11378
Fax: (718) 784-0640

Canada
Prologue Inc.
1650 Lionel Bertrand Blvd., Boisbriand
Québec, Canada J7H 1N7
Tel: (450) 434-0306. Fax: (450) 434-2627

Worldwide
Apa Publications GmbH & Co.
Verlag KG (Singapore branch)
38 Joo Koon Road, Singapore 628990
Tel: (65) 865-1600. Fax: (65) 861-6438

Printing

Insight Print Services (Pte) Ltd
38 Joo Koon Road, Singapore 628990
Tel: (65) 865-1600. Fax: (65) 861-6438

©2000 Apa Publications GmbH & Co.
Verlag KG (Singapore branch)
All Rights Reserved
First Edition 1990
Second Edition 2000

CONTACTING THE EDITORS
Although every effort is made to
provide accurate information, we
live in a fast-changing world and
would appreciate it if readers
would call our attention to any
errors or outdated information
that may occur by writing to:
Insight Guides, P.O. Box 7910,
London SE1 1WE, England.
Fax: (44 20) 7403-0290.
e-mail:
insight@apaguide.demon.co.uk

This guidebook combines the interests and enthusiasms of two of
the world's best-known information
providers: Insight Guides, whose
titles have set the standard for visual
travel guides since 1970, and
Discovery Channel, the world's premier source of non-fiction television
programming.

Insight Guide editors provide practical advice and general understanding about a destination's
history, culture, institutions
and people. The Discovery
Channel and its website,
www.discovery.com, help
millions of viewers to
explore their world from
the comfort of their
own home and also
encourage them to ex-
plore it first hand.

This completely updated edition
of *Insight: Oxford* is carefully struc-
tured to convey an understanding of
Oxford and its culture as well as to
guide readers through its sights:

◆ The **History** and **Features** sec-
tions, indicated by a yellow bar,
cover the history and culture of the
city through informative essays.

◆ The main **Places** section, indicated by a blue bar, is a complete guide to all the sights
and areas worth visiting. Principal places of interest are
cross-referenced by num-
ber to the colour maps.

◆ The **Travel Tips** listings section provides
easy-to-use information
on how to get around,
hotels, shops, restau-
rants and much more.

The contributors

This edition of *Insight: Oxford* was edited by **Sarah Hudson**, a freelance editor living in Abingdon, and builds on the earlier editions, edited by Tony Halliday and Brian Bell.

Jim Ferguson, a freelance writer, Oxford resident and Oxford graduate, has fully updated and revised the text to convey the changes in this cosmopolitan city. He also wrote the features on "Pub culture" and "Festivals and Events".

Mark Davies, who lives on a canalboat and is the author of a book, *Our Canal in Oxford*, wrote the feature "Canal Life".

Tony and **Renée Halliday**, Oxford residents, provided much additional material, in particular on Oxford's Outskirts and Travel Tips.

This edition has retained much of the work of the original contributors, including **Christopher Catling**, who wrote the Places section and whose knowledge of Oxford is long-standing – he used to be taken there for birthday treats. Despite being a graduate of Cambridge University, he still confesses to liking Oxford more as a place to live.

The history chapters were written by **Roland Collins**, a researcher in social history; **Helen Turner**, a former features editor on the *Oxford Times* and an Oxford graduate; and **Ray Hutton**, motoring correspondent of London's *Sunday Times*, who covered the history of Oxford as a top car-manufacturing centre.

Several of the one-page boxes were written by **Yvonne Newman**, a Headington resident who is a freelance writer and lecturer.

Simon Veksner, an Oxford graduate, wrote about "Academic Life" and compiled the Who's Who of Colleges, while **Elisabeth Dunn**, a freelance journalist, covered the perennial discussion of the equality of women at the University. **David Leake**, a gardener at Corpus Christi College, wrote about Oxford's "elusive gardens". The chapter on Warwick in the excursions section was written by **Michael Ivory**.

The wonderfully evocative photography includes the work of **Chris Andrews, Chris Donaghue, Jon Davison, Norman McBeath, Lyle Lawson, Alain de Garsmeur, Glyn Genin, Tony Halliday** and **Mark Davies**. Special thanks for assistance go to **Dr Malcolm Graham**, local history librarian at the Central Library, and to the library staff of **Oxford & County Newspapers**.

The book was proofread by **Sue Platt** and indexed by **Isobel McLean**.

Map Legend

----	County/Unitary Authority Boundary
–•–	National Park/Reserve
✈ ✈	Airport: International/Regional
🚌	Bus Station
■	Parking
●	Tourist Information
✉	Post Office
✝ ✝ ✝	Church/Ruins
✝	Monastery
☾	Mosque
✡	Synagogue
🏰	Castle/Ruins
∴	Archaeological Site
∩	Cave
𝟏	Statue/Monument
★	Place of Interest

The main places of interest in the Places section are coordinated by number with a full-colour map (e.g. ❶), and a symbol at the top of every right-hand page tells you where to find the map.

INSIGHT GUIDE OXFORD

CONTENTS

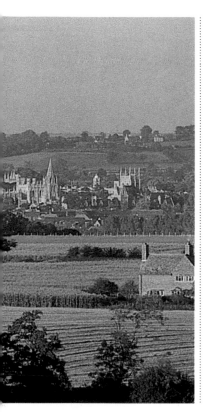

The famous
dreaming
spires

DREAMS AND DISILLUSION

There's always been a tension between Town and Gown.

One is known for a car plant, the other for colleges

It is small wonder that Oxford is one of the world's most anthologised cities. Many famous writers, having attended its university, have tried to recapture on paper an experience that profoundly affected their lives. Often their feelings recall the relationship between child and parent: a complex cocktail of love and resentment, admiration and disdain.

Matthew Arnold, whose poetry immortalised Oxford as "that sweet City with her dreaming spires", captured this ambivalence in a letter to his mother in 1861: "I always like this place, and the intellectual life here is certainly much more intense than it used to be; but this has its disadvantages too, in the envies, hatreds, and jealousies that come with the activity of mind of most men."

In *Wealth of Nations* (1776), Adam Smith was less equivocal, dismissing Oxford as "a sanctuary in which exploded systems and obsolete prejudices find shelter and protection after they have been hunted out of every corner of the world". A century later, George Bernard Shaw was just as beastly: "It is characteristic of the authorities that they should consider a month too little for the preparation of a boatrace, and grudge three weeks to the rehearsals of one of Shakespeare's plays."

Those writers, of course, are equating Oxford with the university, and it is certainly the aura of learning that draws most visitors to the city. But there are many other sides to Oxford: it is a thriving market town, for example, as well as a pioneer of the latest bio-tech research. John Betjeman, an influential architectural critic as well as a poet, once lamented that the car factories "could have been a model for the rest of England, so that visitors to the university, instead of trying to pretend no industrialism was near and bathing themselves in a false twilight of grey Gothic things, would have naturally hurried to see the living beauty of industrial Oxford after the dead glory of university architecture." The failure of such hopes led another poet, W. H. Auden, to moan: "Oxford city is sheer hell. Compared with New York, it's five times as crowded and the noise of the traffic is six times louder."

Yet even the complainers keep coming back, forgiving the city its foibles as they would forgive a venerable but wayward parent. Its allure is elusive, but its myths are powerful, offering to visitors what the writer Peter Ackroyd called "a clutter of broken images" that demand to be seen again and again. ❑

PRECEDING PAGES: academics starting young; the interior of the Sheldonian Theatre; gargoyle on the Church of St Mary the Virgin; a tired bicycle.
LEFT: a meeting of minds.

Decisive Dates

1500BC onwards Bronze Age cattle herders and farmers build large, round grave mounds on Port Meadow. During the Iron Age the landscape is dotted with small, mixed farms.

3rd century AD The Romans establish important potteries in the area.

400 Migrants from Germany and Saxon mercenaries in the Roman army forcibly settle local farms; their descendants live there as peaceable tenant farmers.

635 St Birinius, the Bishop of Dorchester, sets out to convert the worshippers of the Saxon gods Thor and Wodan. The Thames emerges as an important frontier between two Anglo-Saxon kingdoms, Wessex and Mercia.

730 According to legend, Oxford's first abbey is founded by St Frideswide on the site of present-day Christ Church. This may have been the core of the original town.

912 The first written reference to Oxford in the *Anglo-Saxon Chronicle* during the reign of King Edward the Elder, son of King Alfred, who fortifies the town to guard the river crossing into Wessex and protect the surrounding countryside against the Danes.

1071 Robert d'Oilly, Oxford's Norman governor, erects a castle to the west of town.

12th century Oxford attracts scholarly clerics from far and wide. Monasteries bring prosperity and stability. The Thames provides power for the mills, and economy is based on cloth and leather as well as the trades spawned by the emerging university.

1122 St Frideswide's Priory refounded by the Augustinians on the same site.

1129 Osney Abbey built on an island in the west. It becomes one of the largest and most important Augustinian monasteries in England.

c1130 Henry I builds his Palace of Beaumont just outside the north gate, setting the seal on the town's rising importance.

1167 English scholars at the University of Paris are forced to leave and come to Oxford.

1199 King John grants the town his royal charter, and local government, based on the guilds, is free to develop independently.

1200 By this time an association of scholars has been established in the city.

13th century Friars form the various major orders teaching in Oxford. Their students live and work in academic halls dotted around the city. The first colleges are founded by powerful bishops; they are noted for their exclusivity and wealth and cater only for graduates.

1226–40 The city wall is extended and rebuilt.

1349 The Black Death kills one in three people.

1355 St Scholastica's Day. A pub brawl turns into a massacre of dozens of scholars. This event has dire consequences for the future of the town.

1361 John Wycliffe, Master of Balliol, speaks out against corruption within the church. His teachings resonate throughout Europe.

1379 New College is founded as the first college to accept undergraduates. From now on the balance of learning in the town gradually shifts from the academic halls to the colleges.

1400 Oxford is one of the largest towns in England with a population of some 6,000. There are 1,500 students.

1426 Work begins on the Divinity School.

1478 First book (the Bible) printed in Oxford.

1488 Duke Humphrey's Library opened.

1490s Erasmus and Thomas Moore in Oxford, developing Humanist ideas.

1525 Cardinal Wolsey founds Cardinal College (later to be known as Christ Church) on the site of St Frideswide's Monastery.

1536 The university is brought to the brink of destruction by the Dissolution of the Monasteries, but

Henry VIII saves the colleges by adopting them to train the state's most loyal supporters.

1542 Creation of the Diocese of Oxford, with its cathedral at Christ Church.

1555–6 The Protestant Martyrs Latimer and Ridley are burned at the stake in the city ditch (later Broad Street) on 16 October. Six months later, Thomas Cranmer suffers the same fate.

1558–1603 Reign of Elizabeth I. The city is transformed as a new civic pride emerges with increased trade and prosperity. The university expands greatly.

17th century Prosperity is fuelled by the famous glovers and cutlers of Oxford. University buildings begin to dominate the central area.

1602 Duke Humphrey's Library reopened to the public as the Bodleian Library.

1613 Work begins on the Old Schools Quadrangle extension to the Bodleian Library.

1621 The Physic Garden, which was later developed to become the Botanic Garden, is established on the site of the old Jewish cemetery opposite Magdalen Tower.

1642–5 Civil War. Oxford is the royal capital and headquarters of the King's army.

1646 Oxford besieged by General Fairfax and his Parliamentary army. Charles I escapes in disguise and the city surrenders.

1650s A group of mathematicians and scientists, including Christopher Wren and Robert Boyle, meet regularly in Wadham College, before moving to London in 1658 to found the Royal Society.

1664–8 The Sheldonian Theatre, designed by Christopher Wren, is built.

1670s onwards Glove and cutlery industries in decline. The university provides new additions to the already famous Oxford skyline; many existing colleges are radically altered or rebuilt.

1679 Building of the (old) Ashmolean Museum on Broad Street, now the Museum of the History of Science.

1715 Hawksmoor's Clarendon Building completed for the Oxford University Press.

1748 The Radcliffe Camera built according to a design by James Gibbs.

1771 Paving Commission established. Much of old Oxford is destroyed to allow traffic easier access to the city centre.

1790 The Oxford Canal arrives from Coventry bringing cheap coal from the Midlands.

1830 The Oxford University Press moves to its present site on Walton Street. The suburb of Jericho is built to house the Press workers.

1833 John Keble preaches his famous sermon on national apostasy, leading to the foundation of the Oxford Movement.

1844 A branch railway line connects with Didcot.

1853 University Commission is established to reform the university.

1860 The University Museum opens.

1879 The first two women's colleges, Lady Margaret Hall and Somerville, open.

1913 William Morris establishes his car plant at Cowley. In the 1930s, as Lord Nuffield, he becomes the university's most celebrated benefactor in the fields of medicine and science.

1956 A "green belt" is created around Oxford, putting an end to the haphazard development that surrounded the city.

1960s Plans for a link road across Christ Church Meadow are abolished.

1996 Syrian-born businessman Wafic Said offers the university £20 million for the establishment of the Oxford Business School.

1999 Cornmarket Street is completely pedestrianised as part of a controversial new road scheme for the city centre. ❑

PRECEDING PAGES: the eternal search for sponsors.
LEFT: Wadham College, as seen by the noted artist Rudolph Ackermann.
RIGHT: new horsepower in the Morris works.

BEGINNINGS

*The site was first settled in Saxon times, and was named Oxford after
its "oxen ford", probably today's Folly Bridge*

Oxford was a late starter. Shunned by Stone-Age tribes and avoided by the Romans, it had to wait on the Saxons, who always lived and moved by water, to launch it in importance as one of England's great defensive and cultural centres. If that is a simplistic view of local history, then the evidence to the contrary is thin on the ground – and, indeed, in the museums. A few axe-heads, some bronze tools and perhaps the burial mounds of farmers and cattle herders in Port Meadow by the river and in the University Parks are all that remain to span thousands of years.

It is not difficult to see why the site of Oxford was unattractive to settlers. It was low-lying and traversed by the deep streams of the Thames and Cherwell. The Icknield Way, high road to the west, kept well away south to the hills.

The Romans, who hated clay soil for their roads and never settled at fords, bypassed the site to the east and north, building their villas away from the rivers. West of Oxford, they established a pottery industry that became one of five principal centres of Roman Britain, one kiln at Cowley anticipating a different artefact in more recent times: the motor car.

There may be an earlier Oxford down there, under the modern city, buried by the rubble of 1,000 years of rebuilding. Ironically, demolition and excavation for yet another massive re-development in the centre may just provide the missing links the archaeologists are looking for that will give Oxford history an earlier start. The rest is myth or guesswork.

Memphric and miracles

In the Middle Ages assorted worthies were credited with founding Oxford – a legendary King Memphric in 1000 BC, Brutus bringing Greek scholars after the fall of Troy, and, more credibly, Alfred the Great. University College went so far as to forge some deeds to prove its

LEFT: one of the many 10th-century illustrated manuscripts kept in the Bodleian Library.
RIGHT: King Alfred, posthumous victim of forgery.

foundation by King Alfred, and relinquished its claim only in Queen Victoria's time, with red faces all round. Even the origins of the name "Oxford" have been open to interpretation, but its most likely derivation is the obvious one. Why there was a need for oxen to cross the river, however, is another question. That stone-

lined and embanked river crossing may have been where the first settlement grew up. Was it at St Aldate's, the causeway to the river? Recent excavations point to its construction by Offa, King of Mercia from 757 to 796.

Those dates are narrowly beaten for the founder's stakes by the persistent legend of St Frideswide. Daughter of a Mercian king, the virginal Frideswide seems to have resisted the unwelcome attentions of a princely suitor by blinding him with the aid of a well-aimed thunderbolt. Relenting, she restored his sight with water from her own private holy well by the river. At Binsey, to the west of the fringes of Oxford, that well still exists in the churchyard, and is credited by a notice posted on the church door with being "the very beginning of anything at Oxford".

Frideswide, vowed to celibacy, went on to found a priory on a site near the present cathedral. The time: the early 8th century. The place: a gravel spit near where the Thames and Cherwell rivers meet. Nothing except an obituary is recorded of the 400 years of the priory's existence. It was burned down during a massacre of the Danes in 1002.

In the cathedral that replaced the priory, between the choir and the north aisle, is the shrine of St Frideswide. Stand near it and you

are at Oxford's heart and Oxford's beginning. From the fragmented canopy of stone, faces peer through sculptured leaves of ivy and sycamore, oak and vine, a medieval mason's interpretation of the virgin princess's escape from her tormenter to the safety of the forest.

Fact or fiction, St Frideswide is remembered every year on 19 October in a service at the cathedral attended by both Town and University. The body of the saint is no longer there; it disappeared during the upheavals of the Reformation in the 16th century.

Alfred and the Danes

If King Alfred did not found the university, he at least played a prominent part in the development of Oxford as a strategic frontier town in his defences against attacks by the Danes. The natural barriers of the Thames and Cherwell, an established nucleus in the settlement at the gate of the priory, a central position in the kingdom, and access to the important West Saxon port of Southampton combined to make it an obvious choice, and one which was to be of tremendous importance to the growth of civilisation in England.

Alfred's experience in reusing Roman defences at Winchester probably persuaded his son Edward, who succeeded him in 901, to lay out his streets in a similar pattern within rectangular walls, a pattern reflected in today's streets. Certainly, by 912, when Oxford is mentioned in the *Anglo-Saxon Chronicle*, the town was already head of a district. London and Oxford, then known as "Ludenburg and Oxnaford", were held by Edward the Elder, "and all the land pertaining thereto".

Carfax was central to the small, compact town, its walls supported by bank and ditch on the western, northern and eastern sides, with the Trill stream a natural barrier to the south. At first gravel ramparts supported timber walls, but these were later rebuilt in stone. Roads had a surface of pebbles or cobbles and drained into a channel down the middle.

Oxford has come up in the world since those days, however, and the Saxon roads are in places buried more than 12 ft (4 metres) below the modern pavement.

The town, now the sixth largest in England, developed as a sort of Saxon conference centre, but the lives and habits of its ordinary townsfolk can be deduced only from unearthed pots,

ST FRIDESWIDE

The legend of the virgin St Frideswide is shrouded in mystery. One version tells how her father, King Didan, constructed a church for her, where she set up a nunnery. But when Didan died the kingdom passed to Algar, King of Leicester, "a most villainous man and hateful to God".

Unmoved by her vows of chastity, Algar insisted she become his wife. The servants he sent to seize her were struck blind, but she cured them and fled to Binsey wood. As Algar arrived in Oxford, he too was struck blind by divine intervention. He remained blind, while Frideswide performed healing miracles from a hut in Binsey wood before returning to Oxford, where she died in 727.

rubbish holes and cesspits. There seems to have been division of bigger properties to form smaller "hall" houses with first-floor, all-purpose rooms over ground-floor stores, and the width of the main streets, wider even than now, indicates their use as markets for the produce of agriculture and husbandry.

There was an uneasy integration with the Danes, brought to a bloody conclusion in 1002 by the king's order to massacre all those living in Oxford. Seven years later the Danish army sacked the town as

SAXON REMAINS

One building survives from Saxon times: the tower of St Michael's Church, Cornmarket Street, which served the garrison as a look-out against marauding Danes.

include the castle and the eastern suburb near the River Cherwell.

It is also likely that d'Oilly built Grandpont, the first stone bridge (where Folly Bridge now stands), and the stone causeway to it that crossed the marsh for a considerable distance. Within the castle walls d'Oilly erected a chapel to St George, one of the first-known dedications to the patron saint of England, and in the founding of the Secular Canons of St George we can anticipate the beginnings of the university itself.

a reprisal, which may account for the derelict condition of much of the town and its suburbs outside the walls.

The Norman Conquest in 1066 ushered in an even bigger physical change. Robert d'Oilly, the governor, set about the upgrading of the defensive works by building a castle which destroyed an entire western suburb and involved the diversion of the road to the west. Keep and mound were raised and a moat fed from the Thames. Walls were extended to

LEFT: the Battle of Hastings, which played a major part in deciding England's fate.
ABOVE: an 11th-century haymaker.

English power politics were played out here in the castle. When Henry I died in 1135 the throne was disputed between his daughter, Empress Matilda of Germany, and Stephen Blois. In the fighting that followed, Matilda was besieged in the castle for three winter months. Then, taking advantage of the ice-covered river, she escaped. No one saw her go: she was cunningly camouflaged by a white sheet.

Oxford was becoming attractive to royals in spite of St Frideswide's curse on royalty after her misfortune. At Henry I's great palace of Beaumont, just beyond where the Ashmolean is now, Richard the Lion-Heart and probably King John were born. Henry had also built a palace – or, more likely, a hunting lodge – at Woodstock, 8 miles (13 km) from Oxford in the forest of Wychwood.

Following its 11th-century decline, the fortunes of the town were rescued by the growth of the trade in wool and cloth. This brought the formation of trade guilds, of which the weavers and corvesers (shoemakers) were the earliest, and provided the embryo of civic rule. The right to produce, sell and buy goods was strictly controlled. No one could set up a loom within 15 miles (24 km) of Oxford or sell leather without the guild's consent. The weekly market was held under a similarly strict protectionism.

Tom", the abbey's bell, to speak from its own tower at Christ Church. There followed the foundation of Godstow nunnery in 1133, and the Duke of Cornwall's Rewley Abbey near Osney, where the Cistercian monks played an important part within the university.

The scholars arrive

The university was the product of spontaneous combustion, the pursuit of knowledge fusing with the convenience of physical and spiritual community that Oxford provided. From the early 12th century, English scholars, all of them clerks in holy orders, customarily went to the

Prosperity was reflected in the establishment of a number of religious houses. St Frideswide's Priory was re-founded in 1122 on the site of the Saxon church, and was joined seven years later by Osney, which seems to have been established on superstition and magpies. Edith, Robert d'Oilly's wife, was drawn to the noise of "pyes" from a tree by the river. Told by her confessor that "these are not pyes" but souls in torment, she persuaded Robert to bring them relief in the form of a monastery.

Nearly 30 years later Osney was raised to an abbey, the third largest in the country. The magpies are still there in the cemetery by the railway, but the abbey has gone, leaving "Great

University of Paris to complete their education, but, following an unresolved quarrel with the king of France in 1167, King Henry II ordered them home.

Oxford was a natural place for these outcasts to settle. There were already centres of learning in the Augustinian monasteries of St Frideswide's Priory and Osney Abbey, as well as "Masters" lecturing on the scriptures and on Roman Law. There were also mutual advantages for Henry in his palace at Beaumont and for the students gathering at his gates. From this pool of academic talent the king could readily recruit the civil servants who would implement the power of royal government.

Life for the early students at Oxford was organised along the lines of the tradesmen's guilds. Like apprentices, they lived and studied for seven years with their Masters in "Halls". After four years they took their Bachelor of Arts degree, and at the end of the course their Master's degree, which entitled them to lecture. Those who chose to do so hired houses, boarding and teaching their students under one roof. Beam Hall in Merton Street is one of these halls. Most disappeared as colleges gradually took their place.

OXFORD'S "SISTER"

After the hanging of two scholars in 1209, several students were motivated to leave. They went to Cambridge, where they founded Oxford's "sister" university.

Once the quarrel was patched up, stringent penalties were imposed on the town in the form of fines – which were, incidentally, to provide the first university endowment. Controls were introduced for scholars on the price of food and other necessities, and on their house and room rents. Any scholar arrested had to be passed over to the ecclesiastical authority. The university was to have a charter of privileges and Robert Grosseteste, the future Bishop of Lincoln, was appointed at its head as Chancellor.

Town versus Gown

There were ways in which unscrupulous property owners, traders and Masters could abuse their position, and they did, sowing the seeds of conflict between "Town" and "Gown". Murder brought things to a head. In 1209 a woman was killed by scholars, and two were hanged in revenge, the townspeople claiming the right to do so because the country was under an interdict as a result of a quarrel between the Pope and King John.

LEFT: the Quadrangle at Balliol College.
ABOVE: a Vice-Chancellor, Esquire and Beagle. Both paintings are by the celebrated Rudolph Ackermann.

As the university had no buildings, Congregation, the governing body, met in the church of St Mary the Virgin. There were no students either. The first colleges were founded by bishops, catered only for graduates and were exclusively for the wealthy. They were organised like monasteries, with a hall, chapel, lodgings, kitchen and quarters for the Master; the pattern is the same today.

The atmosphere of a medieval college is most nearly captured in Merton. Founded in 1264 by Walter de Merton, it shares the "oldest" title with University and Balliol, both of which look to the Bishop of Durham for their inception. ❏

CUCKOO IN THE NEST

Relations between Town and Gown deteriorated into mob violence.

And relations with the monarchy weren't exactly cordial

From the 13th century, Oxford's 6,000 people became increasingly dependent on the growing university. The most important trades – weavers and cloth merchants, shoemakers, masons, metalworkers, artists in stained glass, manuscript painters and scribes – demonstrate this all too obviously.

As the university's star moved into the ascendant, so that of the town waned. Relegated to the status of a country and market town, it became more and more subservient to the university's needs. As a cuckoo in the town's nest, puffed up with self-importance and royal patronage, the university forced trades and residents out as more and more sites in the central area were acquired for colleges, and wholesale demolition of houses took place.

The plight of the Oxford townsfolk is vividly illustrated in the fortunes of the weavers, whose guild was one of the earliest in England. In the 12th century there were 60 members; by 1270 15 remained; 50 years later there were none.

Poverty and poor living conditions bred disease; in 1348 a quarter of the town's people succumbed to the plague. Labour became scarce and an attempt was made by both Chancellor and Mayor to control wages. Widespread dissatisfaction led to popular demonstrations against authority.

Poor priests

A religious movement that is credited with being partly responsible for the Peasants' Revolt had its origins in Oxford. John Wyclif, Master of Balliol in 1361, spoke against corruption and worldliness in the established Church, sending his disciples into the country to preach to the people in a language they could understand: English. The Lollards, as his "poor priests" came to be called, used a Bible that Wyclif had translated into common English. Support inside the university brought a swift

reaction from both Pope Gregory and the Archbishop of Canterbury. Excommunications followed and some of Wyclif's supporters recanted. By the middle of the next century the movement had withered away.

In the years following the Black Death, relations between Town and Gown deteriorated to

the point where a tavern brawl unleashed pent-up hatred in an explosion of mob violence. It began in the Swindlestock Tavern, since then a victim of road widening at Carfax, on the Feast of St Scholastica in 1355. Fighting started after some scholars threw wine in the landlord's face and followed it with a quart pot. By pre-arranged signal, the bells of Carfax tower were rung to summon the townsmen and the students rang the bell of St Mary's. In the bloody battle that ensued in the streets and in and out of the colleges and hostels, 60 scholars were massacred. The rest fled.

The townsfolk won the battle but lost the war, because the help of the king and the

---

LEFT: the University crest.
RIGHT: John Balliol, co-founder, with his wife, of Balliol College.

Bishop of Lincoln was invoked. Penance was to be done for 500 years. On each anniversary of St Scholastica's Day until 1825, 63 reluctant burghers went in procession to St Mary's to pay a fine to the Vice-Chancellor for those souls lost in the riot.

The university was given control of the market, the price and quality of goods sold, and weights and measures. For the first time "privileged persons" appeared. These were mostly craftsmen, but included people like barbers, who became "servants" of scholars and thereby

LIBRARY RULES

Even leaders like Charles I and Oliver Cromwell had their requests to remove books from the Bodleian Library refused.

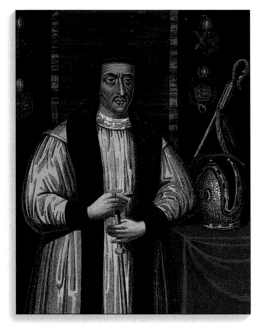

enjoyed special privileges. By the 17th century this hierarchy was to have formed an eighth of the townspeople.

Building the colleges

For 200 years, from 1350, the history of Oxford is the history of the university. New colleges were founded by bishops investing in learning as an insurance for the future power and influence of the Church, king and realm. "Men of learning, fruitful to the Church" was the prescription of William of Wykeham, Bishop of Winchester, for his students when founding New College in 1379. With the land went part of the 12th-century city wall and an obligation

to keep it in good repair that still conserves this valuable link with the city's past.

A clutch of colleges followed: Lincoln in 1427, founded by the Bishop of Lincoln; All Souls, by the Archbishop of Canterbury with Henry VI as co-founder in 1438; Magdalen in 1458 by another Bishop of Winchester. The aims were always the same: to sustain the material superiority of the aristocracy. Brasenose was founded by another Bishop of Lincoln in 1517, and Corpus Christi by the Bishop of Winchester in 1525. Trinity was set up by a civil servant in 1555, and St John's, also in 1555, by a Lord Mayor of London.

Because colleges were by now accepting undergraduates as well as graduates, rich men could buy their sons a university education, and clever scholars could get assisted places. Colleges replaced halls, and by 1543 only 12 halls remained. Two related events were to have far-reaching importance for the growing university. Until the late 15th century, books were scarce and teaching and examinations were oral. In 1478 Theodoric Rood gave teaching and learning a new dimension with the production of his first book on his press in the High Street, a best seller then as now: the Bible.

The other event was the generous gift of books by Duke Humphrey of Gloucester, brother of Henry V, which formed the nucleus of the later Bodleian Library. They were housed over the Divinity School until borrowed, if that is how their removal can be described, by Edward VI. Not until 1602 was a new library formed by Thomas Bodley, the Ambassador to the Netherlands. The lesson had been learned. Then, as now, no book may be taken away.

The severing of the link between the established Church and the Pope in Rome by Henry VIII's assumption of leadership of the Church of England brought the university itself to the brink of destruction. The wealth of the colleges and their essentially ecclesiastical nature made them a prime target when parliament authorised the dissolution of the monasteries in 1536, and their property and revenues were made over to the Crown.

As Franciscans and Carmelites, Cistercians and Benedictines were expelled, the door closed on medieval Oxford. Their property was dispersed among the colleges, the buildings quarried for their stone for new buildings elsewhere and the sites greedily developed.

The pressure on Henry grew as his advisors urged that the university should follow the same fate as the monasteries, but Henry was a scholar and had a personal reason for wishing to see it survive. In 1532 Wolsey, his Chancellor, had founded Cardinal College on the site of St Frideswide's Priory.

After Wolsey's dismissal Henry refounded it as Henry VIII College and after the suppression the college re-emerged as Christ Church. The remnant of the priory church became Oxford Cathedral and went on to enjoy a double life as the college chapel. Henry's epitaph on the outcome was to be: "No land in England is better bestowed than that which is given to our universities."

The Oxford Martyrs

The spread of the New Learning and the Protestant Reformation continued under Henry's son, Edward VI. Translations of the Bible into English began to appear in churches so that everyone who could read could do so in their own language, and the services themselves were conducted wholly in English. In 1549 the first *Book of Common Prayer* was issued and the laws against heresy were repealed. Protestants could now worship in their own faith. But it was a short honeymoon. When the boy king died, that freedom was to be cruelly denied them.

Queen Mary brought what can only be described as a burning zeal to the re-introduction of Roman Catholicism. Following the repeal of anti-papal legislation by a compliant parliament, 300 people met their deaths from 1555 to 1558 by burning at the stake for heresy.

Just why the Queen chose the streets of Oxford for the public humiliation of the three most influential and resistant of the Protestant leaders – Bishops Ridley and Latimer and Archbishop Cranmer – is not at all clear. Perhaps it is of some significance that all three were educated in Cambridge. At first held in the Golden Cross Inn, then in the Bocardo Prison by Northgate, Latimer and Ridley went to the stake in Broad Street. Cranmer, it is said, was forced to watch from his cell as attempts

were made to get him to recant. This he did, but when fastened to the stake his courage and his faith returned, and he thrust into the flames the hand that had signed the recantation.

Oxford's memorial to the martyrs today faces the threat of traffic in St Giles in a Victorian Eleanor Cross that has Cranmer in a niche holding his Bible with "Maye 1541" on the cover, the first year of its circulation. A cross in the road in Broad Street marks the scene of the burnings, and in Balliol College nearby a door blackened by the fire that consumed the flesh of three brave men is preserved.

Another death, that of Mary herself, brought

the burnings to an end in the cooling-off period of Elizabeth I's reign from 1558 to 1603. Another Act of Uniformity made the Church Protestant again, this time permanently. Use of Edward VI's second prayer book was made compulsory, and outward recognition of the new state religion was secured by fines for non-attendance at church.

In this climate of tolerance, learning flourished and the city's population and prosperity increased. While theology was still predominant, other subjects became popular as careers in public life and the professions influenced well-off parents to choose the university for their sons' education. The age of privilege had arrived. ❏

LEFT: Richard Foxe, Bishop of Winchester and founder of Corpus Christi.
RIGHT: Sir Thomas Bodley, founder of the Bodleian.

A TOWN AT WAR

Oxford played a central role in the Civil War between Royalists and Parliamentarians. Afterwards, architecture flourished while learning stagnated

Queen Eizabeth I smiled on "dear Oxford", visiting several times and being welcomed with fulsome expressions of loyalty. To her hosts' orations in Greek and Latin she gave as good as she received – in Greek and Latin!

Oxford will remember the Queen for something that touched the hearts and imaginations of her people. One in particular, Sir Walter Scott, used the story in *Kenilworth*. Amy Robsart, wife of Robert Dudley, Earl of Leicester, was staying at Cumnor House, a few miles from the city. Her husband and Elizabeth were having an affair and Amy was an obvious obstruction to Dudley's marrying Elizabeth when she came to the throne. Servants returning from a fair found Amy dead at the foot of a staircase. At first buried at Cumnor, her remains were later, on Dudley's orders, removed to an unmarked grave in St Mary's. His chaplain, who conducted the service, made what we would today call a Freudian slip in referring to the lady as "so pitifully *murdered*" when he meant to say "so pitifully *slain*". Public opinion had already made up its mind.

Elizabeth and the Bard

Oxford has a rather slender claim to association with William Shakespeare, although John Aubrey, the historian, recorded that Elizabeth's favourite actor/playwright broke his journey every year on his way from London's Globe Theatre to Stratford-upon-Avon to stay at the Crown Tavern in Cornmarket.

Such was his friendship with the innkeeper that he was godfather to his son, and the probability is that Shakespeare was at William Davenant's baptism in St Martin's across the way. With such a start in life, it comes as no surprise that Davenant went on to become a playwright himself and, in 1638, was even made Poet Laureate.

The other connection with Shakespeare lies through the First Folio which the Bodleian Library had acquired. Later it was sold and replaced with a third edition. Not until 1905, when a First Folio was sent to the Bodleian for repair, was it recognised as the original and acquired by subscription.

Town and Gown took their differences into

the 17th century, spilling less blood but spending more money on legal arguments over an ever-increasing number of issues. In 1609 the city complained of proctors' high-handed treatment of citizens, the excessive number of alehouses licensed by the university and the drunkenness and bad manners of its members. Little was resolved, but legal fees accounted for half the city's income.

Fresh disputes

Thirty years later came the last of the great charters reinforcing the university's powers and incidentally breeding fresh disputes. The university gained the right to appoint its own coroners and

---

LEFT: Magpie Lane, painted by Rudolph Ackermann.
RIGHT: Queen Elizabeth I, who reportedly gave as good as she got.

the Chancellor was given the right to veto new building in the town. Dunghills and poor paving would attract fines, and the right to police the streets was bandied about between Mayor and Chancellor.

Behind the walls of their colleges, gardeners were drawing their battle lines with spade and fork, and under the command of Lord Danby made a sortie to the banks of the Cherwell. Here, opposite Magdalen tower they created, in 1621, Britain's oldest botanic garden: the "Physick" Garden at first, since it produced herbs and plants for medicine and was linked with the scientific studies of the Faculty of

Medicine. Lord Danby's bust over the entrance gate nods gratefully to his royal patrons "Charles I and Charles II" in their niches on either side of him, where both are shown by the sculptor as Romans.

Civil War capital

In the struggle ahead Oxford was to be the stage, and King and Parliament merely players. Charles I's connection with Oxford thrust it into the forefront of the conflict between Crown and State that erupted in civil war in 1642.

The miracle is that the city emerged virtually unscathed from the extensive works undertaken to put its defences in readiness for assault, and from the siege that subsequently took place but which was abandoned, without the expected battle ever happening.

The King already had strong support at the university. His Archbishop of Canterbury and chief advisor, William Laud, had been a student at St John's and was Chancellor for a time. He and Charles shared a common dislike for Puritans. On the occasion when the King brought his Queen, Henrietta Maria, and his nephew, Prince Rupert, to open Laud's new Canterbury Quad, the entertainment was so lavish that it cost half what had been spent on the building.

Nearly all the dons and scholars were sympathetic to the Royalist cause. But the townspeople disliked Laud, whom they suspected of being a Papist. Also, they deeply resented the university's control over their affairs and so supported Parliament.

A surprise visit in 1642 from a troop of Royalist cavalry under Sir John Byron brought the citizens out on to the streets and a half-hearted attempt was made to close the gates. After some confusion the Royalists were welcomed in by the scholars. Eleven days later the cavalry went, leaving a divided city to receive a Parliamentary force with Lord Saye at the head. The university was disarmed, the townspeople armed, the head was shot off the Virgin on the porch of St Mary's, and the troops left for what was to be the first great battle of the Civil War.

The Battle of Edgehill made Charles look for a new headquarters, now that London was in the hands of Parliament. Oxford's central position, natural defences and accessibility to areas of support in the west and north made it an obvious choice.

An accommodating Christ Church provided a good substitute palace for Charles, Prince Rupert, his brother Maurice, the young Prince Charles and his brother the Duke of York. Not for some months were they joined by the Queen, who was then billeted in nearby Merton College, a gate being made in a garden wall so that she and Charles could meet easily.

Although the citizens presented the King with money, the Mayor was under pressure to replace aldermen unsympathetic to the Royalist cause. Their Member of Parliament was arrested for subversive activity, and the city was forced to give up its arms.

After an abortive attempt to capture London, in which his army got no further than Turnham Green, Charles went back to Oxford and set about improving the outdated defences. With the help of a Dutch engineer, ditches were dug and ramparts raised by the reluctant citizens and enthusiastic students. The halls and colleges became warehouses for food and supplies, factories for the manufacture of gunpowder and uniforms, and foundries for the cannon. The townspeople looked on aghast as Magdalen Bridge was demolished and a

FUELLING THE TROOPS

To keep the army happy and fed through the winter, sheep, cattle and horses were "removed" from the surrounding countryside.

The burden put on accommodation by the influx of more than 5,000 soldiers with their wives and camp followers can easily be imagined. There were also many visiting courtiers, Members of Parliament sympathetic to the Royalists, their servants and entourage, all needing to be fed and boarded, prisoners of war to be secured, and hospitals found for the wounded from battles elsewhere.

It was inevitable that disease should breed in the filthy conditions of streets and sewers, and there were outbreaks of camp fever and plague.

drawbridge erected in its place, and watched with disbelief as cannon so heavy that they needed 15 horses and 26 men to pull them were brought to the parks near Magdalen.

All this and the maintenance of the garrison required money. The King's answer was to make it. The Royal Mint was brought to New Inn Hall Street, and college plate was pillaged for silver and gold to turn into coin. Unfortunately it did not make enough. City and University were asked for cash "contributions".

LEFT: Oliver Cromwell, who was educated at Cambridge, fought at Oxford.
ABOVE: Ackermann's *Kitchen at Christ Church*.

Just as inevitable was the danger of fire. In 1644 the centre of the city was devastated by a blaze that began in a kitchen and destroyed hundreds of houses.

The Parliamentarians seem to have made rather ineffectual attempts to contain Charles in Oxford. Prince Rupert was able to make excursions as far north as Yorkshire, winning Newark and losing Marston Moor, a battle in which his poodle, Boy, was killed.

With 5,000 men the King slipped away through Port Meadow to Worcester, went on to trounce the Earl of Essex in Cornwall, and was back over the drawbridge five months later to turn down peace overtures from Parliament.

The reaction from Parliament's commander-in-chief, Sir Thomas Fairfax, who had joined forces with Cromwell outside Oxford, was to lay siege to the city. Fortunately for Oxford, but unfortunately for the attackers, Charles had left again and the futility of pursuing the siege was recognised.

The elusive King was able to escape once again after the decisive battle of the war at Naseby, returning to Oxford and a hoping to plan a renewed siege. Looking for guidance in his predicament, he decided to borrow a book on other civil wars from the Bodleian Library, sending a peremptory note. His request was

War wounds

Picking up the pieces was not easy for the university. There were few scholars, but the college buildings and the churches were undamaged. Such was the concern of Fairfax that he set a guard on the Bodleian and had the city policed by his soldiers. For the citizens there were old scores to settle. Council members sacked by the King at the beginning of the war were reinstated and their leader, John Nixon, was elected Mayor.

Farmers and landowners in the immediate vicinity of Oxford complained of damage by Royalist troops to their houses, woods and cat-

refused: the Library *never* lends books, not even to kings.

The last Oxford saw of Charles, who had decided on escape and surrender to the Scots, was as a humble servant with short hair on horseback riding out over Magdalen Bridge in the middle of the night. For the garrison, surrender was near. Sir Thomas Fairfax sent a message to the Governor with the words: "I very much desire the preservation of that place (so famous for learning) from ruin."

With the King's assent, conditions were formally agreed and the soldiers marched out on 25 June 1646. The war was over and Oxford was saved.

tle, and of the loss of income from not being able to grow crops. They found the university inflexible, however, as did those in the city who had suffered during the occupation, and negotiations were abandoned.

Business in Oxford settled down slowly to its only real trade: selling to the university. With this obvious limitation, small shopkeepers were kept small and the only growth was in poverty. The city persisted in its attempts to win better conditions, and in 1684 sought a new charter with the object of extending boundaries, increasing the size of the markets, gaining more control over policing and licensing, and increasing power for the Mayor with the support of additional aldermen. Of course, none of these aims was achieved.

After the monarchy was restored, the Puritan influence soon evaporated from Oxford and serious scholars, as so often in subsequent years, bemoaned the non-academic attitude of their students. Anthony Wood, in his *Life and Times, 1631–95*, wrote: "Why doth solid and serious learning decline, and few or none follow it now in the university? Answer: because of coffee-houses, where they spend all their time; and in entertainments at their chambers, where their studies are become places for victualers, also great drinking at taverns and ale-

the Old Ashmolean Museum. There followed Gibbs' masterpiece, the Radcliffe Camera, the world's first library in the round, and the unique evocation of the Tower of the Winds in the Radcliffe Observatory. Hawksmoor contributed the twin towers of All Souls' College, Gothic outside and classical within. Palladian architecture jostled medieval, and stone replaced brick.

The glory of Oxford was assured; the university's academic achievement anything but. Student sons of the wealthy drank much and learned little. Exams became a farce. The seeds of 19th-century reform and revival were sown in this climate of stagnation.

houses (Dr Lampshire told me there were 370 in Oxford), spending their time in common chambers whole afternoons, and thence to the coffee-house."

But the university also began devoting its attentions to building. A place for grand ceremonial was provided in Wren's Sheldonian Theatre, and a place for the bell from Osney Abbey in Tom Tower. The Clarendon Building found a new home for the Oxford University Press, and the fantastic curiosities collected by Elias Ashmole joined experimental science in

ABOVE: an Oxford book auction in 1747, painted by William Green Jnr.

Delivering the goods

Oxford's self-interested clergy sponsored the city's canal. College heads invested in a proposal which put cheap coal from the Midlands in their hearths instead of sea-coal brought from northeast England and up the Thames. Opened in 1790, the canal survived competition from the Grand Junction Canal and only succumbed with the arrival of the railway, suffering a final indignity when its terminal was filled in for Nuffield College in 1937.

The city and university were less inviting to the railway pioneers. A proposed terminus for the Great Western Railway at Magdalen Bridge in 1837 was opposed and then abandoned. Successive bills before Parliament failed in the face of considerations like the morals of the students and the fear of what might happen if the lower classes could move about more freely. Concessions were made, however, and the railway steamed into Oxford in 1844.

The workshops for the whole of the Great Western could have followed. Town now accused Gown of holding back progress when the university resisted the scheme, but with hindsight it looks as if it was right for once. The works were to go to Swindon, in Wiltshire, instead.

SHOPPING

In the middle of the 19th century the plate-glass window and department store began to appear.

a special dispensation, lingering on at the Butter Bench by Carfax for another seven years.

The new market, open every day, was extended and roofed over in the Victorian "iron" age, then as now the preponderance of butchers a barometer of prosperity. It was also an indication that Oxford's population was increasing rapidly. In the first 40 years of the 19th century it doubled to 24,000.

The character of shopping was changing. Earlier restrictions on the sale of goods other than those produced locally were abandoned.

Housing boom

New enterprises brought workers to the area and a consequent demand for new housing. When the Oxford University Press moved to Walton Street in 1830 it became the principal employer, its employees finding homes nearby in the new suburb of Jericho.

Towards the end of the 18th century the main streets around Carfax were still cluttered with market stalls, just as they had been in medieval times, impeding the free movement of traffic, unhygienic and untidy. Both city and university agreed that a market building was the answer, and in 1774 meat, fish and vegetables were moved to an area behind High Street. Butter had

Factory-made goods were being brought in from London and the Midlands by railway and canal, ousting the work of all except for the specialised craftsmen. Choice became wider, credit was no longer given, and price fixing and tickets replaced bargaining.

Unfortunately for the growing number of retailers, the student population halved in the first half of the 19th century and many shopkeepers found themselves in difficulties. The shops, too, were changing, with shopkeepers no longer living above their premises. ❏

ABOVE: agriculture and academia meet on the outskirts of 19th-century Oxford.

What's Brewing

Oxford had a head start when it came to brewing: it was in the middle of malting barley country and had easy access to pure well water found deep beneath the Thames.

A glass of beer added drama to much of the city's history. Shed a tear for the garrison at Oxford castle, who, it seems, must have gone thirsty from 1255, when their brewhouse collapsed, until 1267 when it was rebuilt. Spare your sympathy for the Chancellor, who had to take on responsibility for the brewing trade after the St Scholastica's Day riots. Reserve your praise for the president of Trinity College in 1600, who observed: "The Houses that had the smaller (*i.e. weaker*) beer had the most drunkards, for it forced them to go into the town to comfort their stomachs." Trinity's beer was best, and they had the fewest drunkards.

Roundly condemn the beer at All Souls' in 1609 which was so good but so strong that it was held responsible for the college's "decriments", whatever those may have been. Weep, too, for the Keeper of the Ashmolean Museum in 1729, who died at Christ Church from "a pretty deal of bad small beer".

From the Middle Ages onwards, most of the monasteries and some of the colleges brewed their own beer. Those without brewhouses obtained permission to use the facilities of those that had. One of these, Queen's, was founded with a brewer among the servants, and brewing was carried on until 1939 in a building that still exists in the Fellows' Garden. Changes in taste and a new building accounted for the end of college-produced beer and left a clear field to the professional brewer.

There were professional brewers in Oxford from the 13th century and the Poll Tax of 1381 identified as many as 32 in the city. Taxes and tolls, price, quality and measures of pollution prevention imposed severe restrictions. Although there were frequent breaches of the regulations, which brought tighter controls by the university, brewers became men of wealth and standing in the community.

Between 1350 and 1500 no fewer than 10 became Mayor, and one was Mayor three times in succession. Among those who took office, John Sprunt, who died in 1419, is commemorated by an engraved brass in St Peter's College Chapel. Unfortunately, for a brewer, it has no head on it.

RIGHT: the age-old tradition of brewing in Oxford.

The brewers came and went, but by the 18th century the leading brewing families of Oxford had begun to emerge. The old-established Swan's Nest Brewery was bought by William Hall in 1795 and, after a partnership with the Tawney family, became Hall's Oxford Brewery Ltd in 1896. Take-overs followed – including the St Clement's Brewery, the Eagle Steam and Hanley's City Breweries.

Local deliveries were made using over 60 horse-drawn drays, and on May Day mornings before World War I they paraded through the city. Hall's were taken over by Allsop's in 1926, then Ind Coope. Now the name Hall's is just a memory, and their brewery is the Oxford Museum of Modern Art.

The last brewery in Oxford, Morrell's, produced its final pint in 1998 after selling up to a housing development company. Brewing had already been going on at its site in St Thomas Street for 200 years before Mark Morrell and his son James set up in business in 1782, producing such classics as Varsity Ale. Today the tradition lives on in the shape of 132 pubs controlled by Morrell of Oxford Ltd, even if the beer itself is brought in from the Thomas Hardy brewery in Dorchester. And the symbolism of the old brewery gates survives, with a pair of rampant lions, each holding aloft a spray of hops like a lover's bouquet, flanking the entrance – a reminder that Morrell's beer was a wedding of malt and hops. ❑

A TIME OF CHANGE

From the religious pressures of the Oxford Movement to the arrival of trams in the streets and women at the university, the city had constantly to adapt

Between 1830 and 1850 one question engaged members of the university to the exclusion of everything else. In the words of a contemporary scholar, Mark Pattison, it "entirely diverted our thoughts from the true business of the place". Such was the Oxford Movement, which started with a church sermon

He noted in his *Diary* that the priest wore "a biretta and a chasuble stiff with gold. The poor humble Roman Church hard by is quite plain, simple and Low Church in its ritual."

Of the leading churchmen associated with the Movement, John Newman, vicar of St Mary's at the time, addressed his readers of the

and left Oxford, with its protagonists, to be debated elsewhere.

It all began on 14 July 1833 when John Keble, Fellow of Oriel and Professor of Poetry, preached the Assize Sermon in the University Church. It stimulated the publication of the controversial *Tracts for the Times*, which gave the Movement the alternative title of "Tractarian". The main thrust of the arguments put forward was in support of a "Catholic" church, but not Roman Catholic, and the most tangible outcome was the revival of ceremonial in Anglican churches.

One in particular, St Barnabas, built to serve the growing working-class suburb of Jericho, was visited by the Rev. Francis Kilvert in 1876.

first Tract as "Fellow-Labourers". After the last Tract appeared he left Oxford, embraced the Roman Catholic Church, and was made a Cardinal in 1879.

John Keble's posthumous contribution to Oxford was the college named after him in 1870. The intention was to provide people of small means with an academic education based on the principles of the Church of England. The chosen architect was William Butterfield, a follower of the Movement, who produced a building in Gothic Revival style.

When the sun fell on its patterned brick, John Betjeman thought it appeared at its worst. Norman Shaw saw Butterfield as "paddling in a boat of his own". His building is certainly unique and striking.

At the beginning of Queen Victoria's reign, the collection of rarities of the rather dubiously acquired inheritance of Elias Ashmole was still installed, neglected and deteriorating, in the Old Ashmolean building in Broad Street. What was needed was a suitable home for the display of these and the university's treasures and works of art, which two timely bequests made splendidly possible. In 1841 Charles Robert Cockerell produced his design for a neo-classical

ALL ABOARD

Passengers on trams were not allowed to smoke or travel in dirty work clothes – *plus ça change.*

to breweries, marmalade to melodrama and town houses to trams.

Tram to North Oxford

There is a romantic idea that the development of the area north of the Martyrs' Memorial that is North Oxford came about when the university allowed dons to marry. The need for large family housing, however, was earlier felt by the city's wealthy merchants and traders.

No doubt St John's College, which had acquired the land as early as the 16th century,

Ashmolean Museum which so magnificently today introduces the wonderful diversity of its contents. Somehow the most significant and compelling of the exhibits is the Alfred Jewel (*see page 160*) – the Alfred who could have been the founder of the university.

Diversity is the essential element of the growth of Oxford throughout the 60 years of Queen Victoria's reign, a diversity of demand from an expanding city that ranged from books

LEFT: Ackermann's *Bachelor of Arts* and *The Astronomical Observatory.*
ABOVE: a dead-heat in the 1877 Oxford-Cambridge Boat Race.

was alive to its potential for development as well. Gothic was the flavour of university architecture; red and yellow brick its chosen medium; gables and gardens characterised the style. Keble College and the Parks' Museum welcomed the villas like hens with chickens. By 1880 most of the houses had been completed, and after 1877 the dons began moving in with their families.

Five years later North Oxford's first trams followed them up the Banbury Road all the way from Carfax for one penny. The horse-drawn single deckers on 4-ft (13-metre) gauge rails also ran from east to west over a specially widened Magdalen Bridge, up the High Street and out to Jericho via Walton Street. Speed was limited to 13 km (8 miles) an hour and further restricted if confronted with a herd of cattle. Worse, a flock of sheep called for a dead stop.

It was the turn of the century before an electric tramway was mooted, and 1913 before the idea was effectively scotched by the motorbus. William Morris, later Lord Nuffield, was refused a licence by the city to run these, but tickets for a ride could be bought in shops. The Tramway Company followed suit, but with buses instead of trams, and eventually won exclusive rights to run Oxford's first official bus service.

Rights for women

The seeds of the slow and grudging acceptance of the equal right of women to higher education were sown not by the university authorities but by central government through the Parliamentary Commissions of 1850 and 1874. Oxford, however, came a conspicuous second to Cambridge in relaxing rules on the admission of women. As early as 1863 examinations had been open to girls at Cambridge, and Girton became the first residential college for women in 1869.

But it was nine years before Oxford followed suit with Lady Margaret Hall, for Church of

Blackwell's bookshop *(see page 121)* is so much one of Oxford's important institutions that you expect it to go back further than 1879, yet it was only then that Benjamin Henry Blackwell started his business at his house in Holywell Street. Demands on space soon forced expansion into other premises.

Down on the river at Folly Bridge, Salter Bros had been quietly contributing to Oxford's sporting prowess and public pleasure since they established the firm in 1858. Boats and college barges were built here, including the eights that took the university to victory over Cambridge, and in 1886 they began the steamer trips that have opened Oxford's fluid asset to millions.

England girls, and Somerville College, the first to place no religious requirements on its entrants (both are now mixed). St Hugh's joined them in 1886 and St Hilda's Hall in 1893, founded by the Principal of Cheltenham Ladies' College for women from that college (and today the only all-female college).

Further concessions were slowly but surely wrung from the university. Examinations were opened to women in 1894, but degrees and equal status for women's colleges had to wait until the 20th century. ❑

ABOVE: Henry Taunt's 1907 photograph of St Aldate's, looking towards Carfax.

The Pied Piper of Christ Church

*A*lice in Wonderland is a love story. It indirectly-expresses Lewis Carroll's feelings for the young daughter of the Dean of Christ Church and reveals his thinly disguised passion for Oxford itself. Growing up brought the first affair quickly to a close – "No thought of me shall find a place/In thy young life's hereafter," he wrote in dedicating *Alice Through the Looking Glass* to her. The other relationship ended only with his death in 1898. In all that time he was scarcely ever away from his beloved Oxford.

Carroll was born Charles Ludwidge Dodgson in Christ Church rectory, Lincolnshire, and entered Oxford's Christ Church at the age of 18 in 1850. He became a lecturer in mathematics and was ordained Deacon. Outside his academic studies he was a keen photographer, developing his own plates in a dark-room he was given permission to build on the roof of his rooms overlooking Tom Quad.

Extremely shy, he was most at ease with children and they became his favourite subjects. His first meeting with the Liddell daughters was in the Deanery garden, where his intention of photographing the Cathedral was diverted by their insisting on getting in the picture.

The friendship with the girls grew, and soon they were posing for his camera in his rooms. Dressed in Chinese costumes or the rags of beggar waifs from the cupboards in his dressing-room, the children began their games of "Let's pretend", and Alice's adventures were about to begin.

During the summer Dodgson took the children on the river, making up stories that lived and died "like summer midges". They rowed to Iffley and beyond, and if time allowed went ashore at Nuneham to picnic in the park of their friends, the Harcourts.

One expedition, on 4 July 1862, took them up-stream to Godstow. The children, as always, pressed their friend for more stories and, when they returned to the Deanery, Alice implored him to write down her adventures. Ever willing to please her, Dodgson began the carefully hand-written book with his own illustrations and gave it to her as a Christmas gift.

Alice's Adventures were so well thought of that Dodgson agreed to their professional publication, and on the advice of John Ruskin, the artist and social reformer, to have them illustrated by a pro-

fessional artist. John Tenniel was chosen, and the author's name changed to Lewis Carroll (Lewis from Ludwidge, Carroll from Charles).

A second book, *Through the Looking Glass and What Alice Found There*, was not published until 1871. The relationship had ended with the end of her childhood, and Alice was now 19. She married a Christ Church man and went to live at Lyndhurst.

From the moment Alice clutches the jar of "orange marmalade" Lewis Carroll starts an intriguing guessing game in identifying Oxford references and characters. Dodgson was currently advertising for sale his brother's orange marmalade. The Cheshire cat is Dinah, Alice's tabby. Lorina and Edith, Alice's sisters,

are the Lory and Eaglet. Her governess, Miss Prickett is the Red Queen, "one of the thorny kind". The Rev. Robinson Duckworth, a friend of Lewis Carroll's, who often went on the picnics, becomes, affectionately, the Duck.

The Dodo is the author himself, and was derived from visits to the new University Museum. The Dormouse's story of three children living at the bottom of a treacle-well leads us to the healing well at Binsey. Deer from Magdalen Park and eels from the wicker traps at Godstow mix fact and fantasy, and along St Aldate's, opposite the college, is the shop where Alice bought her favourite barley-sugar from the old sheep.

You've only to push open the door. ❑

RIGHT: Lewis Carroll in pensive mood.

TRADITION VERSUS PROGRESS

As Oxford developed from a sleepy market town into an important industrial centre, it faced a new range of social and economic problems

Vera Brittain, author of *Testament of Youth*, went up to Somerville College in 1914, an innocent ex-deb who had been born into "that unparalleled age of rich materialism and tranquil comfort", as she describes the Edwardian age. The Oxford that she discovered in the first year of World War I still basked in that mellow security even a decade into the new century.

This was the Oxford of Zuleika Dobson, the eponymous heroine of Max Beerbohm's novel who caused titled undergraduates, besotted with her, to drown themselves in the Isis. Colleges dominated the university, and the university controlled the city that existed to service it. Around the stately quadrangles were narrow, medieval streets containing small businesses and close-knit communities. Public transport was still by horse-drawn trams that were advertised as meeting every train at the sleepy, non-mainline station. In the North Oxford suburb, built to house the large Victorian families of the dons, croquet was played on the lawns, and afternoon tea was served with ceremony.

In 1915, Vera Brittain left Oxford to train as a nurse. In 1919 she returned to Somerville. "It seemed unbearable that everything should be exactly the same when all my life was so much changed." She had lost her brother, her lover, and many friends; 2,700 Oxford men had died in the trenches.

It is invidious to select one name from these thousands, but H.G.J. (Harry) Moseley, who was killed at Gallipoli in 1915, had graduated from Trinity College, and was the most promising of all the physicists of his generation. His work on atomic structure using the relatively new X-rays was in four short years already enough for a Nobel prize to be confidently predicted. His classic equipment has an honoured place in the Museum of the History of Science.

In every college the memorial slabs went up, and the ancient buildings were haunted for those who had survived. The great eccentric

LEFT AND RIGHT: women at work in World War I, as ticket collectors and unpaid social workers.

William Spooner, Warden of New College (*see page 104*), had a plaque erected in the chapel to record the names of college members who had died fighting on the enemy side: "In memory of the men of this college who coming from a foreign land entered into the inheritance of this place and returning fought and died for their

country in the war 1914–1919".

But life went on, and for many the top priority was to live it as on a roller coaster, for as much excitement and risk as possible. Between the wars, Oxford University, so often an exaggeration of the contemporary mood, experienced the excesses of hearties and aesthetes.

Evelyn Waugh's 1945 novel *Brideshead Revisited* offered the fictional version of this lifestyle, and Vera Brittain wrote of her contemporaries: "One and all combined to create that 'eat-drink-and-be-merry-for-tomorrow-we-die' atmosphere which seemed to have drifted from the trenches via the Paris hotels and London nightclubs into Oxford colleges."

A woman's place

Under this hectic surface, a fundamental change had been taking place. Women, admitted to lectures of the university in 1880, and permitted to take exams in 1884, were first given degrees – the ultimate equality – in 1920. Four women's colleges had been founded between 1878 and 1893, so the academic groundwork was well established. It was the post-war emancipation that was gradually to free the female undergraduates to take a more active part in university life.

LOCK UP YOUR SONS!

Under the Intercollegiate Rules of 1924, women could have social dealings with men only with permission, within limited hours and accompanied by a female.

Many of the clubs remained exclusively male, notably the Oxford Union debating society that was founded in 1823, and by mid-century occupied its own premises between Cornmarket and New Inn Hall Street. Its debates were the nursery of a glittering succession of politicians, lawyers and clerics, the most famous of whom were always ready to return in later life as guest speakers. The Union resisted admitting women as members until after World War II. The many other clubs were gradually opened to women,

Christopher Hobhouse, a traditionalist, did not welcome the invasion, and wrote caustically: "They are perpetually awheel. They bicycle in droves from lecture to lecture, capped and gowned, handlebars laden with notebooks and notebooks crammed with notes."

Yet the circumspect invasion of Oxford by women made little impact on male undergraduate life in the inter-war years. The traditional sports and clubs continued. Eights Week still brought throngs of families and girlfriends to cheer on the boat races and socialise on the picturesque college barges lining the riverbank below Christ Church Meadow – now replaced by brick boathouses.

but the majority of male undergraduates had little contact with their female counterparts.

Equally far-reaching changes had been happening to the city of Oxford. By the 1920s, it was no longer a sleepy market town, but an important industrial centre. As early as 1898, William Morris had opened his garage, and the first Morris car came off the line in 1913. By 1923, the Cowley factory's production was over 20,000 vehicles a year.

The area east of Magdalen Bridge had become a town in its own right, owing no allegiance to the university. The industrial age in Oxford had finally arrived.

Between 1911 and 1951, the population of

Oxford grew from 62,000 to 97,000, mostly due to the immigration of industrial workers. Many of these came from the Welsh valleys, creating a strong and obstinately self-contained Welsh community in Cowley, that made its own social life, complete with choirs. The villages close to Oxford – Headington, Marston, Iffley, Wolvercote – also became suburbs of the city.

The industrial expansion of the town caused dismay to many for whom Oxford was Matthew Arnold's "sweet city with her dreaming spires". In 1928, Dr H.A.L. Fisher, Warden of New College, was the prime mover in establishing the Oxford Preservation Trust, whose

greatly between the wars. There were some undoubted improvements in the city centre. The elegant new Elliston & Cavell store was built in Magdalen Street, and the corner of Broad Street and Cornmarket was dignified by the pillared curve of William Baker's furniture shop. Beaumont Street, with its fine 18th-century facades, suffered little from the inclusion of the Playhouse, a piece of infill in the very best of taste.

The New Theatre in George Street, spacious inside and simple outside, was welcome, but the Ritz cinema further west (now the MGM), presents disconcertingly blank walls both to George Street and Gloucester Green.

first act was to raise the money to buy land on Boars Hill and at Marston, in the Cherwell valley, to safeguard these areas from development. The Trust, still active today, owns 350 acres (140 hectares) of land in and around Oxford, and campaigns to preserve the Green Belt so that the historic city, in its ring of hills, may retain its special setting, free of urban sprawl.

A new look

The architectural face of Oxford changed

LEFT: Godley's Own Oxford Volunteers march past the Emperor's Heads on Broad Street in World War I.
ABOVE: a dinner hall in the 1920s.

For the university, there was much new building in the Parks Road area. The Radcliffe Science Library filled with dignity the northern corner of South Parks Road. Opposite, an eccentricity was designed by Sir Herbert Baker: Rhodes House, headquarters of the Rhodes Trust and its scholars. This was aptly described by the writer Christopher Hobhouse as "a Cotswold manor house with a circular temple of heroic scale deposited in its forecourt". Where Parks Road joins Broad Street, another corner site accommodated the New Bodleian Library, a curiously uninteresting building above ground, but fascinating below, where the vast book stacks are linked by conveyor belt under the street to the subterranean reaches of the Bodleian proper.

The commercial building of the 1930s shows how prosperous Oxford had become, even during the Depression, thanks to the motor industry. The university, too, was expanding with the advent of science and medicine, much of the expansion due to the patronage of Lord Nuffield. He endowed poorer colleges, acquired the site round the Radcliffe Infirmary and Observatory to create a medical institute, and in 1936 gave the university £1.25 million for medical research. More funding was poured into the physical sciences, and social science came to Oxford

for the first time with the foundation in 1937 of Nuffield College.

The new boys

The university was gradually changing its character in the 1930s as an increasing number of undergraduates entered with the aid of scholarships. By 1939, about half the student population was grant-aided, leading to a profound change of attitude to studying. For the scholarship boy, Oxford was a place reached through luck and hard work, carrying the obligation to strive for the best degree possible.

It was also a totally unfamiliar environment for some. A Yorkshire miner who won a scholarship described the contrast in *A Pitman Looks at Oxford*, written in 1933 under the pseudonym of Roger Dataller: "Goodbye, University!... Big Tom Tower bell groaning out its plaint... gang of roaring hearties on the tavern doorstep – handkerchief of blackberries on the slope of Cumnor... old port, biscuits, waiters, butlers – white stone, grey stone, greenstone, cloisters – black and white of proctors – sober gait of 'bulldogs'... Now headstocks, coal ranged in many waggons, flicker of pulleys, ochre of fumes, the clatter of clogs."

Yet, despite these changes, public schools still provided the majority of students. The criterion of selection was by no means only intellectual ability. It was considered essential for a college to have its quota of sportsmen and gentlemen, irrespective of their academic quality. As Ronald Knox put it: "They don't do much harm, and when they've finished playing here, they can go out like good little boys and govern the Empire."

But in 1939, Oxford again sent out its young men to fight in another war, at the end of which running the Empire was no longer an option. The Oxford University Air Squadron contributed its quota to the Few who fought the Battle of Britain, among whom was Richard Hilary, author of that great war book *The Last Enemy*.

Medical breakthrough

Oxford made many contributions to the war effort, of which the most dramatic was the discovery of penicillin, which founded the science of antibiotics. Penicillin was described and named in 1929 by Alexander Fleming, but he was not able to make it chemically stable. This was the achievement of Howard Florey and his team, who first used penicillin on a patient in the Radcliffe Infirmary in 1941, the start of a breakthrough in healing of the greatest magnitude. The discovery is commemorated in a formal rose garden between Oxford's Botanic Garden and the High Street, the gift of the American Lasker Foundation in 1953.

Another Oxford contribution to the war was the work of Professor F. A. Lindemann, later Lord Cherwell, Churchill's controversial scientific advisor. He made his home in Oxford, and laid a significant part of the foundations of modern physics at the Clarendon Laboratory.

As Oxford entered another post-war period, the same uneasy mixture of ex-servicemen and women and youngsters straight from school was being shaped through three years in the university's old, inimitable way. It was at this time that the city, having grown to an unwieldy size, began to realise that traffic was a major problem. A planning consultant, Thomas Sharp, was engaged for three years by the City Council to produce a detailed study, which was published in 1948 under the title *Oxford Replanned*. Over 40 years on, one marvels at its confident comprehensiveness, and thinks, if only it were as simple as that to

STUDY, NOT STRIFE

During World War II the government discouraged students from enlisting, insisting on residence of one year for scholarship holders.

cross the river by a new bridge south of Magdalen Bridge. The patient being a city of such fame, the storm that greeted Sharp's proposal was of international proportions, and rumbled on ill-temperedly for the next 25 years.

After a period of shock, the battle lines were drawn. Christ Church, and behind it the university, refused to consider a Meadow Road. But the idea of a relief road, once mooted, continued to occupy the planners' minds, and bore fruit in another route further south, proposed in the 1960s, and called the

manage the growth of a city.

Sharp's study has deservedly become a classic, but its fame rests largely on one of its proposals, the Meadow Road. Sharp wrote: "In the case of Oxford one piece of surgery is required to release the city from a pressure on its spinal column which will otherwise eventually paralyse it." The spinal column was the admired High Street, then ruined by traffic; the surgery was to create a new east/west relief road, running through Christ Church Meadow to

LEFT: the High Street in 1939.
ABOVE: a fish stall in the Covered Market in the early 1950s.

ALEXANDER FLEMING

Sir Alexander Fleming (1881–1955) is most commonly associated with the discovery of penicillin, but the real scientific breakthrough was made by Howard Florey (1898–1968). Florey was a Rhodes Scholar at Oxford before returning in 1935 as Professor of Pathology. Excited by Fleming's discovery that penicillin mould spores killed bacteria, he continued research into antibiotics at the Radcliffe Infirmary and the life-saving medicine went into large-scale production in time to be used effectively in World War II. Fittingly, Florey shared the 1945 Nobel Prize for Medicine with Fleming and Sir Ernest Chain.

Eastwyke Farm Road. This was part of a complex of urban motorways that would have carved up the inner residential areas of the city, and for which approval was actually given in 1969.

At this point it was the turn of Oxford's citizens to protest. A Civic Society was formed, a best-selling booklet called *Let's Live in Oxford* was published, and vigorous opposition was mounted to the motorway scheme at a Public Inquiry. A combination of political factors, lack of money and public protest caused the Eastwyke Farm scheme to be abandoned. A couple of years later, a Labour City Council adopted what was known as the Balanced Transport

stopped the flow of customers. As with so much else in this argumentative city, the debate will no doubt run and run.

The wreckers move in

Though urban motorways did not bring about the wholesale destruction of housing, the new-buildings-for-old enthusiasm of the 1960s produced what some now see as the tragic destruction of the old Oxford. The late Victorian terraces of St Ebbe's, between the city centre and the Thames, were completely pulled down, and in the resulting wasteland a huge shopping centre and multi-storey car park were

Policy, using reduced car-parking, improved public transport and a park-and-ride scheme to contain city-centre traffic.

Attempts to rid Oxford's medieval central streets of ever-growing volumes of traffic culminated in the Oxford Transport Strategy, introduced by the City Council in June 1999. This scheme has at last emptied Cornmarket Street of all traffic, even the buses (between 10am and 6pm) and drastically reduced car access along the High Street and Broad Street. Is it a success? If you like fresh air and a car-free stroll along Cornmarket, you'll probably say yes. But several traders have voiced an unhappiness, saying that stopping the flow of cars has

built. The Oxford Preservation Trust succeeded in saving a small group of 17th-century cottages at the eleventh hour, and these now huddle somewhat incongruously beside the vast Westgate Centre.

The modernisation of Cornmarket actually began in 1957, with the demolition of the Clarendon Hotel. This was replaced by a Woolworth's store, which, although discreetly designed by Sir William Holford in stone, brought the High Street multiples into the centre of Oxford, and was soon followed by the demise of the fine old grocers, Grimbly Hughes, Webbers in the High Street, and Capes of St Ebbe's.

In the 1980s, the Clarendon Centre, another shopping centre, was built to link Cornmarket with Queen Street, a sensible idea marred by crude and inappropriate execution, with the main entrance through the former Woolworth building marked by much-criticised blue-painted metal hoops.

But conservation policies did gain credence, and more sites have been treated with sensitivity. On the corner of Ship Street, for example, a medieval building (now occupied by Laura Ashley) has been restored by Jesus College.

Changes in the university after World War II were no less significant and controversial.

forced to do so by outside forces. The result was the establishment of a committee under the chairmanship of Lord Franks, whose report led to far-reaching changes in the university's structure. The achievements of the 1960s were extraordinary in financial and practical terms. The Historic Buildings Appeal raised over £2 million, making it possible for the grime of centuries to be removed from Oxford's stone, and restoration work on a huge scale to be done.

The College Contributions scheme, which required the richer colleges to provide funds for the poorer, as well as generous outside funding, enabled new building work to the value of

With its usual capacity for pulling a rabbit out of the hat, Oxford suddenly produced a sporting star of international magnitude in Dr Roger Bannister (now Sir Roger, and formerly Master of Pembroke College), who used his knowledge of physiology to famously run the first four-minute mile on the Iffley Road track in June 1954.

There was a strong feeling that the university must modernise its administration or find itself

LEFT: in 1954 Roger Bannister was the first runner to achieve a four-minute mile – in 3 minutes 59.54 seconds. **ABOVE:** in 1978 a former US president, Richard Nixon, was guest at an Oxford Union debate.

£11 million to be carried out. Six new colleges were established: St Catherine's for undergraduates on the pattern of the older colleges, and another five for graduates only. The science area burgeoned, with 4,000 undergraduates and graduate students working there.

Oxford suffered less than many of the newer universities from the student unrest that was a feature of the 1960s. But it did not escape entirely, and its reaction was predictable: a committee on relations with junior members, the Hart Committee, was set up, leading to the creation of a Student Representative Council. Pressure for mixed colleges built up all through that radical decade, and this change was implemented from 1970. Today, all the former men's colleges take male and female undergraduates, and there is only one all-female college remaining, St Hilda's. The ratio today of men to women in the university is three to two.

The 1980s saw none of the spectacular spending of the previous two decades. All academic expenditure was restricted by the Conservative government, and Oxford found itself at odds with Margaret Thatcher, despite the fact that the then prime minister was herself an Oxford graduate

> ### MONEY TALKS
>
> In 1996, businessman Wafic Saïd offered the university £20 million for a new Business School, which is expected to open in 2001.

which was established in 1988, has raised more than £225 million from philanthropic gifts. This money is being spent on securing academic posts as well as maintaining and expanding the university's infrastructure.

But what of the city? The battle is still on between the conservationists, who insist that at least something of the old city should remain intact, and the pressure for more jobs and housing.

Before 1991, few outsiders had ever heard of the Blackbird Leys estate, barely 3 miles

(Somerville College). An attempt to award her an honorary degree was actually voted down. No such snub was delivered to US President Bill Clinton, however. In 1994, a quarter of a century after he had completed his time at Oxford as a Rhodes Scholar, he was awarded his honorary doctorate with great pomp and ceremony.

Fundraising for a new future

Severe spending restrictions remain in force from the government, and the university, keen to expand into new fields of study, is continuously raising money, both at home and abroad.

The Development Programme for Oxford

(5 km) along the Cowley Road from Oxford's famously dreaming spires. In that year the estate achieved national notoriety as law and order broke down and the habit of joy-riding became firmly established as a popular pastime in deprived areas of Britain.

The anarchy at Blackbird Leys did not last long, but it did highlight the fact that even Oxford has its fair share of economic and social problems. Money worries, accommodation worries and employment worries are nothing new here – not even among students. ❑

ABOVE: Turl Street in the 1960s. Congestion has since become a major problem for the city.

Inside OUP

Oxford University Press, known widely as OUP, is the world's largest university press. It publishes more than 3,000 new titles a year, employs some 3,000 people worldwide and has a turnover of over £300 million (US$480 million).

Among its most influential publications is the *Oxford English Dictionary*, first published in 12 volumes and dedicated to Queen Victoria. Today it has four supplements and has been republished in combined form in 20 volumes (£1,650). It also comes in a much-praised CD-Rom version.

As the beginning of each of its books reminds us, "Oxford University Press is a department of the University of Oxford. It furthers the university's objective of excellence in research, scholarship and education by publishing worldwide."

OUP has no board of directors but is controlled by a body of senior Oxford scholars – the Delegates of the Press – and a finance committee. Although it may appear to resemble any large commercial publisher, OUP differs greatly because of its objectives. Like any university press, it is dedicated to serving education and research, but unlike others it has to pay its own way.

OUP is very international in its outlook, maintaining branches and promotion offices in over 50 countries, many with their own substantial publishing programmes. It also publishes in many languages, chiefly in the Indian subcontinent and Africa.

It is more than 500 years since the first book was printed in Oxford, though the date in Roman numerals on the title page actually reads 1468 instead of 1478 – an unfortunate beginning for a press renowned for its high standards of accuracy. The guardians of OUP were often highly eccentric characters, from Archbishop Laud and Dr Fell in the 17th century to Henry Frowde, the first to bear the title "Publisher to the University", in the late 18th and early 19th centuries. His successor, Humphrey Milford, had notoriously unpredictable instincts but seemed invariably to be right, leading to considerable expansion at home and overseas.

OUP has had a succession of homes, including the Sheldonian Theatre and the Clarendon Building, the latter partly financed by the profits from the first edition of Lord Clarendon's *History of the Great Rebellion*. In 1830 it moved to its present home in Walton Street, a series of elegant buildings grouped, in true Oxford fashion, round a quadrangle complete with ornamental pond, lawn and copper beech. It has frequently had a London presence, too: a Bible warehouse in Paternoster Row, and later offices in nearby Amen House. All publishing is now based in Oxford.

Since World War II, OUP has been through various phases of development. In the early years, it concentrated on English literature and scholarly titles, but other academic publishers, such as Macmillan, became prominent and Cambridge shot ahead in disciplines such as archaeology and philosophy. In the late 1970s and early 1980s, OUP launched a catching-up operation to broaden its range and become a major publisher in the main academic disciplines. Its

range is now larger than any other university press.

One of OUP's unusual features is a large and flourishing music department. This not only publishes sheet music and major editions of classical works, but promotes the performance, recording and hire of the work of over 20 contemporary composers.

Although OUP played a major role in the history of printing, including being the first printers in Britain to use the beautifully designed "Fell types", brought over from the Netherlands by Dr Fell, its own printing works closed in the late 1980s. It now outsources all printing, although many important artefacts and papers relating to its history are preserved in the OUP Museum (visits by appointment only, tel: 01865 556767). ❏

RIGHT: no wonder printers have to wear glasses...

THE MOTORING HERITAGE

Many famous names in motoring have had associations with Oxfordshire:
the Morris Minor, the Mini and now the BMW and Williams racing team

The career of William Richard Morris, Viscount Nuffield, has been described by British industrial historians as the biggest success story of the 20th century. His achievement had a profound effect on Oxford and the surrounding area, for it was through Morris's efforts that a major industry – motor manufacturing – was added to what had been a predominantly academic city. He was also one of the great benefactors of his time, distributing some £30 million to various charitable causes before he died in 1963 at the age of 85.

Morris cars were made in the district from 1912 and today the sprawling Cowley factory complex, on the ring road to the southeast of the city, is part of the Rover Group, which was bought by Germany's BMW in 1994 for £800 million (US$1,300 million). A little further out, some of Britain's most famous sports cars were made in the MG factory at Abingdon until it closed in 1981. Nostalgia for the marque lived on, however, and in 1995, as sports cars came into fashion again, Rover began manufacturing the MGF.

The William Morris story

William Morris was born in Worcester in 1877, but his parents were from Oxford and the family moved back to the city when he was a young child. He attended the Church School in Cowley, leaving at the age of 14 to become apprenticed to a bicycle repairer. Within months, and with just £4 capital, he had established his own cycle repair business in a shed behind his parents' house in James Street, Cowley St John.

Rebuilding old bicycles soon led to building new ones, the first order being for an abnormally large frame to suit the towering rector of nearby St Clement's Church. The young Morris became the local cycling champion and by 1901 his exploits and machines were so well known that he was encouraged to open a sales shop at 48 High Street, Oxford, with more

LEFT: original MGS are now collector's items.
RIGHT: Lord Nuffield in his later years.

extensive workshops round the corner in Queen's Lane.

Next came Morris motorcycles, or what would today be called mopeds – bicycles with a small De Dion engine added. Bigger premises, in disused stables at the junction of Longwall and Holywell Street, backing on to the gardens

of New College, were also used for garaging some of the city's increasing number of motor cars, particularly those belonging to rich undergraduates. With his mechanical skill and eye for a business opportunity, it was not long before the Longwall signboard read: "Morris Cycle Works – cycles and motors repaired".

Morris became an agent for a number of British car and motorcycle manufacturers. By 1910 he had given up making two-wheelers and built a new garage on the Longwall site. He began to consider producing a car of his own. It would be a small car of high quality, made in large numbers and sold at a low price. The way to achieve that, he concluded, was to reduce the cost of design, tooling and manufacture by purchasing all the major components from outside companies and simply assembling the cars in Oxford. Longwall was not big enough, so Morris moved out to the suburb of Cowley, to buildings that had once been Hurst's Grammar School (which his father had attended) and become the Temple Cowley military training college.

Appropriately this first car, delivered in 1913, was called the Morris Oxford. It cost £175 and became famous as the first of the "Bullnose"

> ## MARKET LEADER
>
> By the end of the 1920s, Morris was Britain's most successful car maker, producing one third of all the cars in the UK.

out of Cowley – but sales had reduced to a trickle. Faced with a stockpile of cars, William Morris took the bold step of slashing prices by as much as £200 a car – a lot of money then. While others scoffed, he said that sales would double – and he was right. By 1923 Morris was selling 20,000 cars a year; in 1925 demand reached 55,000.

New blood

Initially, the cars were manufactured by WRM Motors, which became Morris Motors in 1919.

Morrises, so-called because of the rounded shape of their brass radiators. The engines and gearboxes were supplied by White & Poppe of Coventry, the chassis frames imported from Belgium, and the bodies made by Charles Raworth & Sons of Oxford. A bigger, second model, with four seats instead of two and a more powerful engine supplied by the US firm Continental, was called the Cowley.

Morris sold 393 Oxfords in the first year and over 900 in 1914; this represented the beginning of mass production in Britain. After World War I, production increased sharply but so did costs and therefore prices. Then came the slump. By 1921, 60 cars a week were coming

Morris Garages continued as a separate enterprise in Oxford city centre and by the early 1920s William Morris was too busy with manufacturing to have much to do with the garages and was happy to leave them in the hands of a manager called Cecil Kimber.

Kimber also had ambitions as a car-maker and designed special, more rakish, bodies for the Morris Oxford and Cowley which were then sold as MG (for "Morris Garages") and carried the distinctive octagonal badge. The MG Super Sports models were so successful that by 1929 a separate MG factory was set up, first in Cowley and then Abingdon, from where the best-selling Midget sports cars emerged. It was the T-series successors to these that, 20 years later, converted a generation of young Americans to lightweight British sports cars.

As the company grew, the original idea of assembling from mostly bought-in components became less attractive and Morris started to make more of the vehicles themselves. The Cowley factory kept on expanding. It even had its own railway halt.

William Morris had been knighted in 1928, became a baron in 1934 and Viscount Nuffield in 1938, the last honour being awarded as much for his generosity to charities as for his success as an industrialist. He chose the name Nuffield

carefully unknotted string from parcels for future use – both habits inherited from his father and his own poorer days as a child. He insisted that an Ericsson telephone, installed in 1913, be retained until it could no longer be repaired, just a year before he died.

Asked to comment on his wealth, Lord Nuffield once said: "You can only wear one suit at a time." His own luxuries were a continuous supply of specially made cigarettes and long sea voyages to distant lands – travel for which he acquired a taste when he visited America to study the production methods of Henry Ford and others.

after the manor house in a small Oxfordshire village near Henley-on-Thames that he had made his home.

Though he became rich beyond dreams, Lord Nuffield was a man of simple tastes. He used the same small and modestly furnished office upstairs in the old school building at Cowley for 50 years; it was part of the Nuffield Press printing company before being converted into a new housing complex in the late 1990s.

His desk always had a pile of neatly sliced used envelopes to use as notepaper and he

LEFT: Morris manager Cecil Kimber with a 1923 MG.
ABOVE: old horsepower outside Morris's original shop.

Money for medicine

Lord Nuffield and his wife Elizabeth had no children and he was determined not to leave his fortune to be decimated by death duties. Medicine was a lifelong interest and in the 1920s he donated sums of money to hospitals in Birmingham, Coventry and London. In 1930 he supported the care of crippled children at the Wingfield Orthopaedic Hospital in Headington and later paid for the hospital to be rebuilt. He funded a new maternity wing at Oxford's Radcliffe Infirmary, and many other medical projects and new hospitals around the country. In 1937, he put up £900,000 to establish a new university establishment, Nuffield College, to the west of the city. However, World War II intervened and the foundation stone was not laid until 1949.

Although he loved Oxford, William Morris had not, in his earlier years, enjoyed friendly relations with the city authorities or the university. He was suspicious of graduates in business and for a long time would not employ anyone who had been through the university. Disagreement with the city council went back to 1913, when he had proposed buses as an alternative to trams to replace Oxford's horse-drawn trams. The council rejected the idea, so Morris bought a fleet of six buses and put them

The ruthless Mr Lord succeeded in restoring the company's fortunes but left in 1936 when Nuffield refused him a share of the increased profits he had generated. Lord swore revenge – and not long afterwards joined Morris's arch-rival, Austin, in Birmingham.

Growing concern

Morris continued to absorb weaker rivals, however; in 1938, the company took over Riley. In 1939, just before the conversion of all their factories to aid the war effort, Morris, MG, Riley and Wolseley were consolidated to become the Nuffield Organisation.

into operation illegally. His audacity paid off, for the bus service was popular, the city was spared ugly and disruptive trams, and he eventually sold the vehicles to the council.

Nuffield's relationships with his employees were less benevolent. He was generally thought a fair, if tough, employer but was notorious for his autocratic style, unwilling to heed advice even from his senior colleagues. By the early 1930s, after the acquisition of many of Morris' suppliers as well as the rival firm Wolseley, the Morris empire was badly in need of reorganisation. Leonard Lord, a forceful character was, to the surprise of many, appointed managing director of Morris Motors in 1933.

THE MINI

In August 1999, 70,000 people and 5,000 Minis from all over the world converged at Silverstone racing circuit to celebrate the 40th anniversary of their legendary car. The Mini was reputedly designed on a restaurant tablecloth by Sir Alec Issigonis as a blueprint for the smallest car for four adults. At its launch, it cost a mere £500. Since then over 5.3 million have been sold. It became a fashion icon in the 1960s, associated with such stars as Twiggy and Peter Sellers, and even starred with Michael Caine in the 1969 film *The Italian Job*. Production stopped at Cowley in 1968, but in 1996 Rover announced that a revamped Mini model was planned for the new millennium.

During World War II, the Cowley plant produced battle tanks, repaired aeroplanes, and made Tiger Moth trainers, as well as engines for military aircraft. An airstrip was built on the factory site.

When peace returned and car production re-commenced, the question of a merger arose once again. Sir Herbert, later Lord Austin, had died during the war. Leonard Lord was in charge at Austin, which had more modern designs and had overtaken Morris' sales. He approached his old boss Nuffield and clearly took delight in

THE MORRIS MINOR

Lord Nuffield reputedly did not like the post-war Morris Minor, which he said looked "like a poached egg". Nevertheless, it became the first British car to sell a million.

From then, the future of Morris and the activity of the Cowley plant became enmeshed in the BMC grand plan. In 1968, after further mergers, BMC became British Leyland.

The unremarkable 1971 Morris Marina was the last car to carry the Morris name. Eventually, after a troubled period of heavy losses which led to government control, British Leyland became the Rover Group and, in 1988, a division of British Aerospace. The new owners concentrated Rover executive car production in the Cowley body plant and

becoming the dominant partner in a deal that created the British Motor Corporation in 1952. Lord Nuffield, by then 75 years old, was appointed chairman of BMC but retired after just six months.

BMC was Britain's biggest motor manufacturer. There was a fusion between Nuffield and Austin products from an early stage, perhaps best exemplified by the most important British small car of the immediate post-war era, the Morris Minor, which quickly adopted an engine that originated at Austin.

shut down Cowley North and South, which included Morris's original buildings. With the help of Honda, Rover's fortunes were reversed. But the Japanese, after heavy investment, were shocked when British Aerospace abruptly sold the company to the Bavaria-based BMW.

While that sale meant the end of UK-owned, large-scale car manufacturing in Britain, the Oxford area still nurtures home-grown success on a smaller scale. Because of the engineering facilities available, it has a new role as a centre of the racing car industry, in which Britain is still a leading player. Reynard, the country's largest racing car maker, is based at Bicester, and the Williams racing team operates from Didcot. ❑

LEFT: the popular Morris Minor (in the foreground).
ABOVE: the even more popular Mini.

THE ACADEMIC LIFE

Dons and students have always encouraged an image of effortless superiority.
But to what extent is this assumption of elitism still justified?

The image of Oxford conveyed in countless films and books has given rise to two great myths. The first is the so-called "Brideshead" image, after Evelyn Waugh's 1945 novel *Brideshead Revisited*, which shows beautiful young aristocrats living a life of eternal summer and champagne in ancient ivy-clad colleges. The 1911 novel *Zuleika Dobson* by Max Beerbohm also paints a similar picture.

The second myth is that of pale intellectuals and palaeolithic dons festering in crumbling cathedral-like libraries, their lives devoted to the study of Homer or Hegel.

Both myths are outdated; but try as it might, the university cannot completely break free from its past. The world still regards it as a bastion of punting and privilege.

Fact or fiction?

Certainly, Oxford is very different from any other university in the world, except perhaps Cambridge – once referred to rather preciously in Oxford as "the other place". To differentiate itself, Oxford has its dons, scouts, tutorial system, Union, Boat Race and balls. But the people who inhabit the place are not, in reality, all that different from students elsewhere.

A recent survey showed that, politically, only one in four Oxford students supports the Conservative party. The most-read national newspapers, according to one survey, are *The Independent*, a middle-of-the-road, rather bland, quality paper, and *The Sun,* the sensation-seeking tabloid. Over a quarter of students admit to being virgins and about three-quarters describe themselves as "very or fairly ambitious".

However, there is a very high proportion of students – around half – who were educated at fee-paying schools, compared with a figure of 20 percent in higher education nationally. What's more, the proportion of entrants from state-run schools is static, and no one predicts

that the trend towards favouring the children of the wealthy will be reversed. Indeed, the retiring treasurer of Somerville, Margaret Thatcher's old college, recently warned parents: "Government assistance in the form of a grant or loan no longer provides sufficient funds to support an undergraduate in Oxford. Parents have to learn

they must take out an insurance policy when the child is two. It's tough, very tough. But you can't expect the state to provide; parents must get that into their heads."

There is also a relatively low percentage of women (41 percent). Mixed colleges were not introduced until the 1970s, and Oxford is still very much a male-dominated institution, with a minority of women dons (only 25 percent).

The myth of Oxford as a book-lined ivory tower is not entirely without foundation either. Academic concerns are still very much a priority; and, although Oxford no longer enjoys the pre-eminent status it once did, university departments find it relatively easy to attract

PRECEDING PAGES: college custodians conferring at Christ Church. **LEFT:** the recipients at a graduation ceremony. **RIGHT:** students at exam time.

funding from industry, especially in the sciences. One university fund-raising group, the Development Programme for Oxford, trades on Oxford's elitist image and has raised over £225 million since it was set up in 1988. So the university must be held partly responsible for propagating its own myth.

The academic life

Oxford's academic reputation is second to none, although its teaching is sometimes criticised for being too intense and too traditional. The intensity springs from the fact that terms are only eight weeks long (compared to at least 10 at most other British universities) and students are required to complete a minimum of one essay or problem-sheet a week, and sometimes as many as two or three. And the rigidly traditional nature of many of the courses is quite exceptional – for example, law students are required to study Roman Law, and English students have to study Anglo-Saxon.

However, the university's famous tutorial system of one-to-one teaching means that most courses are quite unstructured. Science students may have compulsory lectures and practicals, but for Arts undergraduates there is still little formal teaching apart from the one hour a week

THE "OTHER" UNIVERSITY

The name of Oxford University is world-famous, but another institution – Oxford Brookes University (formerly Oxford Poly) – has grown in prominence recently, and now has 14,500 students. Courses are modular, with students examined on core components of their subject at the end of each term, instead of in a single "final" exam.

Brookes does not claim to compete academically with its traditional neighbour and points out that its students come from different backgrounds, with different expectations. Sporting rivalry exists, however, and Brookes supporters are keen to point out that their university rowing team has beaten both Oxford and Cambridge.

spent with a tutor.

The system works brilliantly if the student and tutor are "compatible", but it can backfire badly. The traditional picture of the tutorial – an ancient, book-lined study, an even more ancient don sipping sherry, a timorous student stumbling through his Aristotle – still holds true. But "new-fangled" seminars are becoming increasingly popular.

Lectures can still be solemn occasions. The students rise as the gown-clad don enters the lecture hall. The don then, all too often, mumbles semi-coherently for an hour. Exams are even more solemn. All students taking exams must wear "sub-fusc", a mode of dress descended from 13th-century ecclesiastical costume. It consists of dark suit, gown, white tie and mortar-board for men; gown, white blouse and black tie, skirt and stockings for women.

Students sit a preliminary exam, called Mods or Prelims, in their first year. Finals, which were first set in 1807, are taken in the summer of the third year. Students are awarded a degree, or "Final Honour School", of either a First, 2:1, 2:2 or Third. About 50 percent are awarded a 2:1, which in practice is what most students hope for. In the late 1990s, moves were under way to alter the structure of the Oxford degree radically, with plans to introduce a modular system of assessment and give equal weight to exams in each year of the course, instead of a single hurdle of a final exam. In some subjects students now have the option of writing a dissertation rather than staking everything on the single exam system.

Student life

The student's way of life has remained essentially unchanged for hundreds of years. Training for the ministry as an undergraduate's principal objective began to decline in the 19th century, and over the years new subjects have been added so that there are now 18 separate faculties. But all students' lives are still shaped by the fact that they are members of a college – and that is how they think of themselves, rather than as members of a faculty.

The college has always been much more than just a place of residence; lectures and exams are organised by the university, but the colleges are responsible for a student's weekly tutorials and classes. In addition, the college is the centre of the student's social life. Every college has sports facilities and organised teams in most sports, plus a bar and a Junior Common Room. JCRs, which were first formed in the 1890s, usually provide newspapers and a television set for the use of students. All the colleges have numerous clubs, some of which are hundreds of years old; these can be musical, cultural and academic in orientation or purely social dining and drinking societies. You can guess which have the most members.

Most colleges provide their students with accommodation for at least two years, some of

it in modern buildings, but much of it in the college itself. Living in an ancient college room is a unique experience – romantic, stimulating and extremely draughty. Most students have to "live out" at some stage or another, usually sharing a house with other students. The average rent in Oxford is high (around £80 a week) and the rising price of college accommodation in the 1990s provoked some normally unmilitant students into staging rent strikes.

In addition, the cost of a social life is considerable. One recent survey showed that more than two-thirds of students expected to owe over £3,000 by the time they graduated.

Concerns about the welfare of Oxford students are nothing new. The suicide rate has always been very high, and 43 percent of students claimed to have suffered from bouts of depression or anxiety. There are waiting lists for psychotherapy.

However, all is not doom and gloom. The city's bars, pubs, clubs and cinemas do a brisk trade during term-time, and some are almost deserted during the vacations. If anything, Oxford students are notorious for "japes" – many see alcohol as the easiest antidote to essays. Complaints about student indiscipline are as old as the university itself: Proctors were appointed to enforce discipline as early as 1248.

LEFT: students at exam time. **RIGHT:** taking a break on the lawn at Magdalen College.

The don's life

All teaching at Oxford was originally conducted by clergymen, although this practice ended a long time ago. Oxford academics are still universally known as "dons".

Not all dons actually do any teaching. Many students are taught by postgraduate students, or Junior Research Fellows, who are in most cases appointed for a three-year period. The next step up is a Lecturership, a permanent teaching post at a faculty attached to a particular college.

FAMOUS DONS

Famous "dons", from the Latin dominus (master), have included Lewis Carroll, A.J. Ayer, J.R.R. Tolkien, C.S. Lewis, Iris Murdoch and Mary Warnock.

on TV but too youthful to be accepted as an academic. The "Great and Good don" who has the ear of the Prime Minister is dying out, and in fact many feel the prestige of being a don is beginning to wane in the eyes of the public.

Recent years have witnessed huge changes in the way that most dons work. Largely gone is the old ethos of ivory tower exclusivity and cloistered college life, to be replaced by the pressures of chasing research grants and meeting exacting academic standards. Faculties now have to

A Lecturer can then become a Reader, with fewer teaching duties and more opportunity to concentrate on his or her own research. Readers may become Professors, who are responsible for overseeing a particular subject area, in which they are said to hold a "Chair".

Oxford dons live a fairly comfortable life. Their accommodation is provided by their college, they have the right to dine at High Table, and of course they have long holidays. There are as many different types of don as there are student. Some never leave the library (the "old fogey"). Others appear regularly on television (the "trendy young don"). Then there is the "young fogey", who is too untrendy to appear

prove their worth to government and other funding agencies by producing quantifiable and quality-tested research in the form of books, articles and papers produced by their members. Presentations must be made to bodies such as the Economic and Social Research Council, which funds postgraduate research programmes and enables academics to pursue their specific areas of interest. This means that dons are expected to publish regularly, take part in the international conference circuit and generally market their academic work in a highly competitive world.

Clearly, the stress levels are higher in fields such as technology and computer sciences than in say, medieval French, but the brave new world of academic tendering and the information highway has certainly not left the Oxford dons unaffected.

The university currently has 194 Professors, 91 Readers and 954 Lecturers, but many Chairs have lain vacant through lack of funds. Fewer graduates are seeking to become dons and, of those who do, many decide to leave for the private sector before they are 30, owing to poor prospects and salaries.

College figures

Aside from the don, the scout is probably the best-known Oxford figure. Scouts date back to the early 18th century and have traditionally been attached to a particular staircase of a particular college. As late as the 1950s they performed the role of a manservant, waking up their students in the morning, cleaning their rooms, preparing light meals and running errands for them.

Nowadays nearly all scouts are women and act simply as cleaning ladies or waitresses in hall. The close bond that used to exist between a student and his scout has all but disappeared, though some of today's scouts have their favourites among their students and may perform little extra services for them.

The other familiar college figure is the porter, who fills the duties of receptionist and security guard at the entrance to every college. They are involved in college discipline, and a minority are notorious for their obstinacy and rudeness. Each college is headed by what is variously titled the Rector, Master, Principal, President, Warden or Provost, who is the supreme authority within the college, as well as the face the college presents to the outside world.

First impressions

The chaotic first week of their first term is an experience no one forgets. First-year students, or "Freshers", go through a hectic schedule, dominated by two events: Matriculation and Freshers' Fair.

The Matriculation ceremony is a ritual by which students are officially admitted as members of the university, and is conducted by the Vice-Chancellor in the Sheldonian Theatre.

LEFT: a don in his den.
RIGHT: a women's rowing team in action.

Students dress up in sub-fusc and listen to various Latin formulae. Other important first-week ceremonies include registering at the Bodleian Library, at which students have to swear, among other things, not to "kindle flame" in the building.

But the Freshers' Fair is the craziest, most diverse event of the year. The Schools' building on the High Street is invaded by stalls representing all the different university clubs and societies, hoping to sign up Freshers as new members. There are over 200 clubs to choose from, ranging from the sensible (the Strategic Studies Group, the Industrial Society) to the

surreal (the Pooh Sticks Club, the Heterosexual Decadence Society).

The end of the week is marked by a series of college "subject parties", at which the second and third-year students in each subject ply their Fresher counterparts with large quantities of alcohol. If students can survive the first week, they can survive anything Oxford is likely to throw at them.

Acting, journalism, politics

Talented and/or ambitious students will seek to climb quickly to the top of the organisations that control acting, journalism and politics in Oxford. This has been a traditional preparation for the assumption of real power in later life.

The clique-filled world of Oxford drama is presided over by OUDS, the Oxford University Dramatic Society. Many colleges also have their own theatre groups. The standard of the productions varies, but the best are very good. The summer shows, held outdoors in college quads or gardens, are especially popular, despite the frequent inclement weather. Non-students are equally welcome.

Oxford journalism has long been dominated

JUST AN UGLY RUMOUR

Prime Minister Tony Blair was unimpressed with student politics, and avoided the Labour Club, preferring to spend time with his budding rock group, Ugly Rumour.

political clubs are also well-trodden training-grounds for future politicians; the Conservative Association, for example, can point to Margaret Thatcher as just one of many of its ex-presidents who made the big time.

However, it must be said that Oxford students are generally quite apolitical. A recent survey showed that only 42 percent had attended political meetings or discussions. And, although most students go to plays, read *Cherwell* and *Isis* and attend debates at the Union, only a minority – known

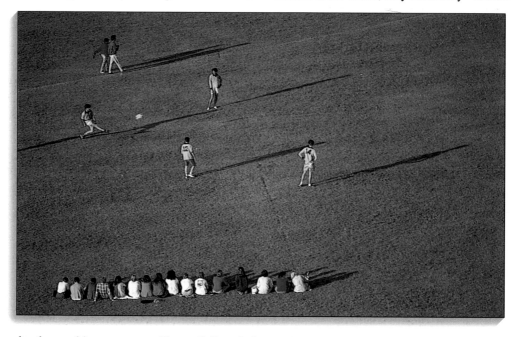

by the weekly newspaper *Cherwell* (founded in 1920) and the literary magazine *Isis* (founded in 1897). Several national newspaper editors were former *Cherwell* editors. Even Rupert Murdoch once worked on the paper. The usual stereotypes are that *Cherwell* is frivolous and *Isis* pretentious, but both regularly win national awards and are worth looking at if you can get hold of a copy (they are both distributed in the colleges' lodges).

But the Oxford Union debating society, by turns frivolous and influential, is by far the best-known student institution in Oxford, perhaps in the world. Five British Prime Ministers were once officers of the Union. The various

to the rest as "hacks" – seek to become actively involved.

Sporting life

Sport is a part of the very fabric of Oxford University, not just because of its long traditions or the nationally renowned events that still take place each year, but also because of the sheer numbers of students who are regular participants in one or other of the great range of sports played.

The highlight of the sporting year is the Boat Race. Held in early April, the race from Putney to Mortlake on the River Thames in London is the focus for the Oxford–Cambridge rivalry which dominates Oxford sport. It was first held in 1829, since when it has been raced almost every year, with the two universities just about neck and neck in their tally of wins. In 1877 it was a dead-heat.

The Oxford versus Cambridge Varsity Matches first began with a cricket match in 1827. They are now held in every sport, and many are given wide coverage in the national newspapers. Two are televised: the Boat Race (second only to football's FA Cup final with 13 million viewers) and the Varsity rugby match, held at Twickenham in December. Training is deadly serious, as those who get to play in a Varsity Match are awarded a "Blue", which is perhaps as equally prestigious as gaining a First Class degree.

Sport is also taken very seriously at college level. Each college produces several rugby, cricket, hockey and football teams who compete in leagues and in an inter-college knock-out competition known as Cuppers, and up to 10 or 12 rowing eights, who compete in Torpids in winter and in Eights in summer, when the winning college is proclaimed Head of the River. Oriel College has a remarkable rowing record, having won the Torpids every year since 1972.

Not all Oxford sport is taken so seriously, however Brasenose College won Tortoise-Racing Cuppers in 1989, their champion tortoise Addington beating Balliol's reigning queen Rosa Luxemburg by "inches". There are also Cuppers matches in Korfball, American football, croquet, Eton Fives, sailing and orienteering. Perhaps all that cycling gives Oxford students a sporting disposition.

The social life

Predictably, Oxford students do most of their socialising at pubs and parties. But for a few weeks every summer they indulge in the unashamed opulence and extravagance of the summer balls.

Some colleges have a ball every year, some bi-annually, and the bigger ones every three years. These are known as "Commemoration Balls" and are the most prestigious – and expensive. There are also minor balls and events, held by the smaller colleges, or by those that see balls as elitist. But are they? Yes, the balls are extravagant: dress is black tie and dinner jackets for men, brightly coloured ballgowns for women – and the revellers enjoy a combination of dancing, drinking and mild debauchery until the obligatory 6am champagne breakfast. And, yes, they are expensive: the equivalent of an average week's wages for a double dining ticket, and anachronistically priced in guineas (£1.05) rather than pounds. And yet the vast majority of Oxford students go to at least one ball during their time at the university, considering them a harmless excuse for dressing up and having a good time.

The summer is generally the most active social season, as it brings students out on to the river to go punting, and out on to the streets to raise money for charity during Rag Week. But long gone are the extravagances of the 1930s when the "gilded youth" of Britain's great families supposedly squandered fortunes in a day and flitted from lunch party to cocktail party to dinner party.

Private dining societies with names like the Disraeli Society and the Russell Club still exist, but today's social scene tends to reflect the wider social mix of today's Oxford. Parties are generally unpretentious and alcoholic – they are also becoming more infrequent as increased

LEFT: all eyes on a football game.
RIGHT: having fun at the boat race.

academic pressure takes its toll. However, Oxford is still alive on Friday and Saturday evenings with groups of students leaving their favourite pubs (the King's Arms, the Turf Tavern, the Bear or the White Horse) and heading for a party, easily recognisable by the alcoholic offering each clutches under his or her arm – today's party invitations invariably include the magic words "Please Bring A Bottle".

Students and the town

The relationship between the university and the city of Oxford has historically been one of hostility and mutual suspicion. This "Town ver-

However, violent clashes are quite rare – except in Cowley. And students would probably avoid the Blackbird Leys area, scene of the famous joy-riders a few years ago. Because of its cheap housing, Cowley is very popular with students, but they do not always mix well with the locals. With Cowley Road itself famous for its curry restaurants, the area's population includes many Caribbean and Asian immigrants, along with a large "alternative" or counter-cultural community.

But there are some institutions whose status doesn't quite fit the Town/Gown stereotype. Principal among these are the numerous sec-

sus Gown" rivalry has been the cause of many deaths in the course of Oxford's turbulent past but nowadays is really restricted to sports' matches between university and city teams and the occasional drunken scuffle outside a pub on a Friday night.

In some ways Oxford is two cities, with certain shops and pubs never visited by students because they are "too townie", and others shunned by locals on the grounds that they are "too full of students". The Bear and the King's Arms are probably the most student-filled pubs, while the Crown on Cornmarket and the O.X. One on Queen Street are still more or less "no-go areas" for students, especially at weekends.

retarial and tutorial colleges, which find it easy to attract both students and teachers because of the proximity of the university. Students at secretarial colleges are universally known to Oxford University students as "seccies" and are often accused (in most cases unfairly) of coming to Oxford more to snare an eligible bachelor than to learn to type.

In the summer, many students make a little extra money by teaching at language schools or giving guided tours to tourists. This is generally considered to be the lowest known form of paid employment. ❑

ABOVE: a formal dinner at a college.

Women:
Who Let *Them* In?

Never let it be said that the colleges of Oxford University do not adapt to changing social conditions while keeping alive traditional ceremonies. One of these is the Christ Church Rain Dance, an elaborate ritual in which a dozen young men gather in an inner quadrangle of the college and sing, at some volume, incantations to their gods. These anthems are accompanied by the symbolic removal of each of the young men's garments until, clad only in socks and shoes, they dance around the quad directing their penises towards the upper windows of the main accommodation block.

This rich and colourful display, threatened with extinction thanks to disciplinary measures, is part of a tradition stretching back to 1981, when women were first admitted to the college.

Oxford's very cautious approach to accepting women in men's colleges means that fewer than one-third of its undergraduates are women. Its attempts to broaden its intake and strengthen its appeal to state school students have, up to now, had the unfortunate effect of *reducing* the number of women, because girls in comprehensive sixth forms are rarely encouraged to fix their sights on the dreaming spires. Balliol, where the Junior Common Room voted to make a special play for state school applicants, has five first-year men to each woman.

The numerical imbalance of students and tutors means that women are likely to be isolated in tutorials. "The whole of Oxford education, especially in Arts subjects, rests on your relationship with your tutor," observed Claire Athis Edwards, a student at Christ Church. "Tutorials are taken in pairs and you hear of women who say that they are completely dominated by their male tutorial partner. The tutor asks *his* opinion all the time. Even if your tutor is not overtly sexist, your male colleagues will have a relationship where they're on first-name terms, they'll go out for lunch together, whereas my relationship with my tutor is very much a teacher-pupil thing."

Individual colleges have their own response to their female undergraduates. Brasenose saw the emergence of The Moosehunters, a group of young warriors who strapped antlers to their heads and crashed around in pursuit of first-year maidens. One Junior Common Room debated a motion that:

RIGHT: female students still cause controversy.

"Women should be hired out on the same basis as college punts."

Colleges are gradually formulating codes to enable women to put their case to various levels of authority. In real life, the procedures are not widely used and the women seem well able to fend for themselves. St Hilda's is now the only single-sex college.

What disturbs some students deeply is the record of women's examination results over the period since Oxford went more or less co-educational. The figures show that in 1958, 8.1 percent of men and 7.9 percent of women got first-class degrees. Throughout the 1960s and early 1970s, the numbers climbed: in 1973, for example, 12 percent of

men and 12.1 percent of women got firsts. The shock came in the mid-1980s when integration was established – if unequally – and it was found that 16.1 percent of men got firsts compared to only 8.9 percent of women. In 1995 the university's equal opportunities committee spent £10,000 studying the imbalance, but this didn't halt the trend: in 1996, 28.6 percent of men were awarded firsts as against 16.6 percent of women.

Some argue that there just aren't enough intelligent women at Oxford to keep the figures up; others believe that Oxford is male-dominated not only in the adversarial tutorial system but in an all-pervasive way. Statistics, as always, provide the basis for dispute, so the argument may well be eternal. ❑

OXFORD'S COLLEGES: WHO'S WHO

Football fans seem restrained compared to supporters of individual colleges.

We cut through the snobbery to assess their strengths and weaknesses

ALL SOULS'

Founded: 1437
Number of students: varies,
graduate students only.

All Souls' is the only Oxford college not to have accepted undergraduate students. It stands on the High Street but can also be reached from Radcliffe Square, from where its famous twin towers are best viewed. The Front Quad has remained virtually unchanged since the college's foundation, as has the chapel, and there is a sundial designed by Christopher Wren, a former All Souls' bursar. To be elected a Fellow of All Souls' is perhaps the highest academic honour in the university.

BALLIOL

Founded: 1263
Number of students: 350
Alumni: Harold Macmillan,
Graham Greene, H.H. Asquith,
Hilaire Belloc, Edward Heath,
Roy Jenkins, Aldous Huxley, Denis Healey.

Occupying a huge area between Broad Street and Magdalen Street, Balliol is one of the oldest, biggest, wealthiest and most prestigious colleges in the university. Balliol's academic reputation is second to none, and its students tend to be dynamic and successful, both at Oxford and in public life. The great scholars Wycliffe and Jowett are associated with Balliol, as is Adam Smith.

The college has a strong political tradition, and went through an especially radical phase in the 1960s. Formal Hall, the saying of Grace and the wearing of gowns have all been abolished. It was also one of the first colleges to begin accepting large numbers of non-public school-educated and overseas students, fostering a cosmopolitan atmosphere. The architecture is serious and uninspired, but the place buzzes with activity.

LEFT: a "mighty fine place", as Samuel Pepys said of Oxford in 1668.

BRASENOSE

Founded: 1509
Number of students: 330
Alumni: Jeffrey Archer, John
Buchan, Colin Cowdrey, William
Golding, Michael Palin, Robert
Runcie.

Situated right in the centre of the city, the college tends to be overshadowed by the surrounding splendour of the Bodleian Library and Radcliffe Camera, although the Old Quadrangle is noted for its colourful sundial. Historically "middle-of-the-road", Brasenose has built up a reasonable reputation for sport – mostly rowing – and on the academic side it is especially strong in Law. It acquired its name from a rather unusual door-knocker ("brazen nose") which now hangs in the hall.

CHRIST CHURCH

Founded: 1546
Number of students: 540
Alumni: Sir Robert Peel,
William Ewart Gladstone,
Anthony Eden, Lord Hailsham,
Auberon Waugh, W. H. Auden.

Originally founded in 1525 by Cardinal Wolsey and re-founded by Henry VIII in 1546, "The House" is Oxford's largest and best-known college (although it is always referred to as just Christ Church). It is the one college *every* tourist visits, if only to be shouted at by the bowler-hatted "Bulldogs" on duty there. The grandiose architecture is imposing to the point of being intimidating, especially Tom Quad, with its famous tower and fountain – and the college even has its own cathedral and picture gallery.

For many years the cradle of the British aristocracy, Christ Church still produces its fair share of bishops and MPs, though there is a slightly wider social mix at the college today. It remains one of the top colleges both academically and in sport, despite not trying very hard at either.

CORPUS CHRISTI

Founded: 1517
Number of students: 200
Alumni: Sir Isaiah Berlin,
William Waldegrave, Matthew
Arnold, John Ruskin, Lord
Beloff.

Sandwiched between Christ Church and Merton, Corpus is the smallest college but boasts a main quad that is among the most beautiful in Oxford – its most notable feature being the famous Pelican Sundial. In 1989 Corpus topped the Norrington Table, the unofficial academic ranking of the colleges. Academic standards have traditionally been very high, but the college is also known for its tolerance and friendliness. In addition, it is the home of the annual tortoise races, the slowest spectator sport in the university.

EXETER

Founded: 1314
Number of students: 300
Alumni: Richard Burton, J.R.R.
Tolkien, Sir Roger Bannister,
Tariq Ali, Alan Bennett, Ned
Sherrin, Russell Harty, William Morris.

One of the three Turl Street colleges, Exeter is an architectural mish-mash of styles, as bits were added on over the centuries. The Victorian chapel tends to look especially odd as only its tall spire is visible from the street, the rest being hidden inside the college. Exeter has historical links with the West Country, and has traditionally been known as an unpretentious, slightly unremarkable college.

HERTFORD

Founded: 1740
Number of students: 330
Alumni: Evelyn Waugh,
Jonathan Swift, John Donne,
Charles James Fox.

A hall for students known as "Hart Hall" was established as long ago as 1282, but Hertford College has had a chequered history and has been plagued by financial problems, which remain to this day. Its most remarkable and attractive feature is the famous Bridge of Sighs (not the one in Venice), which connects the two halves of the college. This attracts hordes of tourists, partly because of its proximity to the Bodleian Library.

JESUS

Founded: 1571
Number of students: 300
Alumni: Harold Wilson,
T.E. Lawrence (of Arabia).

Jesus was founded by Queen Elizabeth I, but much of the money behind the foundation was provided by a Welshman called Hugh Price, and the college retains very strong links with Wales. The joke is that if you run into the college and shout "Jones!" 100 people will stick their heads out of their windows. Architecturally the least interesting of the Turl Street colleges, Jesus has fallen over backwards to keep a low profile over the years – except in 1974, when it became the first of the previously all-male colleges to admit women.

KEBLE

Founded: 1870
Number of students: 400
Alumni: Imran Khan,
Andreas Whittam-Smith.

Keble was originally founded with the intention of making an Oxford education more accessible to people from different social backgrounds. Links with the Church (John Keble was a leading figure of the Oxford Movement) ensure the college retains a strong social conscience. Its buildings have aroused enormous controversy. The main quad is a neo-Gothic palace of red-and-white chequered bricks, with the appearance of a Victorian mental institution. Other quads are all-modern glass and steel – the notorious bar often being compared to a space ship. Local rival St John's College boasts a "Demolish Keble Society", the membership requirement of which is to bring along a brick removed from Keble to your first meeting. It is a dynamic college, traditionally active in sport and politics (both Left and Right), with academic achievement especially strong in the sciences.

LADY MARGARET HALL

Founded: 1878
Number of students: 350
Alumni: Antonia Fraser,
Benazir Bhutto.

Its out-of-town location and beautiful gardens make this college idyllic in summer, though it does look like a prison from the front. LMH was the first "academic hall" for women at Oxford – it became a full college only in 1960 and went mixed in 1978. It is known for its general tolerance, though it has been radical enough to stage an anti-pornography protest.

LINCOLN

Founded: 1427
Number of students: 250
Alumni: John Le Carré,
John Wesley.
One of the most beautiful sights in Oxford is the view up Turl Street towards All Saints' Church (now the Lincoln College library). The college itself is rather small, but very picturesque. It was originally founded as a "small college" in order to create a friendly, cosy atmosphere – a tradition that is still strongly adhered to. Lincoln enjoys long-standing rivalry with the other Turl Street colleges, Exeter and Jesus.

MAGDALEN

Founded: 1458
Number of students: 350
Alumni: Oscar Wilde, Dudley
Moore, Sir John Betjeman, Lord
Denning, Desmond Morris,
Cardinal Wolsey, Edward VIII.
Pronounced "maudlin", Magdalen's academic traditions are as fine as its romantic buildings. They include the tower overlooking Magdalen Bridge from which the choir sings on May Morning (built in the 1490s), Cloister Quad and the Regency New Buildings. The gardens are just as impressive, with over a mile of riverside walks and the famous Deer Park. Magdalen probably captures the spirit of Evelyn Waugh's *Brideshead Revisited* more than any other college, and was for long the favourite choice for the sons of the upper classes. Traditionally weak in sport, the college's strength lies in the Arts, and its members have always been among the most social and outgoing of Oxford students.

MANSFIELD

Founded: 1886
Number of students: 135
Alumni: C.H. Dodd,
Nathaniel Micklem.
Originally a Congregationalist theological college, Mansfield has the advantage of beautiful and tranquil surroundings in a fairly central location off Holywell Street. The

college is historically short of cash and strong in the Arts. In undergraduate life, it contributes more than its fair share to journalism, and its Women's Group has been notably active.

MERTON

Founded: 1264
Number of students: 250
Alumni: John Wycliffe,
T.S. Eliot, Kris Kristofferson,
Robert Morley, Jeremy Isaacs.
Merton is proud to have the oldest quad in the university, large and beautiful gardens and a fine academic pedigree. From the cobblestones of Merton Street to the medieval library in Mob Quad to the old city wall that borders the garden, this college constantly delights the eye. It is noted both for high academic standards and a lively, outgoing collection of undergraduates.

NEW

Founded: 1379
Number of students: 380
Alumni: Tony Benn, John
Galsworthy, Lord Longford,
John Fowles, Richard Cross-
man, Hugh Gaitskell.
New College looks anything but new. In fact, it's one of the oldest colleges in the university, and many of the buildings, including the front quad, dining hall, chapel and cloisters, have survived from the original foundations and look positively medieval. The college has a kind of austere beauty – certainly it is difficult not to be impressed by its size and sheer solidity. It's a prestigious and well-known college, with well-established links to the Civil Service and to Winchester (it was founded by William of Wykeham). Strong in both sport (especially rowing) and academia, New is currently considered to be one of the main social centres of university life.

NUFFIELD

Founded: 1958
Number of students: 90
Alumni: James Callaghan.
Nuffield College stands rather apart from the rest of the colleges on the road to the railway station. Built thanks to an endowment from the motor magnate Lord Nuffield (William Morris), it accepts postgraduate students only, specialising in

research into social, economic and political problems. Visiting research fellows from the fields of business, politics and the trade unions engage in work that the college describes as making "a bridge between the academic and non-academic worlds". Like most postgraduate colleges, Nuffield is a serious sort of place, strong on research facilities and weak on sport and entertainment.

ORIEL

Founded: 1326
Number of students: 275
Alumni: Cecil Rhodes, Sir Walter Raleigh, Cardinal Newman, Beau Brummell, John Keble.
The Oriel rowing tradition is one of the strongest traditions in Oxford. The college has consistently dominated the river, especially in the past 20 years, and was the last college to remain all-male, admitting women only in 1985. The film *Oxford Blues* is considered an accurate portrayal of the college: hearty, traditional and not particularly academic. However, things are beginning to change now that the women have arrived. Oriel Square is a fantastically picturesque place, and is probably the most-filmed location in Oxford.

PEMBROKE

Founded: 1624
Number of students: 310
Alumni: Michael Heseltine, Samuel Johnson, William Fulbright.
A middle-of-the-road college, Pembroke is tucked away behind Carfax, and suffers from being opposite Christ Church. Equally undistinguished in both sport and academia, Pembroke has the doubtful accolade of being the finest darts-playing college in the university. Architecturally it is as unremarkable as the undergraduates it houses.

QUEEN'S

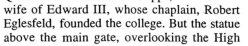

Founded: 1341
Number of students: 300
Alumni: Rowan Atkinson, Brian Walden, Edmund Halley.
Queen's is named after Philippa, wife of Edward III, whose chaplain, Robert Eglesfeld, founded the college. But the statue above the main gate, overlooking the High Street, is of Queen Caroline, wife of George II, who in the mid-18th century funded the building of its two unusual and impressive quads. The college has links with the north of England and is traditionally a sporting college, being especially strong in rugby (with appropriate beer cellar).

ST ANNE'S

Founded: 1893
Number of students: 400
Alumni: Baroness Young, Edwina Currie, Dame Cicely Saunders, Naomi Mitchison.
This former women's college looks like a 1970s polytechnic and many of its students certainly behave like those from a bygone age. Even so, it has developed a fearsome rugby-playing reputation, providing more than half of a recent Blues team. One of Oxford's more "unpretentious" colleges, St Anne's also does its bit for student drama and journalism.

ST CATHERINE'S

Founded: 1963
Number of students: 450
Alumni: Eric Partridge, David Hemery, J. Paul Getty.
Oxford's newest college is an architectural masterpiece or else a sprawling modern monstrosity, depending on your point of view. Designed by Danish architect Arne Jacobsen and situated out of town by the River Cherwell, it is very pleasant in summer. "Catz" has yet to perform a feat remarkable enough to attract the attention of the rest of the university, but the liberal establishment of the college (for example, it has no chapel) makes it popular with students.

ST EDMUND HALL

Founded: circa 1278
Number of students: 350
Alumni: Sir Robin Day, Terry Jones.
"Teddy Hall" is a compact college just off the High Street, whose buildings are an interesting combination of a delightful 17th-century front quad and several 1970s tower blocks. It has always been famous for sport, especially rugby – the college won Rugby Cuppers for nine successive years in the 1980s. It has an extraordinary library with a tall, book-lined

tower: it is in a converted church and students have to cross a graveyard to get to it.

ST HILDA'S

Founded: 1893
Number of students: 350
Alumnae: Barbara Pym,
Hermione Lee.
Just over Magdalen Bridge, St Hilda's lies on the banks of the River Cherwell, with superb views over Christ Church Meadows. It is the only remaining all-women college, but "Hildabeasts" are anything but cloistered, and are known for their active participation in university life. However, its continued single-sex status may have contributed to a decline in academic standards. The buildings are not ugly – even the modern ones.

ST HUGH'S

Founded: 1886
Number of students: 400
Alumni: Barbara Castle, Brigid
Brophy.
St Hugh's is a former women's college which went mixed in 1987. It is sited far out in North Oxford, on the extreme edge of the university area, so St Hugh's students are noted cyclists. The college grounds are said to be quite pleasant, but no one except St Hugh's students have actually seen them.

ST JOHN'S

Founded: 1555
Number of students: 350
Alumni: Robert Graves,
Kingsley Amis, Philip Larkin,
A.E. Housman, Dean Rusk,
Tony Blair.
It is sometimes said that you can walk all the way from Oxford to Cambridge on land owned by St John's. It is the richest Oxford college, and is said to own a fair chunk of Switzerland as well as large tracts of London's West End. The college's extreme wealth means glorious buildings and luxurious accommodation for the students (there are rumours of Jacuzzis). A new block – "a fish tank on stilts" – lets things down. Situated on St Giles (which it also owns), St John's has traditionally been the most academically successful college, consistently topping the Norrington Table, the unofficial academic standings.

ST PETER'S

Founded: 1929
Number of students: 280
Alumni: Edward Akufo
Addo.
St Peter's has long been considered a backwater of Oxford. Situated next to the ex-Oxford Prison, and rooted firmly to the bottom of the Norrington Table, it was mostly noted for the great ugliness of its buildings and the beer-drinking exploits of its students. However, this picture is no longer so accurate nowadays, according to those who have dared enter.

SOMERVILLE

Founded: 1879
Number of students: 350
Alumnae: Indira Gandhi,
Shirley Williams, Margaret
Thatcher, Dorothy L. Sayers,
Iris Murdoch, Esther Rantzen.
Baroness Thatcher's old college is not overly proud of its most illustrious graduate – in 1989 a bust of the Supreme Leader had to be taken off display and stored in a broom cupboard after being repeatedly daubed with graffiti. The college site up the Woodstock Road is grassy and pleasant, its members sociable, outward-looking and very dominant in most of the university's women's sports. Once an all-women college, it is now mixed. Its denizens used to like to point out that "Somerville girls can take care of themselves". Given their alumnae, who could doubt it?

TRINITY

Founded: 1554
Number of students: 250
Alumni: William Pitt the
Elder, Jeremy Thorpe, Terence
Rattigan, Anthony Crosland,
Miles Kington.
Trinity is essential viewing for visitors. The path leading from the wrought-iron gates on Broad Street through the beautiful college buildings to the spectacular gardens is a pilgrimage for every tourist. Generations of Trinity students have spent their summers playing croquet or just relaxing on the lawn, with the result that, despite its long history, the college has never really distinguished itself academically. It is, however, a great place for a picnic.

UNIVERSITY

Founded: 1249
Number of students: 370
Alumni: Willie Rushton,
Clement Attlee, Richard
Ingrams, Percy Bysshe Shelley.
The college is said to have been founded by King Alfred the Great in 812, but this remains disputed – as does the existence of the college ghost, that of one Obadiah Walker, a former Master of the college. What is certain is that "Univ" was the first Oxford college to be founded, and has never ceased to set high standards for its students, whether in the library or on the games field. The college has a particularly strong reputation in the sciences, and Univites have always been very active in university life – perhaps in order to escape the architecture of their own college, which has been likened by some to an Alcatraz on the High Street.

WADHAM

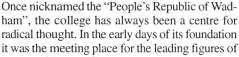

Founded: 1610
Number of students: 375
Alumni: Melvyn Bragg,
Michael Foot, Sir Christopher
Wren, Michael Checkland.
Once nicknamed the "People's Republic of Wadham", the college has always been a centre for radical thought. In the early days of its foundation it was the meeting place for the leading figures of the Scientific Revolution, who went on to form the Royal Society. Today it is known as a left-wing college, the majority of students entering the public sector after graduating. The Parks Road college has a long tradition of political activism – it is the only college to have its own Student Union rather than a Junior Common Room. The college buildings are attractive, especially the original front quad, but the notoriously trendy Wadhamites are more likely to be found in the neighbouring King's Arms than in Wadham.

WORCESTER

Founded: 1714
Number of students: 340
Alumni: Richard Adams,
Sir Alastair Burnett, Rupert
Murdoch.
Secluded Worcester is set in 26 acres (10 hectares) of grounds on the western edge of the university area. It stands on the site of the former Gloucester Hall, a Benedictine foundation of 1283 which was dissolved during the suppression of the monasteries. The college's front quad isn't really a quad at all – the money ran out after only three sides had been finished. However, Worcester is the only Oxford college to possess its own lake – complete with ducks. Its students are consequently a relaxed bunch. ❏

RIGHT: off duty in Turl Street – off to a ball.

HOW THE COLLEGES ARE GOVERNED

Oxford colleges are all different. Some are wealthy, others are poverty-stricken; some have a reputation for academic excellence, others are better known for their rugby. But all undergraduate colleges have a Governing Body of Fellows in charge of almost every aspect of college life.

Some Fellows are more important than others, although key posts, such as Senior Tutor or Dean, are normally filled by one Fellow for two or three years only. The Senior Tutor is concerned with academic achievement, while the Dean has the unenviable task of enforcing discipline. The other top jobs are the Bursar, responsible for finances, and of course, the Principal (or Warden, Master, Provost, President, Dean or Rector). The head of house is elected by all the Fellows and is recruited depending on his or her expertise and connections.

The Governing Body meets regularly to discuss the day-to-day running of the college. Some subcommittees, such as those supervising the college gardens or the wine cellar, are more popular than those dealing with investments or building works. Votes are taken on all issues, and there is often a surprising degree of articulate argument.

One of the Governing Body's duties is to sit in judgment on any student in trouble. There is a procedure for those who fail exams, involving a further test, with the threat of expulsion if the exam is failed again. The old punishments of gating (confinement to college) and rustication (sending out of residence for a term or two) are now obsolete, as are the arcane rules that made attendance at chapel compulsory or imposed curfews. Nowadays, serious disciplinary matters are more likely to involve vandalism or other forms of anti-social behaviour, and students are liable to be "sent down" (expelled) only for serious misdemeanours.

The undergraduates also have regular meetings, under the auspices of the Junior Common Room. Motions, some serious and others frivolous, are debated, with budding politicians trying out their oratorical skills.

PLACES

*A detailed guide to the city, with the principal sites
clearly cross-referenced by number to the maps*

What, precisely, gives Oxford its special appeal? In 1856 the American writer Nathaniel Hawthorne, in his *English Note-Books*, put forward an interesting theory: "The quality of the stone has a great deal to do with the apparent antiquity. It is a stone found in the neighbourhood of Oxford, and very soon begins to crumble and decay superficially, when exposed to the weather; so that 20 years do the work of a 100, so far as appearances go. If you strike one of the old walls with a stick, a portion of it comes powdering down. The effect of this decay is very picturesque."

Despite the subsequent destructive emissions of the internal combustion engine, Oxford's walls have yet to fall down. But the city retains its allure, seldom better expressed than by another 19th-century American writer, Henry James: "I walked along, thro' the lovely Christ Church meadow, by the river side and back through the town. It was a perfect evening and in the interminable British twilight the beauty of the whole place came forth with magical power. There are no words for these colleges. As I stood last evening within the precincts of mighty Magdalen, gazed at its great serene tower and uncapped my throbbing brow in the wild dimness of its courts, I thought that the heart of me would crack with the fulness of satisfied desire."

The setting is equally magical. Oxford is not a large town and you don't need to climb far up one of the dreaming spires in order to spy the green countryside which encircles it. Beyond the town centre traffic-jams and the undistinguished suburbs beckon the Cotswolds, their showpiece villages appearing to grow out of the earth, so perfect is their relationship with the landscape. For some, Stratford-upon-Avon will be a place of essential pilgrimage. For others, the sleepy Thames-side towns will hold more attractions.

Oxford provides a convenient base for exploring this rich part of England – that is, if you can drag yourself away from the dreaming spires. As Nathaniel Hawthorne put it: "The world, surely, has not another place like Oxford; it is a despair to see such a place and ever to leave it." ❏

PRECEDING PAGES: punting on the River Cherwell; the famous dreaming spires; graduation day at Queen's College.
LEFT: Magdalen College spires.

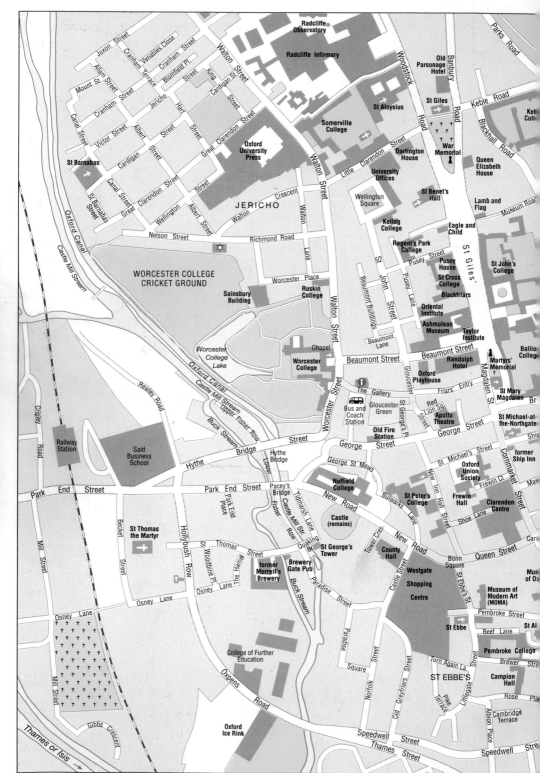

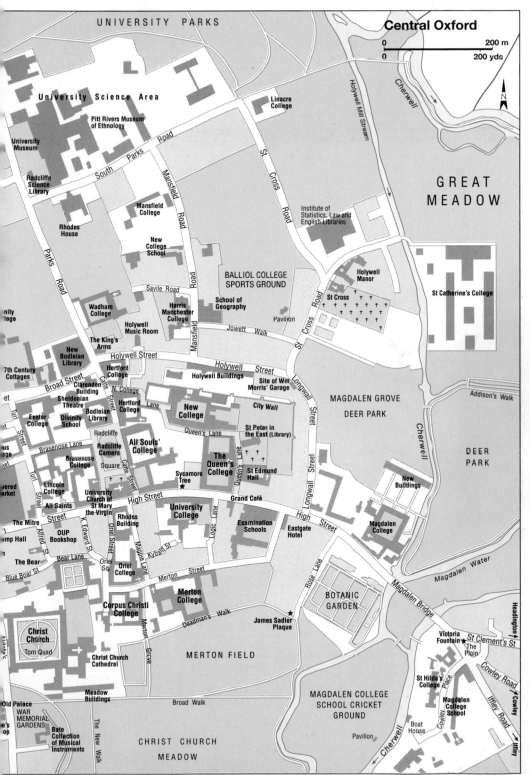

Central Oxford

UNIVERSITY PARKS

University Science Area

Pitt Rivers Museum of Ethnology

University Museum

Radcliffe Science Library

Rhodes House

Linacre College

Mansfield College

New College School

BALLIOL COLLEGE SPORTS GROUND

Institute of Statistics, Law and English Libraries

Holywell Manor

St Cross

GREAT MEADOW

St Catherine's College

Savile Road

School of Geography

Pavilion

Wadham College

Harris Manchester College

Holywell Music Room

Jowett Walk

The King's Arms

Holywell Street

New Bodleian Library

Hertford College

Holywell Street

Holywell Buildings

Site of Wm Morris' Garage

MAGDALEN GROVE DEER PARK

Addison's Walk

7th Century Cottages

Broad Street

Clarendon Building

N. College Lane

Sheldonian Theatre

Bodleian Library

Hertford College

New College

City Wall

DEER PARK

Exeter College

Divinity School

Radcliffe

Queen's Lane

St Peter in the East (Library)

Cherwell

Brasenose Lane

Radcliffe Camera

All Souls' College

The Queen's College

St Edmund Hall

New Buildings

Brasenose College

Square

Cate Street

Lincoln College

University Church of St Mary the Virgin

High Street

Sycamore Tree ★

Grand Café

vered rket

All Saints

Street

Rhodes Building

University College

Examination Schools

Eastgate Hotel

High Street

Magdalen College

The Mitre

OUP Bookshop

K. Edward St.

Oriel Street

Magpie Lane

Kybald St.

Logic Lane

mp Hall

The Bear

Bear Lane

Oriel Sq.

Oriel College

Merton Street

Magdalen Water

Blue Boar St

Rose Lane

Merton College

Magdalen Bridge

Headington ↑

Corpus Christi College

Deadman's Walk

James Sadler Plaque ★

BOTANIC GARDEN

Victoria Fountain ★

St Clement's St

Cowley Road

Christ Church

Tom Quad

Christ Church Cathedral

Merton Grove

MERTON FIELD

St Hilda's College

Cowley Place

Magdalen College School

Iffley Road

Cowley

Old Palace

WAR MEMORIAL GARDENS

e's op

Meadow Buildings

Bate Collection of Musical Instruments

Broad Walk

The New Walk

CHRIST CHURCH MEADOW

MAGDALEN COLLEGE SCHOOL CRICKET GROUND

Pavilion

Boat House

Cherwell

THE HUB OF THE UNIVERSITY

One area of town can be described as the heart of the university.
Lying between the High Street and Broad Street, it includes the
Bodleian Library, the Sheldonian Theatre and the Radcliffe Camera

Map on page 90

A precious and rather feeble Oxford joke is sometimes told about the American tourist who stops an undergraduate in the High Street and asks to be directed to the university. At this point, those in the know are supposed to chuckle over their port for – "as every educated person is aware" – Oxford does not have a central university campus. Like Cambridge, these two ancient universities differ from others in Britain in that they constitute a federation of independent colleges.

And yet, if our American tourist had stopped a helpful student instead of an insufferable prig, he would have been pointed down Broad Street to the heart of Oxford, where there is an impressive group of buildings that might loosely be termed "the University" – in the sense that they provide central facilities for all college members.

Heads of stone

Walking eastwards down **Broad Street**, the eye is drawn to the curious set of railings that separate "the town" from the realm of ceremony and scholarship. Towering above the railings is a series of 13 outsize stone busts, known as the **Emperors' Heads**, or Bearded Ones ❶. They follow the curve of the apsidal end of the Sheldonian Theatre, and were put up in 1669, the same year that the theatre was completed.

Armless busts like these have been used to surmount gateposts since antiquity, and are called "terms", from the Latin *terminus*, a boundary, or "herms" if they represent Hermes, the messenger of the gods. Nobody knows what these splendid giants represent. Max Beerbohm, in his 1911 Oxford-based novel *Zuleika Dobson*, wrote that "they are, by American visitors, frequently mistaken for the Twelve Apostles" – having yet another dig at the poor, untutored tourist from the New World. He also calls them "the faceless Caesars", and perhaps from that developed the current nickname, the Emperors.

Faceless they were until recently; the original terms were replaced in 1868 but with such poor-quality stone that time and the weather soon reduced their features to what John Betjeman called "illustrations in a medical textbook on skin diseases". In 1970, and despite Henry Moore's objection that the eroded heads had their own awesome power, the Oxford sculptor Michael Black was commissioned to carve new heads. After completing the work in 1972, and following exhaustive research into the form of the original heads, Michael Black added his own theory, that the 13 represent the history of fashions in beards.

In any event, the Sheldonian terms make an impressive approach to the buildings beyond, starting with

LEFT: doorway to the Divinity School.
BELOW: Encaenia line-up outside the Sheldonian Theatre.

TIP

It is worth waiting in Broad Street near the Sheldonian on Encaenia Day on the last Wednesday in June to catch a glimpse of at least one "celebrity" en route to collect an honorary degree.

BELOW:
the Sheldonian's golden splendour.

the **Sheldonian Theatre ❷** (open Mon–Sat 10am–12.30pm, 2–3.30pm, entrance fee; closed on Saturday afternoon on performance days and for university events). The theatre was commissioned by Gilbert Sheldon, Chancellor (or honorary head) of the university, in 1662. Sheldon chose as his architect, the young Christopher Wren, who was then 30. Wren had been appointed Professor of Astronomy the previous year and was regarded as one of the most brilliant mathematicians of his day. He had not yet, however, designed any buildings, and the Sheldonian Theatre was the first commission to launch his architectural career. It is fashionable among art historians to describe the theatre as the work of a young amateur, but most of us would give this exuberant building, with its rich, honey-gold coloured stone, far higher praise. It was also revolutionary in its time, for Wren rejected the popular Gothic-Jacobean style and chose instead to follow classical antecedents.

Wren modelled the Sheldonian on the antique open-air Theatre of Marcellus, in Rome. The English weather made it necessary to give it a roof, however, so Wren devised an ingenious timber structure (since replaced) that dispensed with pillars and allowed all 2,000 spectators an uninterrupted view of the proceedings. In place of the open sky, Robert Streeter was commissioned, in 1669, to paint the ceiling with a depiction of the *Triumph of Religion, Arts and Science over Envy, Hate and Malice*.

The Sheldonian was built for university ceremonials, rather than for stage drama, and is still used for this purpose, as well as for concerts and lectures. Here successful students receive their degrees and, at the "Encaenia" ceremony in June, scarlet-gowned dons meet to honour the university founders and bestow honorary degrees upon the worthy and famous (*see also pages 136–7*).

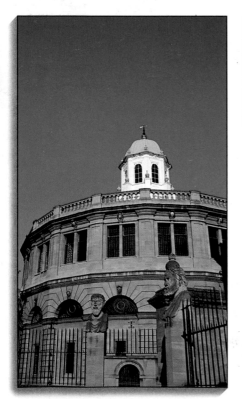

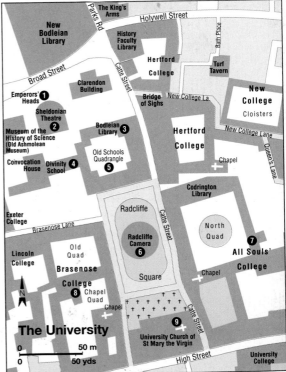

At other times of the year the theatre is open to the public and is well worth visiting for the original woodwork of the Chancellor's throne and the two Orators' pulpits – but most of all for the fine views over the heart of Oxford from the rooftop cupola.

Map on page 90

Early publishing

On the other side of the Sheldonian is the **Clarendon Building**, created to provide the first permanent home for Oxford University Press. Originally, the Press occupied odd rooms in the Sheldonian Theatre, an inconvenient arrangement.

Between 1702 and 1704 the Press published the Earl of Clarendon's account of the English Civil War, and this three-volume *History of the Great Rebellion* proved to be a best-seller. Despite the fact that some of the profits were embezzled by the university Vice-Chancellor, sales of Clarendon's work were sufficient to provide the Press with a new home next door.

The Clarendon, a rather severe classical building, was designed by Nicholas Hawksmoor, Christopher Wren's brilliant pupil, and completed in 1715. The Earl of Clarendon himself occupies a niche on the west wall, where he gesticulates proudly at the building he paid for. Around the roofline are gracious figures, by James Thornhill, of the nine Muses (1717); seven are cast in lead but two are fibre-glass replicas, made in 1974 to replace the originals that had blown down.

The Press moved out of the Clarendon Building in 1830 and the space vacated by the compositors and printers is now filled by part of the Bodleian Library's vast collection of books. As a copyright library, the Bodleian is obliged to accept a copy of every book and journal published in the UK. The result is that space

One of the nine Muses on the Clarendon Building's roof.

BELOW: the degree ceremony moved in 1669 from St Mary's into the Sheldonian.

for books is rapidly running out, despite the more than 80 miles (130 km) of shelving that have been installed just a few feet beneath the surface of Radcliffe Square.

Ancient repository

The cataloguing of books in the Bodleian Library now has a computerised system (OLIS) which allows readers to search through much of the catalogue on screen.

To the south of the Sheldonian lies the **Bodleian Library**  (guided tours included in Divinity School tour, see below; entrance fee), which is entered through a small opening into Old Schools Quadrangle. Before admiring this beautiful courtyard in too much detail, first journey back in time by entering the doors behind the 17th-century bronze statue by Le Sueur of the Earl of Pembroke (a university chancellor) and proceeding through the vestibule into the much older **Divinity School**  (guided tours only of the Divinity School, Convocation House and Duke Humphrey's Library Mar–end Oct, Mon–Fri 10.30 and 11.30am, 2 and 3pm; Sat 10.30 and 11.30am).

Regarded by many as the finest interior in Oxford, work began on this central school of theology in 1426, following an appeal for funds by the university. As it was the most important of all faculties, Divinity required a suitable space, but money kept running out and the room took almost 60 years to complete. Its crowning glory is the lierne vaulted ceiling, which was added in 1478, after the university received a gift from Thomas Kemp, the Bishop of London. Completed by local mason William Orchard, the ceiling is adorned with sculpted figures and 455 bosses carved with biblical subjects, real and mythical beasts, and the coats of arms of university benefactors.

BELOW: the Earl of Pembroke stands proud in the Old Schools Quadrangle.

Candidates for degrees of Bachelor and Doctor of Divinity were not the only people to demonstrate their dialectical skill under this glorious ceiling. It was here, too, that the Oxford Martyrs – Latimer, Ridley and Cranmer – were cross-examined by the Papal Commissioner in 1554, then condemned as Protestant heretics. Until recently, the Divinity School displayed rare manuscripts from the Bodleian collection. Now it is empty, except for an iron-bound chest, with its elaborate lock mechanism, that once belonged to Thomas Bodley, the library's founder. The chest is used to collect donations towards a £10 million appeal for vital restoration work that will eventually allow books back on display in a temperature- and humidity-controlled environment. In the meantime, there is a small display of exhibits, ranging from early copies of Chaucer's *The Canterbury Tales* to Victorian playbills, in the School of Natural Philosophy, on the south side of Old Schools Quad.

In around 1440, a substantial collection of manuscripts was donated to the university by Humphrey, Duke of Gloucester, the younger brother of Henry V. The walls of the Divinity School were built up to create a second storey for **Duke Humphrey's Library** (*see above for guided tours*). The library, with its magnificent beamed ceiling, was first opened to readers in 1488, but was defunct by 1550, largely as a result of neglect and the emergence of book printing (which rendered manuscripts redundant), but also due to the depredations of the King's Commissioners after the dissolution.

It was while he was a student at Magdalen College that Thomas Bodley became aware of this appalling state of affairs. Posted abroad as Ambassador to the Netherlands by Queen Elizabeth I, he used his far-reaching network of contacts to establish a new collection of some 2,000 books to restart the library. The room was restored and opened once more in 1602, and subsequently extended by the addition of the "Arts End". Here visitors can see original leather-bound books dating from the 17th century, some of them turned spine inwards so that chaining them to the shelves (a common practice) would cause less damage. The "Selden End", named after John Selden, who gave 8,000 volumes to the library, was added in about 1650.

Both the "Ends" have beautiful panelled and painted ceilings. Sometimes visitors are also shown the top floor of the library, with its painted frieze of 200 famous men, executed in around 1620 and only rediscovered in the 1960s.

In 1610, an agreement was made whereby the library would receive a copy of every single book registered at Stationers' Hall. Soon Bodley's collection had grown so large that a major extension was required, hence the **Old Schools Quadrangle ❺**. This magnificent piece of architecture is designed in Jacobean-Gothic style (a style that characterises many Oxford buildings of the early 17th century). The quadrangle has a wonderful serenity, and despite being built much higher than college quads it is still light and airy.

The complex was designed to provide lecture rooms on the lower floors, and library space above. Above the ground-floor doorways, painted in letters of gold, are the names of the original schools, or faculties, of the university. Note that the Divinity School facade, covered in panel tracery, is considerably more ornate than the rest of Old Schools Quad – appropriately enough, as Divinity,

A break from college sightseeing.

BELOW: tour in progress in the Divinity School.

THOMAS BODLEY

It was as an undergraduate at Magdalen that Thomas Bodley realised that the university's library was in a critical state of disrepair.

He had spent his youth in Geneva, since as part of a Protestant family he was liable to religious persecution under the reign of Mary I. With the accession of Elizabeth I, he was able to return to England, where, after studying at Oxford, he worked in the diplomatic service. A scholar of Greek and Hebrew, he travelled widely before becoming a fellow of Merton College. On his return to Oxford, the now knighted Sir Thomas Bodley resolved to take action to restore Duke Humphrey's Library. In 1598 he announced that "I could not busie myself to better purpose than by redusing that place [i.e. the library] which then in every part laye ruined and wast, to the publick use of students."

So began the four-year task of restoring Duke Humphrey's room, followed by the extension required to house the rapidly growing collection. Convinced of the need to replace "those ruinous little roomes" by "better built schools", Bodley bequeathed enough money to ensure the completion of the Old Schools Quadrangle, and although only the cornerstone had been laid at the time of his death, it can be regarded as the culmination of his life's work.

Detail of the Tower of the Five Orders

John Radcliffe has more than his fair share of places named after him. The Camera, a square, an observatory, two hospitals, a quadrangle, a library and a road.

BELOW: the Radcliffe Camera.

or Theology, was the principal subject at Oxford until well into the 19th century and the subject for which all other studies were merely a preparation.

Three sides of the quad are regular in composition. James I was on the throne when the building was completed in 1624, and the monarch sits in a niche between allegorical figures representing Fame and the University, in the gate-tower at the east end. This splendidly carved work is called the **Tower of the Five Orders** because it is ornamented with columns and capitals of each of the five orders of classical architecture – Doric, Tuscan, Ionic, Corinthian and Composite – in ascending order. You will find many more heads (binoculars are essential to appreciate them fully) carved in stone all around the battlement line of Old Schools Quad – grotesques and demons, angels and men, all convincingly medieval in appearance but, in fact, the inspired work of masons who restored these buildings in the 1950s. At ground-floor level as you pass through the passageway between the Schools of Music and Natural Philosophy, look for the portraits of two recent librarians, carved into the stone.

The Bodleian Library has always been a reading library, from which no book could ever be borrowed. In 1645, even Charles I, desperately seeking a strategy to thwart the advancing Parliamentarians, was refused the loan of a book, and had to come in and consult one on the spot. In 1939, the **New Bodleian** was completed to take some of the overspill. This fortress-like building opposite the Clarendon, on the corner of Broad Street and Parks Road, has three floors of underground storage beneath Blackwell's bookshop. A conveyor belt beneath Broad Street links the new library to the old.

Emerging to the south of the Old Schools Quadrangle, the splendid sight of **Radcliffe Camera** ❻ rising from a perfect green lawn meets the eye. "Camera" simply means chamber, and John Radcliffe was the physician who, despite his renowned ill temper, made a huge fortune by treating the wealthy – including the monarch, William III. Radcliffe Camera was built after his death in 1714 to house a library devoted to the sciences – just one of the Oxford projects that was funded from his estate.

The gracious round form of the Camera was suggested by Nicholas Hawksmoor, but it was another great 18th-century architect, James Gibbs, who was asked to produce the detailed designs. The building was completed in 1748 and absorbed as a reading room of the Bodleian in 1860. The Radcliffe Camera was just part of a grand 18th-century scheme to open up this part of the city as a public square, to replace the existing jumble of medieval houses. Not all the plan was realised, but it is amazing how the circular Radcliffe Camera appears to fit so naturally into the rectangular square.

The fellows' college

Hawksmoor did, eventually, get his fair share of Oxford commissions, including the great North Quad of **All Souls' College** ❼ (open Mon–Fri 2–4pm; tel: 01865 279379; parties of more than six need permission from the Bursar; free), to the left (east) of Radcliffe Camera. This college, founded in 1438, is unique: it does not admit graduate or undergraduate

Map on page 90

students. Instead, it retains the medieval tradition of restricting membership to "fellows". There are several means of entry: distinguished scholars from all over the world may be elected as visiting fellows, while others sit a highly competitive examination. The system is, in theory, designed to provide facilities for the brightest and best minds to pursue their research, but it has not always been so, and in the 16th century fellowships were bought and sold, and the college was notorious for the drunkenness and corruption of its members.

A century or so later, the winds of reform swept through the college and, as if in a symbolic break with the past, the medieval cloister was cleared away, and new accommodation planned. Then, in 1710, before the work began, Christopher Codrington, a fellow and Governor of the Leeward Islands, died, leaving much of his sugar wealth to the college, as well as a large collection of books. Thus the building plans were changed, and Hawksmoor designed the grand library block and the imposing twin towers of the east side of the North Quad.

The **Codrington Library** (viewing as All Souls' College) is an ingenious piece of work; outside it is all Gothic, while the interior is fully classical – even the windows are Venetian within but with lancets and tracery on the outside. The sundial on the library wall, moved from the chapel, is renowned for its accuracy; Christopher Wren is reputed to be the designer.

The chapel is essentially 15th-century, with its original hammerbeam roof carved with gilded angels and misericords, which include depictions of a mermaid and a man playing the bagpipes. The floor-to-ceiling reredos is a *tour de force*, although the statues are all replacements, installed in 1870, of the originals smashed by Puritan iconoclasts. The surviving 15th-century niches were once brightly painted and even now a few have traces of the original pigment.

Christopher Wren was known in Oxford as a scientist and inventor as well as an architect. His various schemes included new printing techniques and "an instrument to write double".

BELOW: All Souls' College, open to Fellows only.

A brazen addition

At the opposite (west) side of the square is **Brasenose College ❽** (open daily 10–11.30am, 2–4.30pm; tel: 01865 277830; entrance fee for groups only). The college is named after the "brazen nose", a bronze door knocker that once hung on the gates of Brasenose Hall. Anyone who was fleeing from the law could claim sanctuary within the protective walls of the Hall if they could get their hands firmly round the ring of the knocker.

Perhaps because of the protective powers of the brazen nose, a group of students stole the ring in the 1330s and took it with them to Stamford where they intended to establish a rival university. Edward II refused to sanction the breakaway institution, but while some students settled in Cambridge, others returned to Oxford and the brazen nose got left behind. Here it remained, serving as a door knocker, until Brasenose House in Stamford came on the market in 1890. Even then, the college had to buy the whole house to secure the return of the symbolic piece of bronze – now hung behind the High Table in the dining hall.

In the meantime, a new knocker was commissioned for Brasenose, on the occasion of its official foundation as a college, as distinct from the pre-existing academic hall, in 1509. Shaped like a human head, this is now fixed at the apex of the main gate of the college.

Passing through, you enter the Old Quad with its Tudor buildings, completed shortly after the foundation; the third storey, with its fine dormer windows, was added in the early 17th century. The sundial on the right-hand side was painted in 1719. The dining hall, on the left side, is usually open, so that the original brazen nose can be seen. First mentioned in a document of 1279, the Romanesque feline head and ring could have been made as early as the 12th century.

BELOW:
Brasenose's Old
Quad with sundial.
RIGHT: Ackermann's
*Brazen Nose
College.*

Map on page 90

A passageway in the southeastern corner leads into Chapel Quad, with its delightful library, carved with a frieze of exuberant swags, and lit below by pairs of oval windows. This work dates to the mid-17th century and is surprisingly innovative for its date, foreshadowing the 18th-century's Baroque style.

The chapel is of the same date and mixes Gothic with classical motifs. The unusual fan-vaulted and painted roof is made of plaster. In the ante-chapel is a bronze plaque with a Greek inscription celebrating Walter Pater (died 1894), the writer and aesthete. He is portrayed at the centre of a tree whose other branches bear portrait medallions of Plato, Dante, Leonardo da Vinci and Michaelangelo. The implication that Pater was a scion of the same stock as these great artists reminds us that his precious and overblown style was once considered the epitome of fine writing.

As you turn to leave the college, you realise what a splendid view the students and fellows enjoy, being so close to Radcliffe Square. The huge dome of the Radcliffe Camera looms above the entrance tower and the spire of St Mary's church to the right.

Walter Pater inspired a cult following among young writers in the Victorian era, and Oscar Wilde once proclaimed that "there is no Pater but Pater and I am his prophet".

Beginnings of the university

Returning to Radcliffe Square, the huge **University Church of St Mary the Virgin ❾** fronts on to the High Street. It can be regarded as the original hub of the university, for it was here in the 13th century that the first university meetings and ceremonies were held, and all the administrative documents kept. Before entering via its north door, you'll see the sign to **Convocation Coffee House**. There can be few cafés with such a history, for it occupies the space of the former Convocation House, an annex built in 1320 specifically to house the uni-

LEFT:
Brasenose College again – the vista remains the same.
BELOW:
St Mary the Virgin, from the church of the same name.

Map on page 90

Convocation Coffee House

OPEN

Morning Coffee
Lunches
Afternoon Tea

Entrance on
Radcliffe Square Side

The side chapels of Convocation House were once used as lecture theatres.

BELOW: picnickers at St Mary the Virgin church.

versity governing body, which continued to meet here until 1534 when the administration moved to Convocation House at the Divinity School. A library was installed above it, but this was later replaced by Duke Humphrey's Library.

Now, instead of disputatious students sharpening their wits in learned debate, the church is often full of visitors queuing to climb the 188-ft (62-metre) spire-topped **Tower**, which dates to the late 13th and early 14th centuries (open daily 9am–5pm; July–Sept 9am–7pm; entrance fee). The gangway at the base of the spire offers a magnificent view, revealing not only the layout of the city and many of the colleges, but just how much green space there is in the heart of Oxford.

The rest of the church was rebuilt in Perpendicular style in the early 16th century and is really rather dull, except for the eccentric south porch at the High Street side, added in 1637 and designed by Nicholas Stone. Fat barley-sugar columns support the curvaceous pediment and angels surround the central niche containing a statue of the Virgin and Child. Perhaps the Virgin's rather startled look is a legacy of the English Civil War, for her head was shot off by a soldier in 1642 – but replaced 20 years later.

Inside the church, the pillar opposite the pulpit in the north side of the nave has been cut away; this was done to build a platform for the final trial of Thomas Cranmer, Archbishop of Canterbury, in 1556. His fellow martyrs, Nicholas Ridley, Bishop of London, and Hugh Latimer, Bishop of Worcester, had both been executed at the stake the previous year for their support of the Protestant Reformation. Cranmer, however, was given leave to appeal against his sentence, and signed several statements recanting his earlier beliefs. This was not sufficient for his accusers, the Pope's commissioners and the zealous supporters of the Catholic Queen Mary. Cranmer was brought to St Mary's to make a public statement of his errors; but he refused to do so, and instead retracted his former recantations. Likc Ridley and Latimer before him, having been dragged from St Mary's Church he was burned at the stake in Broad Street (he was imprisoned first at Bocardo Prison, by the church of St Michael at the North Gate, and brought to St Mary's for the final verdict).

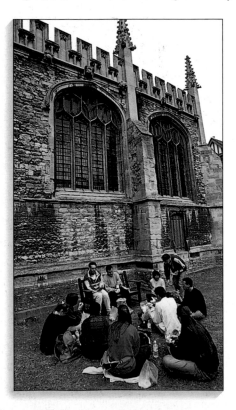

In 1833 St Mary's was again at the centre of religious controversy when John Keble preached his famous sermon here, leading to the foundation of the Oxford Movement. John Henry Newman, Vicar of St Mary's at the time and a leading supporter of the Movement, brought down a storm of indignation for his increasingly pro-Catholic views; his sillier supporters affected an ascetic appearance, fasted on toast and water and smoked Spanish (Catholic) cigars – while some colleges altered the times of compulsory chapel services to keep impressionable students away from Newman's sermons. In the end, he resigned, became a Catholic and ended up a Cardinal – and to this day Oxford remains a centre of High Church Anglo-Catholicism.

Return along Catte Street, looking back to admire Radcliffe Square. The view is at its most splendid from opposite the Bridge of Sighs (*see page 101*). The gateway to the Old Schools Quadrangle, the dome of the Radcliffe Camera and the spire of St Mary's create one of the finest urban panoramas in Europe. ❏

Oxford architecture

Oxford is a city of crazy architectural juxtapositions, reflecting the changing tastes of every age from Saxon times to the present. Gothic, Jacobean, Palladian and neo-Grecian stand cheek by jowl with some of the most quirky buildings to have been constructed: Wren's pepperpot gate-tower to Christ Church, Hawksmoor's bristling All Souls' and Nicholas Stone's twisting columns fronting the porch of St Mary's.

All that binds this haphazard mélange together is the colour of the limestone, an aristocrat among building materials. The oolite once quarried in the hills around Oxford is very accommodating. When freshly dug, it is plastic and easily carved into any shape. Once dry, it is a strong, hard-wearing material, ranging in colour from honey gold to white, with shades of pink and blue. The Normans, themselves from a limestone region, were the first residents of Oxford to see the potential of this versatile stone.

As English masons grew in confidence, they developed their own variations on the Gothic style. Early English, characterised by tall, pointed lancet windows, clusters of shafts in place of monolithic columns and capitals carved with stylised leaves, is well exemplified at Christ Church Cathedral.

Merton claims to have established the pattern for collegiate buildings both in Oxford and further afield, with its enclosed quadrangle surrounded by communal dining hall, library, naveless chapel and accommodation wings.

The Perpendicular style was invented in Gloucester in the 1350s, along with the fan vault, England's greatest contribution to Gothic architecture. Oxford has several splendid examples: the vestibule of Christ Church Hall and the Divinity School – the latter a late example, completed in 1488.

In the 17th century, Oxford developed its own hybrid Jacobean-Gothic style, exemplified by the Old Schools Quad and Wadham. These buildings retain Gothic features – traceried windows, blank arcading and stone vaulting – alongside classical columns and entablature, and it has been argued that the reluctance to let go of the Gothic represented a deep-seated conservatism.

Yet, within less than a century, the best-known architects of their age were to give Oxford some of Europe's most radical and adventurous buildings. Wren's Sheldonian Theatre, Gibb's Radcliffe Camera and Hawksmoor's Clarendon Building transformed the city from a place of reserved cloisters to a city of boisterous and assertive buildings.

The architectural rot set in in the 19th century when zealous proponents of the neo-Gothic style swept away many medieval buildings and replaced them with their own "perfected Gothic", often in harsh brick.

Our own age has done even worse, with its taste for concrete and steel, but stoneworking skills still survive and modern masons have left their mark in the form of humorous gargoyles: a rugby player on the frontage of Brasenose, or a bespectacled librarian in the Old Schools Quad. Ironically, Oxford's ancient quarries closed at about the time that the tradition of carving was revived; today's masons import their limestone from France. ❑

RIGHT: the Bridge of Sighs at Hertford College.

AROUND NEW COLLEGE

Map on page 102

*Span the entire history of Oxford by taking in the site of a
pagan well, a Norman crypt, the medieval town walls
and the birthplace of Morris Motors*

On the east of Catte Street, linking the two halves of **Hertford College**
(pronounced "hartford") ❶ (open daily 10am–5pm; tel: 01865 279400;
free), is the ornate aerial corridor known as the Bridge of Sighs, after the
famous Ponte dei Sospiri in Venice. Although it is now a much-photographed
landmark, the bridge's erection was strongly opposed when it was built by Sir
Thomas Jackson in 1913–14. The other buildings of the college are Jackson's
design, too, put up after 1887 and remarkably varied in their use of Italian,
French and English Renaissance motifs.

Hertford is a college that only just survived to see the 20th century. The original Hart Hall, named after Elias de Hertford, dates from the late 13th century.
For centuries it was embroiled in disputes with its predatory neighbour, Magdalen Hall, which wanted room to expand, and took every opportunity to take
control of the impoverished Hart Hall. Magdalen achieved its objective in 1813
– only to be destroyed itself by a fire in 1820. It was then decided to refound the
college, calling it Hertford and combining the properties of Magdalen and Hart
Halls with funds donated by the banker Thomas Charles Baring in 1874.

The principal buildings, with their neo-Palladian details, lie on the south side
of New College Lane. Traditional English cream teas can be enjoyed in the historic Dining Hall (daily except Monday 2.30–4.30pm).

The site on the north side, linked by the **Bridge of
Sighs** ❷, was acquired in 1898 and is interrupted on
the Broad Street frontage by the History Faculty
Library, originally built as the Indian Institute by Basil
Champneys, beginning in 1883. Hindu deities and
tiger heads carved in stone on the facade, and the elephant weather vane, mark its original use.

LEFT: the Bridge
of Sighs.
BELOW:
a string quartet
in the cloisters
of New College.

Ghostly lane

Pass under the Bridge of Sighs and into the dark,
narrow and traffic-free New College Lane. This lane
is the result of the replanning of the northeast quarter
of town in the late 14th century, when many early
medieval dwellings were replaced by residential colleges. The original street pattern was obliterated, leaving New College Lane to wind its way between the
high college walls.

Immediately on the left, a narrow opening between
two houses, St Helen's Passage (formerly Hell Passage), leads through to the **Turf Tavern** (*see page
107*). Further along on the left, a plaque on a house
wall indicates the home of astronomer **Edmund
Halley** (1656–1742). Having calculated the orbit of
the comet that now bears his name, and carried out
many scientific investigations, Halley was appointed
Savilan professor at Oxford in 1703. He built an
observatory at his home, still visible on the roof.

"New" foundation

The lane turns sharp right, between the cloister walls of New College on the left and the New College warden's barn on the right. Round another bend and straight ahead stands the gate-tower of **New College** ❸ (this entrance open Easter–Oct daily 11am–5pm; in winter use Holywell Street, open daily 2–4pm; tel: 01865 279555; entrance fee in summer). The narrow gate-tower, with statues of the Virgin, an angel and the founder, William of Wykeham, belies the spaciousness and grandeur of what lies beyond.

Wykeham, Bishop of Winchester, founded the college in 1379, having acquired land in the northeast corner of the city wall, which, according to contemporary accounts, was "full of filth, desolate and unoccupied". Building work proceeded speedily – in part because Wykeham was a very wealthy man. The range of buildings surrounding the Great Quadrangle was largely completed by the time of Wykeham's death in 1404. What is more, most of it has survived intact, although a third storey was added to the accommodation range in 1674.

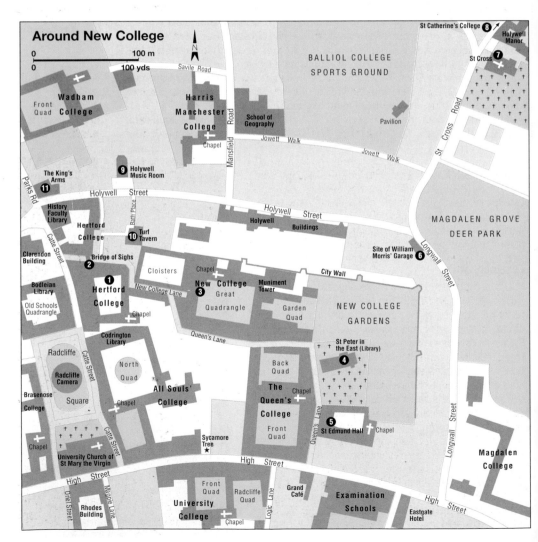

Around New College

On the left of the gate-tower is the spacious chapel, a fine example of Perpendicular architecture. A dramatic stone figure of Lazarus, struggling to break free of his funeral bonds, dominates the ante-chapel and was carved by Sir Jacob Epstein in 1951. It stands beneath a controversial window designed by Sir Joshua Reynolds and painted by Thomas Jervais between 1778 and 1785 (the two artists appear as shepherds in the Nativity scene). Sir Horace Walpole called it "washy" and Lord Torrington described the figures of the Virtues as "half-dressed languishing harlots". As models, Reynolds used society beauties of the day, including Mrs Sheridan, wife of the playwright; she appears as the Virgin.

There is no glass in the east end of the chapel; instead, a great 19th-century stone reredos rises from floor to ceiling, filled with life-sized statues of apostles, saints and martyrs. The hammerbeam roof is also Victorian, by Sir George Gilbert Scott, as is the stone sedilia (group of three seats) to the left of the altar, one of which is used to display the founder's gilt and enamelled episcopal staff.

Scott also designed the woodwork of the choir stalls, but incorporated original armrests and 38 misericords that provide a glimpse of 14th-century life, with bishops preaching, acrobats tumbling and monsters with multiple heads.

On the left, as you emerge from the chapel, is the cloister, dominated by a vast and ancient holm oak tree, that evokes medieval Oxford with its original 14th-century waggon roof and atmosphere of tranquillity.

At the northeast corner of the Great Quad is the **Muniment Tower**, again with statues of the Virgin and Wykeham. The steep staircase within leads to the hall, lined with 16th-century linenfold panelling under Scott's roof of 1877.

The wall above the high table is hung with portraits of former benefactors and Wardens (heads of college). Among them (bottom right) is the white-haired

Map on page 102

The look on all students' faces after exams are over.

BELOW:
New College gate can be somewhat forbidding in winter.

GHOSTS ON NEW COLLEGE LANE

Walking down New College Lane at night, you would be excused for believing the persistent rumours that this dark, narrow alleyway is haunted. Many stories of strange noises and inexplicable apparitions have been reported over the years, not least claims that ghostly horses can be heard trotting down the Lane.

Ghost experts believe that this phenomenon can be traced back to the Civil War, when the lane was the assembly point for a Royalist force preparing to ride out of the city to confront the Parliamentarians. Crammed into the narrow street, the mounted troops would have made a formidable sight, with hooves ringing on cobblestones, horses snorting and steel weapons clashing as the men anxiously awaited the command to set off. Curiously, these are precisely the sounds that many people have heard centuries later, evidence perhaps that the troops' collective psychic energy sank into the Lane's high walls.

Other sightings of a strange glowing blob between New College and Hertford are treated less seriously, especially since students are known for practical jokes. Both New College and Queen's claim their own ghosts, the former in the shape of the legendary Dr Spooner. Details of Ghost Tours from the Tourist Information Centre (01865 726871).

Many of Spooner's verbal gaffes were, in fact, intentional, as he confessed to a friend that he liked "to raise a laugh".

figure of William Spooner, elected in 1903, whose habit of transposing the initial letters of words gave rise to many humorous "Spoonerisms". Many are thought to be apocryphal, made up subsequently to nurture the myth. There is no evidence, for example, that he once proposed a toast to "our queer Dean". It is also said that he expelled one undergraduate with the words "Sir, you have tasted two whole worms, you have hissed my mystery lectures and you were found fighting a liar in the quad: you will leave at once by the town drain."

An archway in the Great Quad east range leads through to the Garden Quad, lined with 17th-century neo-Palladian buildings and separated from the gardens beyond by a curvaceous wrought-iron screen – a replica of the original designed by Thomas Robinson in 1711. The gardens contain a substantial stretch of Oxford's medieval town wall, which dates from 1226 when the original timber defensive walls of the town were rebuilt. The college was made responsible for maintaining it under the terms of the original land purchase; as a result it is one of the best-preserved examples of a town wall in England.

The tree-covered Mound, in the northeastern angle of the wall, looks like a Norman castle motte but was thrown up in the 16th century as a prospect from where to view the gardens.

Saxon church

Exit the college via the New College Lane gatehouse, and turn left under the archway and round another bend into **Queen's Lane**. Traffic-free, the walk along Queen's Lane is enlivened by Michael Groser's series of corbels on the New College buildings to the left, carved in the 1960s with harvest mice, beetles, frogs, lizards and other zoological subjects.

BELOW:
New College, with part of the ancient city wall.

Beyond the sharp right-hand bend in the lane is the church of **St Peter in the East** ❹, whose 11th-century tower is one of the oldest in Oxford. Originally dating from Saxon times, the present church is now the library of neighbouring St Edmund Hall, but visitors can gain access to the cavernous 11th-century **crypt**, one of the finest in Oxford by asking for the key at St Edmund's porter's lodge. During the war local residents used the crypt as an air-raid shelter, though Oxford was never actually bombed. A torch is useful for those who want to study the details: the capitals are carved with dragon-like beasts. In summer in the churchyard, St Edmund Hall students study beneath the yews. One of them commemorates James Sadler, the "first English aeronaut", whose inaugural balloon flight took off from Christ Church Meadow on 4 October 1784.

James Sadler's gravestone is a place of interest for any balloonist.

Medieval hall

St Edmund Hall ❺ (open daily dawn until dusk; tel: 01865 279000; free), with its small, flower-filled quads, achieved independent status as late as 1957. Before that, it had been controlled by Queen's College, next door. It is, however, the only surviving example in Oxford of the medieval halls that pre-dated the foundation of the colleges. By tradition, it dates to the 1190s, when St Edmund of Abingdon taught here, and therefore has every right to be considered Oxford's oldest educational establishment.

Everything about St Edmund Hall is built on a diminutive scale, including the chapel, on the east side of the Front Quad. Note that the pillars supporting the 1682 door pediment are carved to resemble a stack of leather-bound books. Fans of pre-Raphaelite artists William Morris and Edward Burne-Jones should check with the lodge for permission to see some of their stained-glass work in

BELOW:
student digs, a fun alternative to living in college rooms.

The cemetery behind St Cross Church is well worth a visit. Look out for the grave of the Oxford shopkeeper Theophilus Carter, reputedly the model for Lewis Carroll's Mad Hatter in "Alice in Wonderland".

BELOW: St Catherine's College is set apart from other colleges.

the chapel, together with original cartoon drawings. There is also a bold modern altar painting of *Christ at Emmaeus* (1958) by Ceri Richards.

Birthplace of the Morris Oxford

The narrow confines of Queen's Lane finish as it emerges on to the High Street. Immediately on the right is Queen's College (*see page 127*), while on the corner on the left you can rest your legs at Queen's Lane Coffee House. This is one of Oxford's oldest coffee houses, established in 1654, where students still linger for hours over hearty breakfasts or mugs of coffee.

Turn left here and continue for a short stretch along the High towards the traffic lights at Longwall Street. At No. 48 is a shoe shop, once the bicycle repair shop of William Morris, where the famous mechanic began his career. To follow Morris' career further, turn left again into **Longwall Street**. Just around the first corner on the left is the building that housed the **garage ❻** in which Morris built the prototype of the "bullnose" Morris Oxford in 1912, a project that was to launch him on the road to fame and fortune and launch Oxford into the industrial era. Though the garage was converted to residential accommodation in 1981, there is an information window with further details on the career of Morris, later Lord Nuffield (*see pages 53–7*).

Adjacent is Holywell Street, but first continue north along the main road to the **Church of St Cross ❼** on the right. The present church was founded in the 11th century on the site of an ancient chapel of St Peter in the East, which was established beside a pagan Saxon holy well (hence "Holywell"), and became an important place of pilgrimage. The only surviving Norman part of the church is the chancel, but the 13th-century tower has a fascinating feature, namely the **sundial clock**. The grave of Kenneth Grahame, author of *Wind in the Willows*, is in the churchyard. The key to the church is available from the porter of the neighbouring Holywell Manor; sadly, the ancient holy well is no longer there.

The real "new" colleges

Opposite the church are the huge brick cubes of the **Law Library** (1964), while a turn right into Manor Road brings you to a classic example of 1960s architecture, **St Catherine's College ❽** (closed to the public), designed by Danish architect Arne Jacobsen and completed in 1964. While modern architects rave over its pioneering "functional" style, most find the plain yellow-brick buildings dull. However, the landscaping, also planned by Jacobsen, is now mature and does much to compensate – especially the long vista between the Cherwell and the water gardens, backed by the splendid trees of Magdalen College meadows.

On the corner of South Parks Road is another "new" college, **Linacre** (ask at the porter's lodge to visit; tel: 01865 271650). It was founded in 1962 for students studying for higher degrees, notably graduates of universities other than Oxford.

Back towards the centre, Holywell Street is one of Oxford's quietest and most charming streets, closed to traffic and lined with pastel-painted, timber-framed houses and Cotswold-stone vernacular; most are now

Map on page 102

student lodgings. New College's imposing Holywell Buildings, with the college's main entrance are also here, on the left.

Music and mead

On the other side of the street is the **Holywell Music Room** ❾ (tickets from the Playhouse box office; tel: 01865 798600), opened in 1748 and reputedly the world's oldest surviving concert hall. Restored in 1959–60, it can seat 250 and has acoustics that do particular justice to solo recitals and chamber concerts.

In Holywell Street, too, you can see how effectively the town wall marked the limits of the city, for, apart from the 17th- and 18th-century houses of Holywell Street itself, everything to the north belongs to another age, part of the 19th-century expansion of the city.

Near the western end of Holywell Street, on the left, is **Bath Place**, a narrow, cobbled alley with many right-angled bends, leading past ramshackle houses – former slums but now picturesque leaning cottages backing up against the town wall. Follow it through to the rambling **Turf Tavern** ❿ (open Mon–Sat 11am–11pm; Sun 12–10.30pm). Recently renovated, the Turf is a splendid, low-beamed English tavern. Its foundations date to the 13th century, though most of the present building is 16th century. At the back is an attractive beer garden, and along the alleyway is another terraced area, tucked up against the exterior wall of New College cloisters.

Another venerable Oxford watering hole is at the end of Holywell Street on the right: **The King's Arms** ⓫ (open Mon–Sat 10.30am–11.30pm, Sun to 10.30pm) is a pub much frequented by students, particularly in June when they gather here to celebrate the end of their exams. ❑

TIP

The Turf Tavern serves a hot rum punch in the winter months – ideal for drinking by the braziers.

BELOW: the Turf Tavern is popular with both students and townies.

A THIRST FOR KNOWLEDGE

Oxford is a city of learning, of course, but also a city of drinking, as can be seen from its many pubs, ranging from medieval inns to modern theme bars

There are pubs to suit all tastes in Oxford. Pubs for students, of course, but also establishments that cater for other inhabitants of the city.

George Street is now almost entirely comprised of places for eating and drinking, many of them catering for a young, non-student clientele, and the street is animated – to say the least – on Friday and Saturday evenings.

But there are also plenty of more traditional and sedate pubs. Some of their names reveal their historic connection with a particular trade or profession: the Bookbinders Arms in Jericho (publishing), the Waterman's Arms on Osney Island (canal haulage), the Bullnose Morris in Cowley (named after the first vehicle produced by William Morris, founder of the motor-car industry in Oxford).

Each suburb or inner-city neighbourhood has its local, complete with loyal regulars, but there are some pubs that have strong associations with the famous, and sometimes the infamous, some of whose drinking habits were as pronounced as their literary or artistic talents.

CALLED TO THE BAR

William Shakespeare, so tradition has it, used to stop off at the Crown Tavern in Cornmarket on his way from London to Stratford, and many other writers have followed his example.

Meanwhile, the pubs in Broad Street near to the Bodleian Library have offered refreshment to generations of scholars and authors, from Oscar Wilde, an Oxford graduate, to Colin Dexter, creator of Inspector Morse.

◁ **THE MITRE**
The historian Anthony Wood told in 1690 how one Fellow of All Souls' died at the Mitre after immoderate drinking.

RICHARD BURTON ▷
The Welsh actor often came to perform at Oxford's Playhouse, and was nicknamed "Beer Burton", for none too subtle reasons.

◁ THE TURF TAVERN

Difficult to find down a warren of narrow lanes near New College, the hard-drinking Welsh poet Dylan Thomas used to quench his thirst in the ever-popular Turf Tavern.

△ C.S.LEWIS

The celebrated author C.S. Lewis used to meet J.R.R. Tolkien, author of *The Lord of the Rings*, for drinks at the Eastgate Hotel on High Street.

INSPECTOR MORSE ▷

Inspector Morse, the fictional detective created by Oxford-based writer Colin Dexter, loves Oxford pubs. The Trout and the Eagle & Child have appeared in the TV series starring John Thaw (left).

◁ THE EAGLE AND CHILD

The "Inklings", a group of literary cronies including C.S. Lewis and Tolkien, used to meet in the back bar of this unspoiled pub on St Giles.

◁ THE BOOKBINDERS ARMS

This friendly pub in Jericho has associations with Inspector Morse. You can visit it on a Morse guided tour, as the detective visited many pubs!

KINGSLEY AMIS ▷

A contemporary of Philip Larkin at St John's College, novelist Kingsley Amis was a jazz fanatic while at Oxford and a regular at the King's Arms in Broad Street.

A GHASTLY, GHOSTLY INN

The Mitre Inn on the High Street has been a pub in continual use since 1310.

It has always had strong religious connections and in the 17th century was a hotbed of Catholicism, when secret Masses were held on the premises. This affront to Protestantism led to a riot in 1688 as mobs smashed every window and went in search of other Catholics.

One of the worst chapters in the city's long history of religious intolerance occurred here during Henry VIII's Dissolution of the Monasteries. A secret tunnel then linked the Mitre with buildings across the High Street and it seems that Henry's soldiers drove a group of monks under-ground and then bricked up both ends of the tunnel.

It is said that the monks' screams can still be heard today in the dead of night.

AROUND BROAD STREET

This area more than any other illustrates the contrasts between Town and Gown, combining peaceful college quads with the bustle of the Covered Market, Carfax and Cornmarket

Map on page 112

The route begins at the southern end of broad St Giles', at the neo-Gothic **Martyrs' Memorial ❶**. Erected by public subscription, to the designs of Sir George Gilbert Scott from 1841 to 1843, it contains statues of the martyrs Latimer, Ridley and Cranmer, and an inscription stating that they died for maintaining sacred truths "against the errors of the Church of Rome". The Oxford Martyrs were burned at the stake in the town's north ditch, now Broad Street, just around the corner, where a cross in the road opposite Balliol College marks the site of their execution. Latimer and Ridley went to the stake first, in 1555. Latimer offered the following words of comfort to his desperate colleague before both were consumed by the flames: "Be of good comfort, Master Ridley, and play the man. We shall this day light such a candle, by God's grace, in England, as I trust shall never be put out."

Immediately to the south of the Martyrs' Memorial the road splits into two and the **Church of St Mary Magdalen ❷** occupies the island in the middle. Usually locked, this church is a centre of Anglo-Catholicism, and the congregation remains loyal to the memory of Charles I, celebrating the Feast of King Charles the Martyr on 30 January. The north aisle, funded out of money left over from the building of the Martyrs' Memorial, is an interesting early example of Gothic Revival architecture, and was designed by Gilbert Scott in 1842. Scott was a keen supporter of the Oxford Society for the Study of Gothic Architecture, founded in 1839, whose members believed that this medieval style was morally better than the pagan classical.

LEFT: the Carfax quarterboys.
BELOW: the Martyrs' Memorial.

Charity, charm and history

Broad Street is aptly named, though it was originally known as Horsemongers Street after a horse fair held here from 1235. Narrow at each end and wide in the middle, it has a feeling of spaciousness, emphasised by the grounds of Trinity College on the north side, which are separated from the street by a wrought-iron gate. The far end is dominated by the Sheldonian Theatre and Clarendon Building and much of the south side is distinctive for its colourful facades above some interesting shops including **Oxfam** (Oxford Committee for Famine Relief), the first permanent shop to be opened by the charity in 1948.

Here, too, is **The Oxford Story ❸** (open Apr–Oct daily 9.30am–5pm; July and Aug 9am–6.30pm; Nov–Mar 10am–4pm; entrance fee), a museum primarily devoted to the history of the university. After a brief introduction in a "common room", visitors are propelled through the ages on a motorised medieval desk, experiencing the sights, sounds and smells of this 800-year-old institution (children's and foreign-language commentaries are available).

*Balliol College,
bastion of liberal
traditions*

Adjacent to the Oxford Story, at No. 11 Broad Street, is **Thornton's book-shop** (open Mon–Sat 9am–6pm), a rambling antiquarian bookshop, no longer quite so idiosyncratic since "improvements" were made in 1985 to meet fire regulations. It is now possible to reach the upper floors without climbing over stacks of unsorted books.

Academic prowess

At the other side of the street is **Balliol College** ❹ (open daily 2–5pm; tel: 01865 277777; entrance fee), a college that has produced a greater number of eminent men – in particular statesmen and politicians – than any other. These include Lord Jenkins of Hillhead, and prime ministers Harold Macmillan and Edward Heath.

The liberal traditions and academic strengths of the college in its heyday were due to the reforming measures of Benjamin Jowett (Master 1870–93), who believed that his students should not merely be filled with facts but educated for life. His self-proclaimed mission was to "innoculate England with

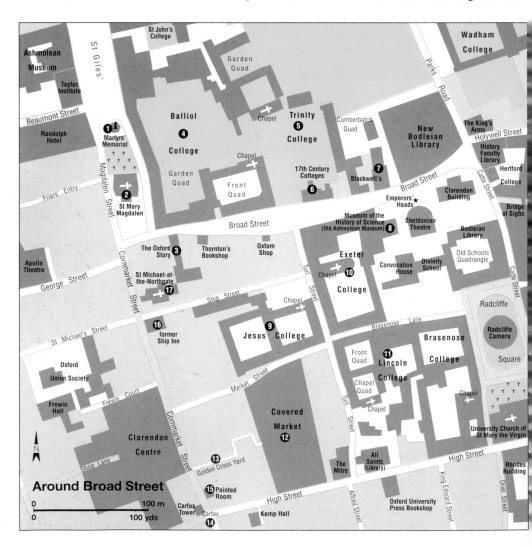

Around Broad Street

0 _____ 100 m
0 _____ 100 yds

Balliol" – which he sought to do by encouraging his charges to devote their lives to public service. But Jowett wasn't the first Balliol Master to espouse progressive ideas: back in 1361 the religious reformer John Wyclif spoke out against corruption and worldliness within the established church. His teachings resonated throughout Europe.

Jowett also supervised the near-total rebuilding of the college and, sadly, it is difficult to find much of merit in the result. William Morris, who watched the demolition of the medieval Balliol buildings with dismay, later founded the Society for the Protection of Ancient Buildings with the avowed aim of seeking means to repair and protect old buildings rather than replacing them.

The Fellows of Balliol, however, thought the buildings too decayed to be rescued. They had stood for a long time; Balliol claims to be the oldest Oxford college (also a claim of University College and Merton) on the grounds that John Balliol founded it in 1263, as penance for insulting the Bishop of Durham; the statutes, drawn up under the patronage of Balliol's widow, Dervorguilla, date to 1282.

The college was never very wealthy, however, until some ancient estates in Northumberland were discovered to be a rich source of coal. Three major Victorian architects were employed in the rebuilding that resulted – Salvin, Butterfield and Waterhouse – yet all produced second-rate work.

The Front Quad, entered from Broad Street, contains the former hall, now the library, and one of the few surviving pre-Victorian buildings, last remodelled in the 18th century. The chapel, Butterfield's work of 1856–57, was once lavishly decorated with Gothic furnishings – too ornate for the taste of Balliol dons who had them removed in 1937. The silver-gilt altar frontal commemorates college members who died in World War I.

Map on page 112

A forbidding and puritanical person, Benjamin Jowett had a long, platonic relationship with Florence Nightingale, with whom he corresponded for many years.

BELOW: Balliol College Hall.

OXFAM

The Oxfam shop in Broad Street was the first permanent charity shop to open in the United Kingdom. Today the Oxford-based aid agency has a network of more than 800 retail outlets, selling goods from developing countries and items donated by supporters to raise money for its work with the poor throughout the world.

The Oxfam story began in 1942 when Greece was occupied by the Nazis. The Allies had imposed a blockade, and neither food nor medicines could reach the civilian population. As Greeks began to die of hunger and disease, the Oxford Committee for Famine Relief was established to send emergency supplies. The first "Greek Week" of fund-raising netted £12,700. The success of this venture encouraged Oxfam's founders to carry on their work, and important aid was sent to the Middle East and Korea in the 1950s, as well as Biafra, the Congo and India in the 1960s.

As Oxfam grew, it opened offices in almost every poor region in the world, sending not only aid but also expertise, encouraging communities to find their own solutions to their poverty. Today, with an annual income of over £90 million and a staff of 1,300 (plus 30,000 volunteers) in the UK, the charity works in 70 countries and lobbies for an end to unfair trade and the debt crisis in the Third World.

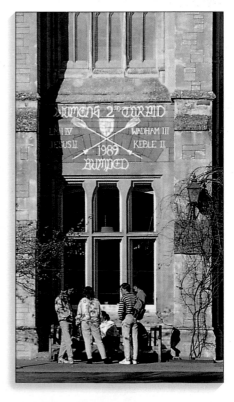

The chapel exterior, partly clad in ivy and Virginia creeper, is built in alternating bands of buff and red stone and is best appreciated from the Garden Quad. Here things begin to improve slightly: a group of trees and rose beds softens the appearance of the ill-harmonised buildings, and the steep flight of stone steps up to the porch of the dining hall – the work of Waterhouse, 1876 – makes a dramatic statement.

Open house

Adjacent to Balliol is **Trinity College ❺** (open daily 10.30am–noon, 2–5pm; tel: 01865 279900; entrance fee). Unlike in most other Oxford colleges, the Front Quad is not closed off, and its tree-filled lawn almost invites visitors to enter, which they do through a small entrance between the wrought-iron gates and a row of humble **17th-century cottages ❻**, which were rebuilt in 1969.

A path leads northwards across the lawn to Durham Quad, so called because it occupies the site of the original Durham College, founded in 1286 by the monks of Durham Abbey. When the monasteries were dissolved by Henry VIII, the property was purchased by Sir Thomas Pope, a wealthy Treasury civil servant, and he re-founded the college in 1555.

Durham Quad is fronted by the elegant Baroque chapel – so much like Wren's City of London churches that the design has been attributed to him, although any college records that could prove or disprove this theory are missing. Certainly the chapel, which attracts the highest eulogies from architectural historians, was the first in Oxford to break away from the Gothic style. Completed in 1694, the tower is carved with fruit and flowers, and the pinnacles consist of allegorical figures representing Theology, Medicine, Geometry and Astronomy.

Tradition has it that the grand wrought-iron gates of Trinity College on Parks Road will be opened only when a Stuart monarch returns to the British throne. In fact, the "gates" are railings and therefore will always remain closed.

BELOW: Trinity College Gardens.

Inside, the panelling, stalls and screen, carved with figures of the Evangelists, are principally of juniper wood, with walnut veneer. The beautiful reredos, all cherubs and foliage, is certainly good enough to be the work of the great 17th-century master of wood carving Grinling Gibbons. The centrepiece of the plaster ceiling is painted with an Ascension by the Huguenot artist Pierre Berchet.

A passageway on the north side of Durham Quad leads through to the peaceful Garden Quad. Here the north range, of 1668, is known to be Wren's work, but 19th-century alterations have obscured his design beyond recognition.

Four handsome lead urns form a prelude to the college garden, to the right, entered through a wrought-iron gateway, made as a World War II memorial. The expansive gardens stretch all the way to Parks Road, creating a fine vista that is closed at the far end by 18th-century wrought-iron railings. By taking the central path and turning right, you reach a group of buildings added in the 19th and 20th centuries, tucked into the rear of Blackwell's bookshop. The paving of Cumberbatch Quad, built 1964–68, forms the roof of the Norrington Room.

Students hurry past Blackwell's to a ball.

The heart of publishing

Blackwell's ❼ (open Mon–Sat 9am–6pm, Tues 9.30am–6pm, Sun 11am–5pm), on Broad Street, was opened in 1879 by Benjamin Henry Blackwell. The original shop was tiny, and even today the initial impression is of an average-sized provincial bookshop. Downstairs, however, is the underground **Norrington Room**, an enormous space stacked with shelves devoted to truly every topic under the sun. The pre-eminence of Blackwell's in Oxford is reflected not only here, but in other premises in the city, including the adjacent well-stocked Map and Travel Shop; Blackwell's Too Shop (children's books), next door to the

BELOW: the Norrington Room, an underground treasure beneath Blackwell's bookshop.

Theology

The Turl Bar is definitely popular with students, who generally agree with its sentiments about beer!

BELOW: Turl Street epitomises old Oxford.

Oxford Story; the Music Shop at 23 Broad Street; and the Art Shop, just across the street. *(See profile of Blackwell's, page 121.)*

Over to science

Before leaving Broad Street, go back to the Emperors' Heads *(see page 89)*. Just to the right is the **Old Ashmolean Museum**, built between 1678 and 1683 to house the "cabinet of natural curiosities" inherited by Elias Ashmole from the Tradescants. Designed, perhaps, by Thomas Wood, it picks up motifs and ideas from Wren's building alongside, and is equally ornate.

The contents of the museum were transferred to the newly built Ashmolean in Beaumont Street in the late 19th century and the building now houses the **Museum of the History of Science ❽**, a comprehensive collection of early instruments reopened in September 2000 after restoration. The museum may at first seem daunting, with its cases packed with complex astrolabes, quadrants and armillary spheres, but there is much to enjoy, even for the non-scientist.

The ground floor has a collection of very early photographs, dating from the experimental period of the 1840s; they include one of John Ruskin's views of Venice, used as reference material by the artist for his own hand-drawn illustrations for his pioneering work on Renaissance architecture, *The Stones of Venice*. There are also some novelties among the exhibits: George III's ornate silver microscope and an extraordinarily elaborate machine turning handwriting into minuscule engravings,which can be seen only under a microscope.

In the former chemistry laboratory in the basement, a blackboard covered with Einstein's neatly chalked theorems is carefully preserved, a memento of his first Oxford lecture on the Theory of Relativity, given on 16 May 1931. It is partnered by an assortment of gruesome medical and dental instruments, early radios, gramophones and phonographs, and a display on the war-time work of Oxford scientists racing against time to prepare penicillin for large-scale production, using improvised materials such as milk churns and tin baths.

Explorers, writers and Methodists

Between the Art Shop and Blackwell's Too Shop on Broad Street, **Turl Street** marks a boundary of sorts between Town and Gown, for most of the colleges lie to the east and the shops and markets to the west. The street is thought to be named after a pedestrian turnstile or twirling gate that stood in the city wall at the Broad Street end. Looking south, you can see how the street gradually narrows to its original medieval width.

Down Turl Street, on the right, is **Jesus College ❾** (open daily 2–4.30pm; tel: 01865 279700; free). It is said that college porters hate being on duty on Christmas Day because of the constant stream of telephone calls from pranksters ringing to ask "Is that Jesus?" – to which, if the answer is yes, the caller responds by singing "Happy Birthday to you".

Jesus is also known as the Welsh college because it was founded, in 1571, by Brecon-born Hugh Price, and took many of its students from the grammar schools of Wales until 1882. T.E. Lawrence, "Lawrence of Arabia", was one of the non-Welsh alumni, admitted

Map on page 112

in 1907, although he resided only a term in college and spent most of his time studying medieval military architecture in a summer house built for him by his parents in the garden of their North Oxford home (2 Polstead Road). There is a bust of Lawrence in Jesus College Chapel.

The chapel itself, consecrated in 1621, contains a High Victorian altar reredos so out of keeping with the surviving 17th-century woodwork that it is usually curtained off from view. In the same north range of the first quad, the Principal's Lodging has a delicate shell hood of 1700 over the doorway.

Exeter College ⑩ (open daily 2–5pm; tel: 01865 279600; free), opposite Jesus, was founded in 1314 by the Bishop of Exeter, Walter de Stapledon. Much of the college now looks Victorian, due to rebuilding, and the first quadrangle is dominated by the over-large chapel. This was built from 1854 to 1860 to the design of Sir George Gilbert Scott, and the resemblance to a miniature French cathedral is no accident – Scott borrowed freely from the Sainte Chapelle in Paris.

The interior is bathed in the rich colours of stained glass, even on a dull day, and the sense of opulence is enhanced by the mosaic work of the apse. On the right of the altar, the large tapestry of the *Adoration of the Magi* was made in 1890 by the firm founded by William Morris, and designed by Burne-Jones. The two artists met in 1853 as fellow students at Exeter College, and their shared interest in the ideas of Ruskin and the pre-Raphaelites led them to devote their lives to the revival of medieval arts and crafts.

Another Exeter man was J. R. R. Tolkien, author of *The Lord of the Rings*, who much enjoyed the magnificent chestnut trees of the Fellows' Garden, beyond and to the rear of the front quad. The vast tree, "Bishop Heber's chestnut", seems as ancient as the college itself, and members of the Exeter boat

In order to demolish the former chapel of Exeter College, dating from the 17th century, Gilbert Scott had to blow it up with gunpowder.

BELOW: stained glass in Exeter College Chapel

TOLKIEN

John Ronald Ruel Tolkien was born in 1892 in Bloemfontein, South Africa, but was brought up in Birmingham, England. Both his father and mother died when he was young, and he and his brother came under the care of a stern aunt and a local parish priest.

A natural linguist, Tolkien had studied Greek and Latin and was interested in lesser-known languages such as Finnish even before he went to Exeter College in 1911. There he specialised in Old English and also developed his childhood habit of inventing private languages. After World War I, a spell working on the *Oxford English Dictionary* and a teaching job at Leeds, Tolkien returned to Oxford as Professor of Anglo-Saxon. A turning-point came when he met the young writer C.S. Lewis, who encouraged him to publish what he had thought was an unpublishable manuscript – *The Hobbit* (1937). The huge success of this book was followed in 1954 by *The Lord of the Rings*, the trilogy that won him cult status.

But such was Tolkien's following and so insistent were his fans, especially in the psychedelic days of the 1960s, that he was forced to escape Oxford for the anonymity of Bournemouth. He eventually returned to rooms in Merton College, where he died in 1973.

club watch its growth in spring with interest. It is said that if the foliage of the branches, arching over the garden wall, succeed in touching Brasenose College opposite, Exeter will beat its neighbour in the Bumping Races. The magnificent **view** from the top of the garden wall (accessible by stone steps and a walkway) provides a fresh perspective of Radcliffe Square (*see page 94*).

Lincoln  (open Mon–Sat 2–5pm, Sun 11am–5pm; tel: 01865 279800; free) is the last of the colleges fronting on to Turl Street. It was founded in 1427 by the Bishop of Lincoln, Richard Fleming, but he died four years later, leaving the college with little income and few endowments. Because it remained relatively poor, many of the original 15th-century buildings escaped "improvement", and much of the charm of the Front Quad is its unspoiled character.

The Chapel Quad, to the south, was added in the 17th century. The chapel exterior (1629) is conservatively built in the Perpendicular style of the previous century, but the fine carved woodwork inside is much more typical of its age. The richly coloured stained glass, showing prophets, apostles and biblical scenes, is attributed to the prolific German artist Abraham von Linge, who arrived in Oxford in 1629 and proceeded to leave his mark on other college chapels as well, notably University and Queen's.

One of the ironies of Lincoln College is that, founded during an age of heresy specifically to train priests in orthodox church teachings, it nevertheless elected John Wesley to a fellowship in 1726. Members of the Holy Club – nicknamed "the Bible moths" and "Methodists" because of their regular and methodical devotions – used to meet in his college rooms, in Chapel Quadrangle. Another room in the Front Quad, erroneously thought to have been Wesley's, was restored as a memorial by American Methodists in 1925.

One 17th-century Rector of Lincoln left an annual bequest of £10 to pay for champagne and strawberries for college heads and professors each year before Encaenia. The "Creweian Benefaction" is still appreciated by its beneficiaries today.

BELOW: Lincoln College quadrangle

A paradise for gourmets

Brasenose Lane, shaded by the chestnuts of Exeter, has a leafy, rural feel and the cobbled gulley down the middle marks the line of the original open sewer. Undergraduates use the lane as an unofficial cycle path. The lane ends on Radcliffe Square with the Radcliffe Camera and Brasenose College (*see page 94*).

Opposite Brasenose Lane, Market Street leads westwards to arrive at the north entrance of the **Covered Market** , where no quarter is given to the sensibilities of vegetarians, who will find haunches of meat, plump turkeys and blood-dripping game of every kind, hung in great quantities outside the butchers' stalls in true Edwardian style. The market was originally built in 1774 as part of the Paving Commission scheme to rid Oxford of its untidy and often foulsmelling street markets. Fish and meat sellers, later to be joined by butter and fruit retailers, were brought into one place under the supervision of a beadle.

The present structure dates largely from the 1890s, when the market was rebuilt and roofed over. It retains its turn-of-the-century atmosphere, and it is possible to buy a great range of locally produced "poor man's meats" – haggis, brawns, faggots, raised pies, black puddings and Oxford sausages – not to mention fresh fruit and fish, cheeses and rich pastries. There's also a high-class delicatessen and a pasta shop, as well as

Map
on page
112

cake shops and tea shops all vying for custom alongside smart boutiques and florists. The market wouldn't be the same without its traditional "greasy spoon" café, but there also several more upmarket eateries.

You can exit either on to High Street or via **Golden Cross Yard** ⓭, an enclosed courtyard surrounded by timber-framed ranges dating from the 16th to 19th-century. The buildings were meticulously restored in 1987 to create a stylish precinct. The courtyard was originally formed in the Middle Ages for the Cross Inn; indeed an inn may have existed on this site as early as 1193. During the 16th century the inn was used by travelling companies of players and it is said that Shakespeare stayed there on occasion. The first floor of the Pizza Express occupies the former bedroom accommodation of the inn and contains the major fragments of two painted rooms, the Crown Chamber and the Prince's Chamber.

The city's focal point

Head through the 15th-century archway of Golden Cross Yard into **Cornmarket Street**, Oxford's main shopping thoroughfare, pedestrianised in 1999. Though severely blemished by the wholesale destruction of many of its fine buildings, it still has a number of historic attractions.

The busy crossroads at the southern end is known as **Carfax** ⓮, after the Norman *Quatre Vois* (four ways). This is the ancient heart of Saxon Oxford, where the four roads from north, south, east and west met. The prime attraction is **Carfax Tower**, all that remains of the 13th-century St Martin's Church which was pulled down as part of a road-widening scheme in 1896 and was itself built on the site of an earlier, late-Saxon church. The east side of the tower, which can be climbed for fine **views** of the city (open late Mar–late Oct 10am–5.30pm,

The Covered Market has its own style and atmosphere.

LEFT: Carfax Tower.
BELOW: pressure salesmanship on Cornmarket Street

Map on page 112

A busker entertains locals and tourists outside Carfax Tower.

BELOW: the Saxon St Michael-at-the-Northgate Church.

Nov–early Mar 10am–3.30pm; entrance fee) is embellished with **quarterboys** which strike the bell every 15 minutes (replicas of those taken from the original church), as well as the original church clock. Note above the gateway to the right of the tower the sculpture of St Martin giving his cloak to the beggar. Also on Carfax stood the Swindlestock Tavern, where, on St Scholastica's Day (10 February) 1355, an argument between scholars and the landlord developed into a riot, resulting in the deaths of many scholars. The site of the tavern is indicated by a plaque in the wall of the Abbey National Bank.

On rare occasions, perhaps early Sunday morning, you can stand beneath Carfax Tower and enjoy an uninterrupted view of the beautiful High Street, or look down St Aldate's to the great pepper-pot tower of Christ Church (*see page 153*).

Shakespeare's godson, William Davenant (himself a playwright), was christened in St Michael's Church (*see below*) in 1606, and Shakespeare is known to have stayed regularly with Davenant's father, landlord of the Crown Tavern. This building, just across the street (No. 3 Cornmarket), was changed almost beyond recognition in the 1920s, but the **Painted Room** ⑮ on the second floor (above the betting shop and open during office hours) has well-preserved mid-16th-century wall paintings of fruits and flowers.

Continue until you get to the corner of Ship Street. Here is the former **Ship Inn** ⑯, one of Oxford's finest timber-framed buildings. Originally built in 1389 as the New Inn, it was recently restored by Jesus College to its 18th-century appearance, and is now occupied by Laura Ashley. At the other side of Ship Street stands the **tower** of the church of **St Michael-at-the-Northgate** ⑰. Built as a look-out against the Danes, this sturdy tower (open Apr–Oct 10am–5pm, Nov–Mar 10am–4pm; entrance fee) is Oxford's oldest surviving building and dates to around 1050, exhibiting characteristic late Saxon features.

The tower was built up against the north gate of the city walls, part of the fortifications of Edward the Elder's original Saxon town. The gate (dismantled by the Paving Commission in the late 18th century) was enlarged in 1293 to create a prison known as the Bocardo. Scholars debate whether Bocardo simply means "boggard", a privy, or whether it derives from the medieval logician's term for a syllogism, implying a difficult trap from which to escape. The Oxford Martyrs Cranmer, Latimer and Ridley were all imprisoned here before being taken outside the city wall to be executed (*see page 111*). Their cell door is in the tower.

St Michael's Church was substantially restored after a fire in 1953 but some fine 15th-century glass has survived, including a window showing Christ crucified on a lily flower (symbolising purity). The medallions in the window above the altar are the oldest examples of stained glass in Oxford, dating from 1290. The font is late 14th century. The treasury in the tower is used to display a beautiful silver chalice of 1562, a lustful sheela-na-gig (a late 11th-century erotic stone carving) and a charter of 1612 bearing the great seal of King James I.

Continue north into Magdalen Street, with Debenhams on the left and St Mary Magdalen on the right, to arrive back at the Martyrs' Memorial. ❏

Blackwell's

Blackwell's is one of the most famous bookshops in the world. It first opened in October 1879 and is situated at the end of Broad Street, in one of the most beautiful parts of the city, surrounded by Trinity, Balliol, Exeter, Hertford and Wadham colleges and opposite Wren's Sheldonian Theatre.

Benjamin Henry Blackwell's shop was just 12 ft (3.6 metres) square and was criticised by many for its situation – furthest from the city centre and with two well-established bookshops opposite. Frederick Macmillan, proprietor of the publishing house of Macmillan and forebear of Harold Macmillan, who was prime minister and Chancellor of Oxford University, said: "Well, Mr Blackwell, we shall be pleased to open an account with you but I fear you have chosen the wrong side of the street to be successful."

This pessimism was soon disproved. Blackwell's devotion to books – he characterised bookselling as "the infinite capacity for taking pains" – quickly became legendary. Professors, dons and undergraduates hastened to his door. The shop was originally so small that, when more than three customers came in, the apprentice had to be sent outside.

Right from the start the tradition was established that customers should be allowed to browse among the books, undisturbed by the staff. The custom continues today.

Naturally enough, famous literary figures have always been among the customers and the shop itself has been the subject of many writings. In *Summoned by Bells*, John Betjeman wrote:

*I wandered into Blackwell's, where my bill
Was so enormous that it wasn't paid
Till ten years later, from the small estate
My father left.*

Other well-known customers have included Hilaire Belloc, A.E. Houseman, Oscar Wilde, George Bernard Shaw and Lewis Carroll.

Blackwell's gradually expanded in order to meet the steadily increasing business and took over more space behind the shop. After World War II some departments were moved to nearby premises. The most notable part of the expansion was the development of a vast underground room, the Norrington Room, opened in 1966,and named after the president of Trinity College, under which it extended.

Still a family firm, Blackwell's is also a publisher in its own right. Benjamin Henry Blackwell began publishing poetry in the 1880s, and this was continued by his son, Basil, publishing early works by many writers who subsequently became famous, among them Tolkien and Robert Graves. From these small beginnings, two major publishing companies have grown: Blackwell Publishers, which specialises in humanities, and Blackwell Scientific Publications, which concentrates on scientific and medical titles. Sir Basil Blackwell, known to all as "the Gaffer", was awarded a knighthood in 1956 for his services to bookselling.

Today, Blackwell's has nine bookshops in town ranging from travel and arts to children's books, as well as one at Oxford Brookes University and another in the academic centre of the John Radcliffe Hospital. ❑

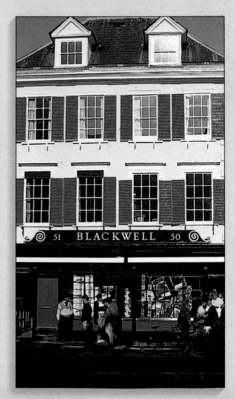

RIGHT: Blackwell's main store has its front on the original site of Blackwell's bookshop.

THE HIGH

High Street, known as "The High", has a grace and elegance unmatched elsewhere in the city, inspiring Nikolaus Pevsner to describe it as "one of the world's greatest streets"

High Street is different from other streets in central Oxford in that it is curved. This is because the layout of the original Saxon town was out of alignment with the crossing point of the River Cherwell to the east, at the site of Magdalen Bridge. So beyond the original east gate (where St Mary the Virgin Church now stands) the road, then nothing more than a track, began a gentle curve down to the river. Over the centuries, not only colleges but also inns and shops were built, resulting in the charming street we see today.

History in the making

The High Street has always been busy, with local and long-distance traffic. In the 18th and 19th centuries, the coach-and-four to London departed with ever-increasing rapidity from coaching inns such as the Angel and the Mitre. Since the arrival of motor vehicles, there have been attempts to limit the numbers of vehicles, including a radical (thankfully abandoned) scheme to construct a link road from St Ebbe's across Christ Church Meadow. In 1999, the most radical shake-up to Oxford's transport scheme in decades closed the western end of the High to Longwall Street to all traffic except delivery vans and buses.

The Carfax end is the commercial end, mostly taken up by shops and the facade of the Covered Market (*see page 118*). But there are interesting details worth examining. Starting on the south side, at No. 137, is Savory's fragrant pipe and tobacco shop, in a medieval building that was once the Fox Inn. Also take a look at the sign above the silversmiths at **No. 131**, a white dog with a giant watch in its mouth. Just here a small alley, one of many that delineated the original medieval plots along this part of the street, leads down to the Chequers Inn, a tavern dating from the 15th century with many interesting features. The next alley along is signposted to the Chiang Mai Kitchen, a Thai restaurant housed in the beautiful **Kemp Hall ❶**. Built by an Oxford alderman in 1637, this is a fine example of the numerous timber-framed houses that sprang up all over Oxford during the great rebuilding of the city in the 16th and 17th centuries. The timber door with its projecting canopy is original, as are many of the windows; the interior is also very well preserved.

Back on the High Street, the next building of interest is **No. 126**. With its elegantly curved windows and fine proportions, this is the best-preserved example of a 17th-century facade in Oxford. But the building itself actually dates back a lot further, for it is known to have been owned by a bell founder before being taken over by St Frideswide's Abbey in 1350. This is the story of many of the buildings along the High Street – medieval in origin but given new facades later.

LEFT: the elegant, curved High Street. **BELOW:** the historic Mitre, once a coaching inn.

Cross the road at the traffic lights to arrive at the **Mitre ❷**, now housing a restaurant and tearoom but once a popular student inn (open Mon–Sat 10.30am–11.30pm, Sun noon–10.30pm; tel: 01865 244563). It was built in about 1600 over a 13th-century vault, which sadly can no longer be visited. Nevertheless, the Mitre remains full of history, enlivened by anecdotes of ale-supping clergy. The German clergyman Pastor Moritz relates in his *Travels in England* (1795) that he was taken there by a companion and found it full of convivial parsons debating whether or not a passage in the *Book of Judges* ("wine cheereth God and man") meant literally that God was a wine tippler. A sign in the lobby recalls The Mitre's role as a coaching inn.

The original tower of All Saints' Church was declared unsafe in 1660 and local residents were encouraged to leave their homes. It took another 40 years to collapse.

An eclectic mix

The Mitre stands on the corner of Turl Street (*see page 116*), and on the opposite corner stands the former **All Saints' Church ❸**, now used as a library by Lincoln College. The splendid tower was rebuilt after the original tower collapsed in 1700, partly to the designs of Nicholas Hawksmoor. Beyond this is the High Street frontage to Brasenose College (*see page 96*), which, despite looking positively medieval, was built only in the latter part of the 19th and early 20th centuries.

On the south side is a fine run of buildings with 18th-century facades. The Regency bow-fronted shop window of Hall Bros, University Tailors is used to display silk-lined academic gowns and clothing embroidered with multi-coloured college crests. **No. 117/118** has a fine Art-Nouveau shop window, while next door at No. 116 are the premises of the **Oxford University Press Bookshop ❹** (open Mon–Sat 9am–6pm), which sells only the books that the Press publishes. Further down, beyond King Edward Street, **Nos. 106** and **107**

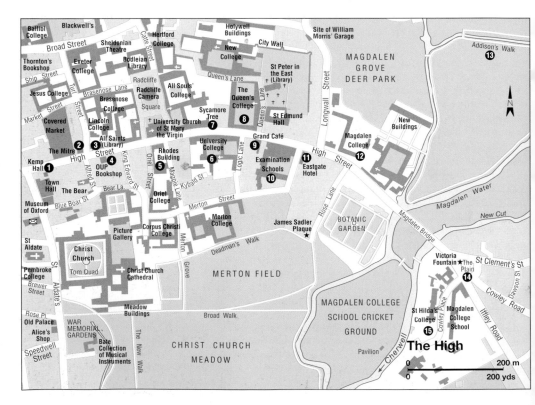

(The University of Oxford Shop and A-Plan Insurance) are particularly interesting. Together they were originally **Tackley's Inn**, built in 1320 and subsequently rented out for use as an academic hall. A-Plan may allow you through to the back of their premises to see the 16th-century roof structure of the hall as well as a large medieval window. The cellar is regarded as the best medieval cellar in Oxford.

On the other side of Oriel Street, opposite the University Church of St Mary the Virgin (*see page 97*), is the **Rhodes Building ❺** of Oriel College, built in 1910 from funds bequeathed by Cecil Rhodes, the South African statesman who made a fortune in Southern Africa after completing his education at Oriel and ultimately gave his name to Rhodesia (now Zimbabwe). Rhodes also endowed Rhodes Scholarships at Oxford, one of the most notable beneficiaries being Bill Clinton.

Continue along the south side, cross Magpie Lane past the Barclays Old Bank buildings. Opposite is All Souls' College (*see page 94*). Dating from the 14th century, this is the oldest surviving part of the college, though it was refaced in the 19th century. A line of grotesque sculptures runs beneath the parapet.

Changing statues

Still on the south side, we now come to the long frontage of **University College ❻** (closed except by special arrangement). The claim that "Univ" was founded by King Alfred was invented by medieval lawyers, but it did not stop the college celebrating its millennium in 1874. Even without this fiction, Univ is respectably ancient: William of Durham, who had fled from Paris after a row between the kings of France and England, left funds for its foundation in 1249,

Map on page 124

The OUP bookshop is a relative newcomer to The High.

BELOW: the magnificent Rhodes Building.

Shelley cultivated a reputation for extreme eccentricity while at Oxford, wearing outlandish clothes and sporting spectacularly long hair. Known as "Mad Shelley", he complained that "they are very dull people here".

and on this basis it can claim to be the oldest college. None of the original buildings remain, however, the college having been rebuilt from substantial benefactions in the 17th century in the now familiar Oxford Jacobean-Gothic style.

The range facing the High is in two parts, firstly the **Front Quad** (with main entrance), completed in the 1670s, and beyond the **Radcliffe Quad**, almost an exact copy completed 40 years later. The gate-towers contain, respectively, the statues of Queen Anne (which replaced a statue of King Alfred in 1700) and Queen Mary. On the inner face of the front quad is a statue of James II, wearing a toga, one of only two statues in England of this unpopular Catholic king. It was erected in 1676 by the then Master, Obadiah Walker, who supported the monarch's religious views.

Before reaching the main range, you may have noticed a small dome peeping above the wall. This covers the **monument to Percy Bysshe Shelley**. Shelley spent less than six months as an undergraduate at Univ, having been expelled in 1811 for his joint authorship of a pamphlet on *The Necessity of Atheism*. Some 80 years later, in 1894, Lady Shelley presented the monument to the college. Designed by Edward Onslow Ford, it was intended for the poet's grave, in the English Cemetery in Rome, but was found to be too large. The life-sized sculpture of the naked, drowned poet (he perished off Livorno in 1822), supported by winged lions and the Muse of Poetry, is shockingly pathetic. It can be reached via a passageway in the northwest corner of the Front Quad.

Another attraction of the college is the **Chapel**. Although refurbished by Sir George Gilbert Scott in 1862, it still retains its original, finely detailed stained glass, designed by the German artist Abraham von Linge, his last known work and full of exotic details. The ante-chapel contains fine monuments by Flaxman,

BELOW: Shelley's vulnerable memorial.
RIGHT: University College.

PERCY BYSSHE SHELLEY.
BORN AUG 4. 1792.
DIED JULY 8. 1822.

including that of Sir William Jones (died 1794), judge in the Calcutta High Court, who is shown compiling his digest of Hindu law.

On the north side of the High, directly opposite the gatehouse of University College's front quad, stands a lone **sycamore tree** ❼, whose presence endows the High Street with a rural flavour. As the only landmark that can be seen from both ends, it has long been regarded as Oxford's most significant tree and has even been described as one of the most important trees in Europe.

Map
on page
124

On to Queen's

To the right of the tree runs the beautiful baroque facade of **Queen's College** ❽ (access only with an official guided tour booked at the Oxford Information Centre; tel: 01865 279121; entrance fee). Facade is perhaps the wrong term, for the High Street front is no more than a screen, with a handsome domed gatehouse, containing a statue of Queen Caroline. All this work was once attributed to Nicholas Hawksmoor, but is now thought to be by the local Oxford mason William Townesend, and was completed around 1735.

Queen Caroline occupies pride of place because she donated substantial funds to the 18th-century rebuilding of the college, which swept away all the original buildings. The college is, however, named after Queen Philippa, wife of Edward III, whose chaplain, Robert of Eglesfeld, founded it in 1340. Queen's still marks the memory of its founder with an ancient ceremony whereby dinner guests are presented with a needle and thread – the French for which (*aiguilles et fils*) is a pun on Eglesfeld's name. The more famous Boar's Head Feast, celebrated in December, commemorates a Queen's student who is said to have killed a wild boar by thrusting a copy of Aristotle's works down its throat.

The sycamore tree opposite "Univ" has a special importance.

BELOW: Queen's College, the sixth Oxford college to be founded.

Frank Cooper's marmalade remains a breakfast favourite.

As one passes through the centre of the Front Quad, the north range ahead has the hall on the left and the chapel on the right. The latter, consecrated in 1719, reused the colourful stained-glass windows from the old chapel, designed by Abraham van Linge in 1636, and is notable for the bold and exotic foliage framing the biblical scenes.

Beyond lies the Back Quad, with its splendid library of 1696 on the left, lit by a great expanse of glass, through which the stucco frieze and ornate bookcases may just be glimpsed. A narrow passage to the left of the library passes between high walls into a tiny rose garden known, for reasons now forgotten, as "the Nun's Garden".

Food, glorious food

Opposite Queen's, connecting the High with Merton Street, is **Logic Lane**, so called because there used to be a school of logicians at the High Street end. Cross Logic Lane and continue along the south side of the High. **No. 84**, with its elegant windows and Corinthian columns, was once the grocery shop belonging to Frank Cooper. It was here, in 1874, that Cooper began selling jars of surplus marmalade produced by his wife, Sarah Jane, from an old family recipe on her kitchen range. It proved so popular that a factory had to be constructed on Park End Street. Although the firm sold out and moved in 1974, the marmalade is still manufactured under the original label. The premises now house the **Grand Café** ❾ (open Mon–Sat 9am–11pm, Sun til 10.30pm), a friendly, Edwardian-style café, with high ceiling, marble, mosaics and chandeliers.

BELOW: the Grand Café has an eclectic menu.

Next door, at **No. 83**, are offices of the Oxford Bus Company, worth mentioning on account of the delightful first-floor Venetian window.

TRANSPORT ON THE HIGH

Oxford's High Street was once described by the eminent architectural historian Nikolaus Pevsner as "one of the world's greatest streets". It has, however, had a protracted battle with traffic since the advent of the motor car.

Pictures from the 19th century depict a broad, elegant and largely empty thoroughfare, but archive photos from the 1950s onwards show a gradual build-up of traffic and traffic jams. The street has always been an important artery for the city's flow of people and vehicles. In the age of horse-drawn transport, the High was the site of several important coaching inns, notably the Mitre, the Eastgate and the long-disappeared Angel Inn. As cars and buses became more commonplace, however, the street began to suffer from pollution and congestion, and several schemes, including a tram system, were proposed as antidotes to the motor car.

The 1999 Oxford Transport Strategy finally banned private cars from the High for large parts of the day, allowing buses, taxis and, of course, bicycles to continue to use the street. Local traders complained loudly that the ban had a negative impact on their business, but the City Council insisted that a traffic-free High Street (and Cornmarket) would attract more rather than fewer shoppers.

Stress and statistics

Next comes the massive block of the **Examination Schools** ⑩, built on the site of the Angel, one of Oxford's most important coaching inns (in 1831 it was operating 11 daily coach services to London and 13 others to all parts of the country). Introduced only in the late 18th century, the first written examinations were held in the Divinity School, before moving to the various rooms of the Old Schools Quadrangle. But by the second half of the 19th century a new, purpose-built edifice was required. This was built in 1882 to replace the Old Schools, now inadequate to accommodate all the students attending lectures and sitting examinations.

The building was designed by T. G. Jackson in neo-Jacobean style with classical and Gothic elements, and the result, especially the High Street facade, has sometimes been described as heavy-handed – designed, perhaps, to intimidate the hapless exam candidates. Students can be seen entering and leaving the building in the main exam month of June, all dressed in "sub-fusc" garb without which they are not allowed to sit their exam. The end of the examination ordeal can be a messy affair as students celebrate with champagne, flour bombs and streamers.

The High Street facade of the Examination Schools building is impressive, but the most beautiful side of the building, with its fine courtyard, overlooks **Merton Street** around the corner. On the same corner stands the **Eastgate Hotel** ⑪. It was at this point, in the middle of the street, that the east gate through the medieval town wall stood until its demolition at the hands of the Paving Commission in 1772. There has been an inn on this site since 1605, but the present hotel was built in 1899 in the style of a 17th-century town house.

Map
on page
124

The Eastgate Hotel once served as a major coaching inn.

BELOW: Examination Schools, the students' least favourite building.

Opposite, at No. 48, is a shoe shop which was once the bicycle repair shop of William Morris. Continue as far as the Longwall Street traffic lights, where you cross the road and proceed towards Magdalen College, whose famous tower dominates the eastern end of the High Street.

Golden glow

Magdalen College ⑫ (pronounced *maudlin*) (open daily 2–5pm; tel: 01865 276000; entrance fee) was founded in 1458 by William Waynflete, Bishop of Winchester and Lord Chancellor of England under King Henry VI. It was on the site of the Hospital of St John the Baptist, some of whose buildings still survive as part of the college's High Street range. Built outside the city walls, Magdalen had lots of space in which to expand, and its grounds encompass large areas of meadow, bounded in the east by the River Cherwell.

Completed in 1505, the **Bell Tower** is famous for the Latin grace sung from the top by the choristers every May Morning. The tradition probably dates back to the tower's inauguration in 1505. Nobody is certain whether it has continued in unbroken succession since that date, but the ceremony was in full swing in the 18th century, when spectators were pelted with eggs by undergraduates from the tower. Today, when the Magdalen College School choristers sing from the top of the tower at 6am on 1 May, the ceremony initiates a morning of revelries: bells ring out, Morris men dance, and students take their lovers off by punt for champagne breakfasts along the banks of the River Cherwell.

During the Civil War, the tower was used as a vantage post by the Royalist forces who had established themselves in the city after the Battle of Edgehill in 1642. But while Magdalen, along with the rest of the university, lent its full

TIP

On May Morning at Magdalen it may be difficult to hear the choristers among a large and noisy crowd, but many pubs open specially to serve breakfast as well as beer.

BELOW: beautiful Magdalen College and its Bell Tower.

Map on page 124

support to Charles I, it did not support the unpopular James II, who attempted to make the college a Catholic seminary. In 1687 James briefly had his own man (Bishop Parker) installed as college president and had Mass, run by Jesuit appointees, set up in the chapel. With the advance of the Protestant William of Orange, however, James promptly did a U-turn and had the original Fellows reinstated on 25 October 1688, an event still celebrated in Magdalen as Restoration Day. But it was too late for the unfortunate king, who soon lost his crown and spent the rest of his life in exile in France.

Enter the college via the porter's lodge on High Street and take the diagonal path across **St John's Quadrangle**. To the right, you enter the low **Muniment Tower** of 1485, which shelters the west doorway to the **Chapel**, carved with figures of St John, Edward VI, Mary Magdalene, St Swithun and William of Waynflete. Originally built in 1480, the chapel was completely redesigned in the early 19th century. But with its stone vaulting and ornamental screens, it is still worth seeing, especially by candlelight at choral evensong. The ante-chapel contains some medieval stalls with carved misericords, a good selection of monuments, including that of the founder's father, Richard Patten (died 1450), and – the most interesting feature – sepia stained-glass windows.

The passageway leads through to the delightful **Cloister Quadrangle**, the 15th-century core of the college. With its vaulted passage, the quad still looks very ancient, though the north and east wings had to be rebuilt in the early 19th century after attempts were made to have the Cloisters cleared to make way for the New Buildings (*see below*). The allegorical figures on the buttresses, called "hieroglyphicals", were added in 1508. One is free to speculate what they represent, for nobody really knows – though in the 1670s, Dr William

The Magdalen crest

BELOW: detail of Magdalen College Chapel.

Some students find time to relax away from their books.

BELOW:
Addison's Walk,
looking towards
Magdalen tower.

Reeks produced a 60-page treatise arguing that they symbolised the virtues (sobriety and temperance) and vices (gluttony, lust and pride) of academic life. The grotesques of the cloister walls include more dark, mysterious subjects, and several that are explicitly erotic – a surprising fact, given that most are the work of Victorian carvers.

A narrow passageway in the north range of the cloister debouches into a vast expanse of green lawns, with the stately colonnaded **New Buildings** straight ahead. Completed in 1733, this was intended to be part of a huge neoclassical quadrangle. Fortunately, the money ran out and only one range was ever built.

Opposite the New Buildings turn along the path to the left, where the massive **plane tree**, planted in 1801, is a direct descendant of a hybrid that was developed by Jacob Bobart in the Botanic Garden (*see page 143*). It is worth following this path a short way in order to look back, southwards, over the fine jumble of towers, pinnacles and Cotswold-tiled roofs of the college – Oxford's dreaming spires in miniature.

Open spaces

To the north, beyond the fence, is **Magdalen Grove**, winter home of the college herd of fallow deer. The grove once looked considerably more leafy than it does at present. Massive elm trees, planted in around 1689, unfortunately succumbed to disease and were felled in 1978. The deer have been here since the early 18th century, when they were introduced to supply the college with venison. Even today surplus animals are occasionally culled and served up in the hall.

In the other direction, through the wrought-iron gates, is a bridge over a branch of the Cherwell River. Here, if you watch on a sunny day, you are quite

likely to see brown trout, or even larger fish, such as perch or pike, basking in the clear, warm waters below, ready to dart back into the shadows created by the overhanging chestnut tree branches beyond if they are disturbed.

Map on page 124

Across the bridge the narrow path turns left to follow a raised bank beside the Cherwell, with Long Meadow, summer grazing home for the Magdalen deer, to the right. The raised causeway, almost completely enclosed by a tunnel of tree foliage, was partly created out of the remains of Civil War defensive embankments. It is known as **Addison's Walk** ⓭, after Joseph Addison (1672–1719), poet and *Spectator* essayist, whose rooms in Magdalen College overlooked these meadows.

The walk was not laid out in its present form, nor named after Addison, until the 19th century, but the name is appropriate since Addison was a pioneer of naturalistic landscape design, arguing in his *Spectator* essays that the works of nature are often superior to the artificial creations of man.

Ironically, the verdant beauty of the walk was almost changed for ever by one of Addison's later followers. Humphry Repton proposed, in 1801, to dam the Cherwell and create an artificial lake out of the meadows. We must be thankful that the plan was not executed, for the meadows are now famous for a far more beautiful sight than a blank sheet of water: in late April, or early May, the grass is filled with the graceful nodding flower heads of purple and white snake's head fritillaries, one of the largest colonies of these rare wild flowers in Britain. Almost picked to extinction in the 19th century, the Magdalen fritillaries have been carefully protected since 1908. The grazing fallow deer are part of a careful management programme, introduced to the meadows to keep down the buttercups that were threatening to crowd out the vulnerable fritillaries.

BELOW: there are supposed to be 40 deer in Magdalen Grove, one for each of the original number of Fellows.

OSCAR WILDE

Perhaps Magdalen College's most flamboyant old boy was Oscar Fingal O'Flahertie Wills Wilde, who was a student here between 1874 and 1878, causing controversy in almost everything he did. Already armed with a degree from Dublin, Wilde was a brilliant and precocious Classics scholar who effortlessly won a double First as well as the prestigious Newdigate Prize for poetry.

The young Wilde relished his time at Oxford, likening it to Athens, where "the realities of sordid life were kept at a distance". At first, he was a keen sportsman, taking part in rowing, boxing and shooting, but gradually he adopted a more mannered, aesthetic posture, pretending to be lazy during the day but in fact working hard throughout the night. Legend has it that he provocatively asked for extra paper after only one hour of a three-hour finals exam and then walked out half an hour before the end – only to be awarded the highest marks in the entire year.

But it was Oxford, too, that contributed to his downfall, as he met Lord Alfred Douglas ("Bosie") on a visit to the city. Their openly homosexual relationship led to his imprisonment in Reading Jail and his eventual exile and early death in Paris in 1900. He always remembered Oxford as "the most flower-like time of one's life".

At the northern end of Addison's Walk, there are views across to the modern buildings of St Catherine's College (not accessible from this point). The path turns to the right and, at the eastern angle, a bridge over the Cherwell provides access to Magdalen's **Fellows' Garden**. This delightfully secluded area demonstrates just how much space the college has at its disposal. It is particularly delightful in spring when the ornamental trees are in flower and the grass is covered in daffodils and anemones. To complete the circuit, return to the bridge and turn left, following the riverbank to Magdalen Bridge and right to return to the college grounds.

Go back to the entrance via the cloisters and then the **Chaplain's Quadrangle**. To the left the Bell Tower soars heavenwards and to its right is the oldest bit of the college, part of the 13th-century hospital incorporated into the High Street range. Passing from the Chaplain's Quadrangle into St John's Quadrangle, you'll notice on the left wall an outside **pulpit**, from where a service is conducted once a year on the Feast of St John the Baptist (24 June), a tradition that dates back to the earliest days of the college.

Exit Magdalen, and on the opposite side of the street you'll see the main entrance to the Botanic Garden (*see page 143*).

Continue along the High to **Magdalen Bridge**. The first bridge to cross the Cherwell at this point was a timber construction built in 1004. It was replaced by a stone-built structure in the 16th century, but this was demolished during the Civil War and replaced with a drawbridge. The present bridge dates from 1772. Part of the major programme of road improvements instigated by the Paving Commission, it has since been widened a couple of times to cope with the ever-increasing volume of traffic.

BELOW:
punts for hire at
Magdalen Bridge.

Back to civilisation

At the other side is the triangular junction known as **The Plain** . This busy junction marks the divergence of St Clement's, Cowley and Iffley roads, fanning out to the suburbs of Oxford. Isolated in the island in the centre stands the **Victoria Fountain**, which was originally used as a drinking trough for horses. It was unfortunately constructed two years too late to commemorate Queen Victoria's Diamond Jubilee in 1897. Until its destruction at the hands of the Paving Commission in 1772, the church of St Clements had stood on this site.

Off to the right, in Cowley Place, is the **Magdalen College School**, originally founded in 1480 but relocated to this new site in 1894. A bit further down is **St Hilda's College** ⓫ (open daily 10am–5pm; tel: 01865 276884; free), founded in 1893 but occupying a fine 18th-century house that enjoys fine views of the Cherwell and Christ Church Meadow.

St Hilda's is the only remaining all-woman college at Oxford. Its founder was the formidable principal of Cheltenham Ladies' College, Dorothea Beale, and she named the new institution after the 7th-century Abbess of Whitby, who had been the first great educator of women in England. Miss Beale stated, in documents relating to the aims of the college, that "I want none to go for the sake of a pleasant life", and the strict chaperonage system, along with measures such as iron grilles fitted on the hall windows, were all designed to prevent encounters between ladies at the college and members of the opposite sex.

A contemporary wit penned a few immortal lines of protest on behalf of Miss Beale's charges: *Miss Buss and Miss Beale/Cupid's darts do not feel./How different from us/Miss Beale and Miss Buss.*

Walk across Magdalen Bridge for a superb view of the High Street. ❑

The Victoria Fountain on the Plain was donated by Morrells Brewery in 1899.

BELOW: studying is a serious business.

TOWN AND GOWN THROUGH THE YEAR

The rhythms of university life have little impact on the city, but once a year on a May morning, the whole of Oxford celebrates the coming of summer

With its three-term calendar and time-honoured diary of events and ceremonies, the university has an annual rhythm all of its own.

Each term witnesses the ritualistic conferring of degrees on successful students, the various gatherings of gowned academic notables and the occasional feast days which have long been celebrated by individual colleges.

Less appealing to most undergraduates is the inevitability of examinations: Finals in Trinity (Summer) Term and Prelims or Mods at the end of Hilary (Spring) Term.

For rowing enthusiasts, the highlights of the year are the inter-college races known as Torpids (seventh week of Hilary Term) and Eights Week (fifth week of Trinity Term). It is around this time, in May and June, before students depart for the long summer vacation, that the university lets its hair down with post-exam May Balls and endless other parties.

EVENTS IN THE CITY

The city has its own annual fun events: the Lord Mayor's Parade over the Easter weekend, and St Giles' Fair in early September.

A more recent innovation is the City Council's series of Fun in the Parks days, with fairs, music and multicultural activities around the city. They usually take place on Bank Holidays in spring and summer and are well attended by the non-student population.

But perhaps Oxford's annual high point takes place early on 1 May, when crowds from all walks of life assemble at Magdalen Bridge to hear the choristers welcome the advent of another summer.

▽ **ST GILES' FAIR**
The 18th-century St Giles' Fair was a toy and craft fair, but today the two-day event offers hair-raising roller-coaster rides, garish prizes and sticky candyfloss.

▽ **MAY DAY**
May Day is an excuse for revellers of every description to stay up all night and continue the festivities into the next day.

◁ **DEGREE CEREMONIES**
Led by the university's Chancellor, dignitaries who are to be awarded degrees proceed with pomp and ceremony, dressed in academic regalia.

YOU *SHALL* GO TO THE BALL

Most colleges hold a lavish party at least every other year at the end of Trinity Term. Officially known as "Commemoration Balls", these extravagant events celebrate the end of exams and the prospect of a lengthy summer vacation.

The dress code for undergraduates and their guests is traditional and rigorously enforced: dinner jackets and black bow ties for men, ball gowns for women. Tickets are very expensive (£100-plus for a double), and the richer colleges compete as to who can organise the most luxurious food and the best entertainment. Big-name bands often appear, paid for by the inflated ticket prices, while champagne and good food are *de rigueur*.

Understandably, security is tight, as gate-crashers attempt to scale college walls to join in the fun. Those with stamina carry on until dawn, when champagne breakfast is served, and some even set off on punting expeditions.

While undoubtedly enjoyed by those involved, college balls do not find favour with all Oxford residents, some of whom object to the noise and the ostentatious extravagance of the students.

△ **ENCAENIA**
Encaenia is the university's most colourful academic ceremony. In June visiting dignitaries from politics and the arts are presented with honorary degrees.

△ **EIGHTS WEEK**
Eights Week, lasting four days in late May, has been around since 1815 and provides rival college rowing teams (eights) with the chance to compete against one another.

▷ **MAGDALEN CHORISTERS**
The traditional ceremony of May Morning begins at 6am, when choristers from Magdalen College School sing an invocation to summer from Magdalen College Tower.

SOUTH OF THE HIGH

*Discover an old tavern and some venerable colleges,
including Merton, on the way to the Botanic Garden,
one of Europe's finest and Britain's oldest*

Map on page 140

This route starts at Carfax and heads east, but soon forsakes the High Street for more evocative back streets. Merton College is especially important, as many of its features provided the model for later college foundations.

From Carfax, cross over to the south side of the High Street and proceed east as far as Alfred Street. Turn right to arrive at the **Bear ❶** (open Mon–Sat noon–11pm, Sun to 10.30pm), one of Oxford's oldest pubs (there has been a pub on its site since 1242), and full of genuine charm. Enclosed in its tiny, panelled rooms, with their smoke-kippered ceilings, are over 7,000 ties displayed in cabinets on the walls and rafters – from the Cheltenham College Mind Games Society to the East of Suez Golfing Club. You are still liable to have your tie added to the collection, although the tradition of cutting off those of unsuspecting customers seems (fortunately) to have faded. There is excellent pub food, and in summer you can eat outside in the adjoining yard.

LEFT: Corpus Christi College and its famous sundial.
BELOW: during exams students are required to dress appropriately.

Oriel and Corpus Christi

Walk east along Bear Lane to arrive in Oriel Square, with its 18th-century houses. At the southwest corner is the Canterbury Gate of Christ Church (*see page 157*). **Oriel College ❷** (closed to the public), founded in 1324, originally occupied a house called La Oriole, because of its prominent upper bay window (medieval Latin: *oratoriolum*).

Nothing medieval survives now, but Oriel does have a splendidly ostentatious Front Quadrangle, built from 1620 to 1642 in the Jacobean-Gothic style. This form of architecture is peculiar to Oxford and combines beautifully shaped gables with traceried windows of medieval appearance. Dominating the quad is the staircase entrance to the hall, with its open strapwork cresting, and its inscription *Regnante Carolo* making a bold statement of Royalist support for Charles I. In the niches above are statues of Charles I and Edward II (Oriel's founder, Adam de Brome, was one of Edward's civil servants) as well as a matronly Virgin and Child.

Adajcent to the Canterbury Gate, at the beginning of cobbled Merton Street, is the entrance to **Corpus Christi College ❸** (open daily 1.30–4.30pm; tel: 01865 276700; free). Founded in 1512 by Richard Foxe, Bishop of Winchester, this small college has always been somewhat radical. Foxe, a friend of the great humanist Erasmus, encouraged the study of "pagan" classical texts in Latin and Greek, so aligning the college with contemporary Renaissance thought. In 1963, the college took the radical step of allowing women to dine as guests in hall: they were not finally admitted as students, however, until 1979.

The intimate Front Quad of the college contains a famous **sundial** of 1581, topped by the emblem of

This postbox on Merton Lane has seen plenty of homesick student correspondence.

the college, a pelican wounding her breast to feed her young, a symbol of Christ's sacrifice. The plinth below is inscribed with a perpetual calendar from 1606. A passageway on the left leads to the chapel, with its colourful Arts and Crafts window depicting St Christopher, designed by Henry Payne in 1931.

Visitors should not leave without also seeing the small college **garden** behind the Fellows Building. Dominated by a magnificent copper beech, the garden provides a fine view of Christ Church Meadow, with the Fellows Garden of Christ Church in the foreground. The view from the raised platform at the back is even better, and you can see down into the secretive Deanery Garden of Christ Church, where Lewis Carroll first got to know young Alice.

Along to Merton

Beyond Corpus Christi is the tower of Merton College Chapel. Founded in 1264 by Walter de Merton, Lord Chancellor of England, **Merton College ❹** (open Mon–Fri 2–4pm, Sat–Sun 10am–4pm; tel: 01865 276310; free) claims to be the oldest college in Oxford. Two other colleges dispute this primacy: University College, on the spurious grounds that it was established by Alfred the Great, and Balliol, which was certainly in existence as a community of scholars by 1263 but was not formally endowed until 1282. It is generally accepted, however, that the statutes of Merton served as the model for all the other colleges of Oxford and Cambridge. Like other early colleges, Merton was an exclusive institution with a privileged minority of mostly graduate Fellows.

Merton Chapel, parallel to Merton Street, dates to 1290. The massive gargoyles that leer from the battlements are another example of brilliant modern masonry – put up in the 1960s to replace the eroded stumps of the originals.

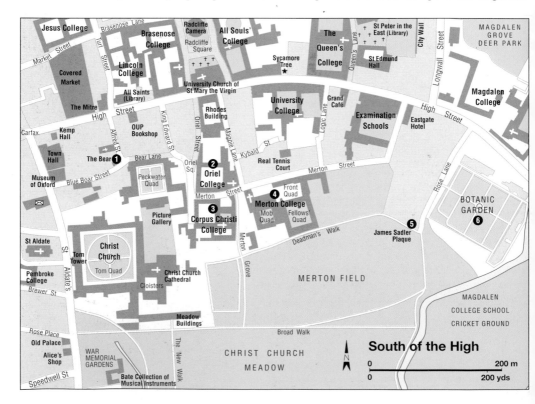

The statues of Walter de Merton and Henry III in the **gate-tower** are also recent, but the mysterious woodland scene carved above the arch is 15th century. It probably depicts St John the Baptist in the wilderness – but it is a wilderness populated by numerous rabbits and bears, while the fruit-filled trees are crowded with a chorus of nesting birds. In the foreground, Walter de Merton kneels before the *Book of Seven Seals* from the Revelation of St John (perhaps a reference to the fact that Merton was founded for the study of theology), while a lamb and a unicorn, representing Christ, look on.

Pass through the entrance into the Front Quad, which lacks the calm regularity of some others in the city. With buildings dating from the 13th to 19th century, it is typical of the piecemeal development of the early colleges. Straight ahead is the Hall, the first building on the site to be completed, but virtually rebuilt in 1794 and again in 1874 when Gilbert Scott added the fine roof. Remarkably, the original 13th-century door, with its ornate scrollwork, has survived.

To the left of the Quad is the **Fitzjames Arch**, built by the Warden (head of the college) Robert Fitzjames in 1497. He had a horoscope cast in order to find the most propitious date on which to begin building, and his astrological interests are reflected in the signs of the zodiac carved in the vault of this arch. It leads through to the 17th-century **Fellows' Quadrangle**.

Merton has some very special features that provided models for later foundations. Principal among these is the **Mob Quad**, reached by going through the arch to the right of the Hall and turning right. Enclosed by 14th-century buildings, this is the oldest quad in Oxford. The origin of the name is not known, but members of Merton like to think that the characteristic form of the Oxford and Cambridge enclosed quadrangle owes its origin to this group of buildings.

Map on page 140

An old tradition stipulates that each new Warden of Merton has to knock on the gates of the college before being admitted to his post by the Fellows.

BELOW: Merton College, as seen by Loggan in 1675 in his *Oxonia Illustrata.*

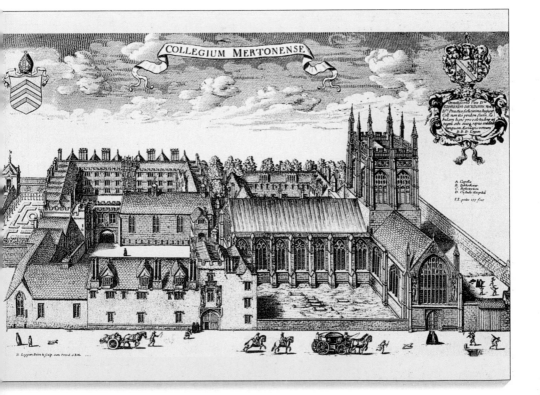

Merton Chapel's magnificent east window

Its form is probably based on that of a medieval inn. The north and east ranges (for accommodation) were completed first, in 1311, followed by the south and west ranges, built to house, on the first floor, the **Library**, the most perfect example of a medieval library in England (guided tours with the verger for a maximum of five people are available Mon–Fri 2–4pm; entrance fee).

The entrance is in the southwest corner of the Mob Quad, where the ancient oak door is believed to have been taken from Beaumont Palace, the Royal Palace of Henry I that once stood on Beaumont Street (*see page 162*). The library itself is up a flight of stone steps. Though its medieval structure remains intact, substantial alterations were carried out subsequent to its completion in 1379. The wooden ceiling, for example, is Tudor, while the panelling and plasterwork date from the late 16th and early 17th centuries. The library still has an original 14th-century reading stall, with chains to protect the valuable manuscripts from theft. Among the many exhibits is one of the locked chests in which the manuscripts were originally stored. Books came later, as did the bookshelves, a feature introduced from Italy and Germany. An astrolabe, an instrument for measuring the altitudes of stars and reputed to have belonged to Chaucer, is sometimes shown to visitors.

The west wing is adjoined by the **Max Beerbohm Room**, full of drawings by the famous caricaturist (1872–1956), who studied at Merton and wrote *Zuleika Dobson* (1912), a satire on Oxford undergraduate life.

BELOW:
lost in thought
in cosmopolitan
Oxford.

To the north of Mob Quad is Merton's splendid 13th-century **Chapel**. Again, the plan of the chapel, consisting of an ante-chapel, screen and choir, set the pattern for all the other colleges – although this form evolved by accident: Walter de Merton intended a massive building, with an extensive nave, that was never

ANYONE FOR TENNIS?

In Merton Street, opposite Merton College's porter's lodge, stands one of England's 25 Real Tennis courts. Real Tennis has been played on this site since the late 16th century, and the present court dates from the late 18th century. The word Real is probably derived from Royal, but now mainly emphasizes the sport's difference from more conventional lawn tennis. Its roots go back to medieval monastery life, when monks would play a sort of handball in their monastic cloisters.

Known in French as the Jeu de Paume (literally "the palm game"), the sport evolved into a more intricate affair involving rackets, a net and a complicated set of rules. What differentiates Real Tennis from the better-known lawn variety is that it must be played inside. Players deliberately use the walls for particular shots, as in squash, while at the same time hitting the ball over a net. The ball is solid rather than pneumatic, made of tightly-bound tape, and is rather like a soft cricket ball. Rackets are asymmetrical and heavier than those that are used for lawn tennis.

The two resident professionals welcome visitors between 9am and 6pm on weekdays (tel: 01865 244212; entrance fee) and will be happy to explain the sport's distinctive history and rules.

built, probably because of lack of funds and space. Even so, the choir alone is huge and lofty. The magnificent east window, with seven lancets, meeting to form a wheel with 12 spokes at the apex, is one of the finest in Europe.

Nearly all the windows retain original late 13th-century glass, representing apostles and saints in gorgeous colours. The choir screen is made up of pieces salvaged from one designed by Christopher Wren, sadly broken up in 1851. Of the many monuments to Fellows and benefactors, the finest is to Thomas Bodley (died 1613) on the west wall; the founder of the Bodleian Library (*see page 92*) is surrounded by allegorical figures representing the arts and sciences.

As one re-emerges into cobbled Merton Street, there is a good view of Magdalen College tower to the east. On the left is **Logic Lane** which leads through to the High Street.

Walks and gardens

Exit Merton and retrace your steps to the left as far as the wrought-iron gateway (open daily until 7pm) leading along the attractive **Merton Grove** between Merton and Corpus Christi. A turnstile at the end provides access to the broad expanse of Christ Church Meadow. Immediately on the left is **Deadman's Walk**, following the old city wall to the east. It was along this path that funerals once processed to the old Jewish cemetery, now the Botanic Garden. It's possible to turn left here, but for better views continue south, past Christ Church Fellows' Garden, to the **Broad Walk**. To the right is the enormous neo-Gothic Christ Church, from where the delightful tree-lined **New Walk** provides a detour past Christ Church Meadow to the Thames and the College Boathouses (*see page 198*). The main route goes left along Broad Walk, a wide avenue once planted with elm trees. The stump of one giant remains, but old age and Dutch elm disease killed them off in 1976; plane trees have been planted in their place.

When you get to Rose Lane, turn back a little along Deadman's Walk. In a wall on the right, a **plaque ❺** commemorates James Sadler, who was born in 1753 (*see page 105*), as the "first English aeronaut who in a fire ballon made a successful ascent from near this place on 4 October 1784 to land near Woodeaton". The views experienced by Sadler as he rose above the spires of Oxford must have been stunning. On the right is the side entrance to the **Botanic Garden ❻** (open daily 9am–5pm, 4.30pm in winter; entrance fee), incorporating the fine archway paid for by the founder, the Earl of Danby, which contains his statue as well as that of Charles II in the niche to the right and Charles I to the left.

At around 5 acres (2 hectares), the Garden is small but packed with interest. It was founded in 1621 by Henry Danvers, Earl of Danby, and is the oldest physic garden in Britain (third in the world). The first head gardener was a retired German soldier and publican called Jacob Bobart, but he understood what was required to create a good growing environment. He ordered 4,000 loads of "mucke and donge" to be spread on the original 3-acre (1.2-hectare) site to raise it above the Cherwell floodwaters, and built the 14-ft (4.3-metre) wall that still encloses the garden.

Map on page 140

TIP

Cycling is not allowed in Christ Church Meadow, and it is difficult to squeeze through the entrance at the Botanic Garden side with wheelchairs or prams.

BELOW: the Botanic Gardens in Oxford are Britain's oldest.

Map on page 140

The Botanic Garden contains the world's largest collection of plants belonging to the euphorbia genus – not always spectacular, but extraordinary in their diversity.

BELOW: punts on the River Cherwell can be hired at Magdalen Bridge, opposite the Botanic Garden.

The fourth side is enclosed by laboratory buildings and the massive stone triumphal arch, designed by Nicholas Stone as the main entrance in 1632 (the statues of Charles I, Charles II and the Earl of Danby were added later, at the end of the century).

Within this sheltered, well-drained and fertilised plot, Bobart laid out a series of rectangular beds, each one devoted to one of the principal plant families. This arrangement, designed to serve the scientific objectives of the garden, has survived, although the regularity is softened now by the many fine specimen trees that have grown up between the beds.

At the far end of the central path, on the right, is a huge yew tree, sole survivor of an avenue of yews planted in 1650 by Bobart. Beyond, the triangular New Garden, enclosed in 1944, contains a lily pond, bog garden and two rockeries for lime-loving plants. Another part of this garden is planted with roses illustrating the development of hybrid varieties in the 19th and 20th centuries. From the central pond, the **view** through the arch to Magdalen Tower on the other side is magnificent.

The gardens can look bleak in winter, but the massive **glasshouses** (open daily 10am–4pm) provide an instant change of climate as well as the sight of luxuriant palms and lotuses, ferns and alpines, and a special collection of carnivorous plants. A stroll along the Cherwell here is delightful, the river crowded with people in punts in the summer.

Exit the gardens via the main entrance and cross over the High Street, past Magdalen's High Street frontage, with its impressive array of grotesques and gargoyles, completed in 1981. Just beyond, steps lead down to a landing stage, the main one in the city for those wishing to try out punting (*see page 205*). ❑

An Insider's Guide to Elusive Gardens

Few cities in the world contain, within so few square miles, so many gardens and open spaces. There are two explanations. First, the colleges jealously guard their individual gardens and refuse to build on them; second, the rivers Cherwell and Isis almost encircle the city and have provided along their banks a ring of flood meadows which also form a barrier to building.

In contrast to the Botanic Garden and University Parks, it is not always possible to see the colleges and their gardens. However, most colleges do have set opening times (*see Travel Tips, page XX*). Further restrictions are usually only applied during exam times, and occasionally during vacations.

The gardens are run almost as eccentrically as the university itself. In each college a Fellow or group of Fellows directs the college gardeners. Traditionally each appointed Fellow had some particular enthusiasm. For example, the "Keeper of the Groves" at St John's, who favoured rhododendrons and their allies which sulk in Oxford's alkaline soil, had a huge pit dug, lined with concrete blocks and then filled with peaty soil to keep these plants happy. A Fellow of Wadham had a liking for rare Chinese trees. The garden committee at Christ Church, under the influence of one member, banned yellow flowers. The gardener at All Souls' once found himself planting a particular plant in one bed under the direction of one committee member, then having to replant it elsewhere at the whim of another, and so on...

The gardeners are a mixed bunch. Some come from other parts of Britain, lured by the variety, the supposed prestige, and the general ambience of the city. Others are hoping to escape to a world where their distracted dreams will rarely be interrupted. But a new drive for efficiency is encouraging many colleges to get rid of their aged retainers in favour of contract gardeners who drive from college to college – smart and tidy, perhaps, but without the personal touch.

RIGHT: escape to peace in the Botanic Garden.

The gardens of St John's, the richest college, are probably the grandest. The path twists and turns between carefully tended shrubs and groves of trees, providing a wonderful blend of the formal and the natural.

Another fine garden is at New College. It has probably the longest and deepest old-fashioned herbaceous border, and is dominated by the Mount, an avenue of clipped trees and elaborate parterres of box. The gardens of Worcester College have a willow-fringed lake, their beauty endorsed by Lewis Carroll in *Alice's Adventures in Wonderland*.

One feature that does unite the colleges is the lawn. There are basically two types: those you can walk on and those displaying the ubiquitous command KEEP OFF THE GRASS. It is on the informal lawns that the outdoor life of the college takes place: tea in the afternoon, Greek tragedies on summer evenings, croquet, bowls and frisbee-throwing. Essays are attempted, discarded and made into paper darts skimming over the grass. After the exams, elegantly attired students stroll across them on their way to summer balls. ❑

CHRIST CHURCH AND BEYOND

*Here can be found the origins of the city, the only
college with a cathedral, recurring echoes of
Alice in Wonderland and alternative art*

Map
on page
150

The road heading south from Carfax is called St Aldate's. It was here, down towards the river, that the first Oxford settlement is thought to have been established, beside the Abbey of St Frideswide. St Frideswide's Abbey provided the core of the massive college of Christ Church, part of whose rich folklore includes the tales told by one of its dons, Charles Dodgson (Lewis Carroll).

Heading down St Aldate's, you pass the **Town Hall** ❶ on the left, a fine neo-Jacobean building, opened in 1897, with Queen Victoria seated in the apex of the central pediment. It was built to the greater glory of the City Council, reflecting Oxford's newly-found status and self-confidence after it was declared a county borough in 1889. Above, the three-tiered belvedere on the roof is topped by a weathervane in the shape of a horned ox – for Oxford was originally called Oxenford. Tea dances are still regularly held in the Town Hall Assembly Room, beneath a large and incongruous painting of the *Rape of the Sabines* by Pietro da Cortona (1596–1669) and portraits of former mayors and members of parliament. The Town Hall contains the city archives, and as Oxford was never bombed or burned the records are particularly complete.

PRECEDING PAGES:
Tom Quad, part of
Christ Church.
LEFT: Mercury's
statue at Christ
Church.
BELOW: the
Museum of Oxford
on St Aldate's.

Old art and new art

Round the corner, in Blue Boar Lane, is the entrance to the former library, built at the same time as the Town Hall and now housing the **Museum of Oxford** ❷ (open Tues–Fri 10am–4pm, Sat 10am–5pm, Sun noon–4pm; entrance fee). The museum has an easy-to-digest history of the city's development. Displays highlight its history from prehistoric times to the industrial age, with exhibits ranging from reconstructions of Roman kilns to the legend of St Frideswide, and from the origins of the university to the development of car production at Cowley. Best of all are the reconstructions of Oxford houses, contrasting the working-class district of Jericho *(see page 165)* with the stylish drawing-rooms of North Oxford's villas decorated in the latest William Morris textiles, and the reconstruction of a 1930s living room in the newly-built Morris Motors suburb of Cowley. Other highlights are the Keble College Barge, an example of one of the ornate floating boathouses of the late 19th century from which spectators watched river races during Eights Week. The most macabre exhibit is the skeleton of Giles Covington, an Oxford Freeman who was convicted of murder and executed in 1791.

The Town Hall building enlivens an otherwise dull stretch of street – the 1879 **post office** on the right is of interest only for the brass-bound wooden posting box in front. **Pembroke Street**, the first turning on the right, provides a better flavour of old Oxford,

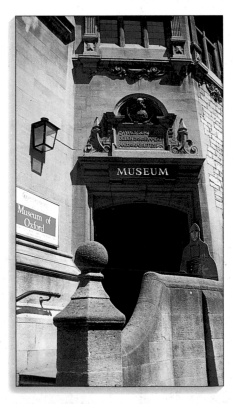

MUSEUM

Museum of Oxford

MOMA has a great shop, with interesting books and wacky calendars and postcards.

before Victorian improvers and modern developers set to work – lined as it is with jettied and bay-windowed houses painted in pastel colours.

It leads to the **Museum of Modern Art (MOMA) ❸** (open Tues–Sun 11am–6pm, Thur until 9pm; entrance fee), occupying a former brewery warehouse on the right-hand side of the street, which mounts highly regarded exhibitions of contemporary work. The **Moma Café** is a good place to rest the legs. On the other side of St Ebbe's Street, in **Pennyfarthing Place**, is the **Church of St Ebbe's ❹**, dedicated to a 7th-century Northumbrian abbess. The church was demolished and rebuilt in 1816, but the 12th-century west doorway, ornamented with beakheads, has survived.

Back now to St Aldate's, where the eponymous evangelical church stands back from the main road, in leafy **Pembroke Square**. **St Aldate's Church** was virtually rebuilt in 1832, and is the centre of the city's lively young evangelical congregation – services are noisy affairs, at which hymns are sung with much *joie de vivre* and to the accompaniment of guitars and tambourines.

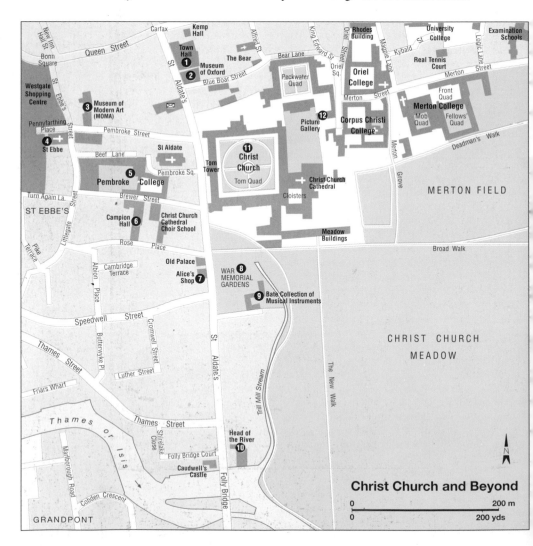

Christ Church and Beyond

Pembroke and Campion Hall

The square also provides access, on its southern side, to **Pembroke College** ❺ (visitors wishing to look around should first enquire at the porter's lodge; tel: 01865 276444). The college was founded in 1624 by King James I, and his statue occupies a niche in the tower of the Hall, which occupies the right-hand side of the Chapel Quad and is reached by means of a steep, stone staircase. The hammerbeam roof and tall Perpendicular windows all look convincingly 15th century, but the hall was actually built in 1848 by John Hayward. The chapel, on the opposite side of the quad, was completed in 1732 and the stalls and screen are of that date – but the richly painted ceiling and the Renaissance-style stained glass is all the work of Charles Kempe, a former student of the college; it was carried out between 1884 and 1900.

Opposite Pembroke Square looms the magnificent **Tom Tower** of Christ Church, by Wren. To the north are the first-floor rooms in which Charles Dodgson, creator of *Alice's Adventures in Wonderland*, last resided while at Christ Church. Dodgson, a mathematics don at the college, made friends with Alice, the daughter of the Dean, while taking photographs of the cathedral from the Deanery garden, and together they plunged into their own fantasy world.

Because there is no public access to Christ Church through the entrance under Tom Tower, continue for the moment down the right-hand side of St Aldate's. For another diversion, turn right into Brewer Street. The buildings on the left house **Christ Church Cathedral Choir School**, and the delightful music of boys rehearsing for evensong is often carried on the breeze. Further down, on the left, is **Campion Hall** ❻, a rather austere building of 1935 and Oxford's only example of Sir Edwin Lutyens' architecture. Campion Hall was founded

Map on page 150

The great essayist and source of quotations, Samuel Johnson, went to Pembroke College in 1728. Although he was a brilliant student, his money ran out and he was forced to leave before taking a degree.

BELOW: "Blue Button" guides give excellent tours.

Alice's Shop is devoted to souvenirs related to Lewis Carroll's Alice in Wonderland.

BELOW: the War Memorial Gardens at Christ Church.

in 1895 as a place of study for Roman Catholic priests. The chapel has a striking set of Stations of the Cross painted by Frank Brangwyn.

The friendlier-looking garden wing of Campion Hall, built in Cotswold vernacular style, can be seen by turning left into Littlegate and left again into Rose Place. At the end of Rose Place, on the right, is the **Old Palace**, built for the first Bishop of Oxford in the 16th century. The oriel windows, supported by carved wooden grotesques, are dated 1628.

Alice, gardens, music and bridges

Back in St Aldate's, the little shop on the right (No. 83) is **Alice's Shop ❼** (open Mon–Sat 10.30am–5.30pm, Thur til 7pm, Sun 11am–5.30pm). It is here that Alice Liddell used to buy her favourite barley sugar, before setting out on river trips with Charles Dodgson. In *Through the Looking Glass*, Alice visits the shop and is served by a bad-tempered sheep, and it was drawn in that book by Sir John Tenniel as "the Old Sheep Shop".

Directly opposite is Christ Church Cathedral rising beyond the **War Memorial Gardens ❽**. Laid out in 1926, the colourful raised perennial beds provide access to the public entrance to the college, through the **Meadow Building**.

Because of the way the official route round Christ Church is organised, starting at the Meadow Building and finishing in Merton Lane, before entering visitors may first want to continue down St Aldate's towards the Thames. On the left-hand side, south of the Gardens, a gateway leads to the University Music Faculty, with a sign indicating the **Bate Collection of Musical Instruments ❾** (open Mon–Fri 2–5pm, Sat during term-time 10am–noon; entrance fee). Established from a donation by Philip Bate in 1963, the collection is an unrivalled

survey of woodwind instruments, added to by many donations of brass instruments, pianos and harpsicords, as well as a fine gamelan from Indonesia.

Further down, with the redeveloped district of St Ebbe's on the right, lies **Folly Bridge**, thought to be on the site of the first crossing point or "oxen-ford" over the Thames, created in the 8th century to serve the expanding Saxon community. Remains of a more substantial causeway (Grandpont), built here by the town's Norman governor, Robert d'Oilly, can be seen if you pass under the bridge in a boat. The present bridge dates from 1827. From Folly Bridge, visitors can enter through the turnstile gate behind the **Head of the River** pub ❿ and walk along the Thames to the **College Boathouses** (*see page 198*).

Splendid Christ Church

Christ Church ⓫ (entry through Meadow Building, Mon–Sat 9am–5pm, Sun 12.45–5.30pm; tel: 01865 276150; entrance fee) was founded as Cardinal College in 1525 by Thomas Wolsey, Henry VIII's all-powerful Lord Chancellor, on the site of a priory thought to have been founded by St Frideswide as long ago as 730. According to accounts of her life, written in the 12th century, she refused to marry the king of Mercia and fled to Binsey, where she hid for three years in the woods, working as a servant to a swineherd. When the king tried to take Frideswide by force, he was struck and blinded by a lightning bolt.

The earliest Oxford settlement may have been a lay community serving St Frideswide's; Saxon tools, artefacts and items of clothing have been found during excavations in St Aldate's. But the first truly historical reference comes in a royal charter of Ethelred the Unready, compensating the community for the burning down of its church by the Danes in 1002. A new Augustinian priory,

Map on page 150

The Head of the River is the largest pub in Oxford and is named after its position by the finishing line for university rowing races. The winning team (or eight) is known as the Head of the River.

LEFT: one of the cloisters at Christ Church. **BELOW:** a Christ Church custodian.

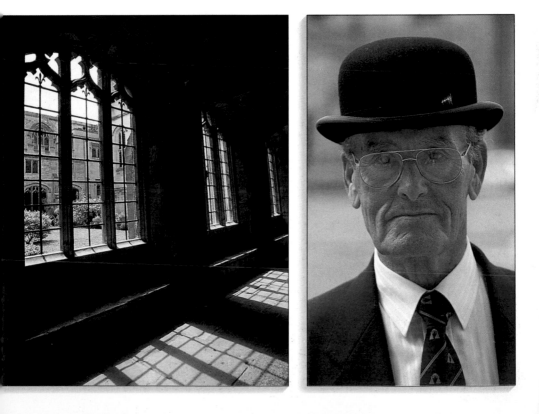

Edward Burne-Jones is famous for his beautiful stained glass at Christ Church.

BELOW: the fan-vaulted ceiling above the staircase at Christ Church.

dedicated to the saint, was re-established here by the 12th century, and by the time Wolsey came along it had been greatly extended. Wolsey dissolved it, using the endowments to found his new college, originally called Cardinal College. But his grand scheme came to an end in 1529 when he fell from grace after failing to secure the speedy annulment of Henry VIII's marriage to Catherine of Aragon. Henry rescued the church and took over the college, refounding it as King Henry VIII's College in 1532. Ten years later, Oxford was made a diocese and the priory was elevated to a cathedral, which Henry then combined with the college, renaming it Christ Church in 1546. Thus the church here is unique in being both a college chapel and a cathedral.

Having entered Christ Church, follow the visitors' trail to the **Cloisters**, which date from the 15th century. Wolsey destroyed the west and south sides of the cloisters, as well as three bays of the priory church, to make way for Tom Quad (*see facing page*). Through the first doorway on the right the Old Chapter House, with its Norman doorway and tall Early English lancet windows, now houses a souvenir shop as well as a collection of cathedral and college treasures.

Enter the **Cathedral** via the next door on the right. Begun towards the end of the 12th century, when Norman architecture was giving way to the new Early English style, the old priory church part of the cathedral is rather disappointing from an architectural point of view. The aisles are too squat when compared to the size of the columns, and the small pairs of rounded arches fit too awkwardly into the main ones.

By contrast, the 15th-century **Choir** with its lierne-vaulted ceiling – similar to that of the Divinity School – is magnificent. To the north of the choir is the reconstructed canopy from St Frideswide's tomb.

In the **Latin Chapel**, to the north, is a Burne-Jones window of 1858, depicting the life of the saint, including a depiction of St Margaret's Well at Binsey (the "Treacle Well" from *Alice's Adventures in Wonderland – see page 203*). This is one of Burne-Jones's earliest works, and the crowded scenes are full of dramatic detail – especially where the king of Mercia is struck by a red-hot thunderbolt – though the calamine-lotion colour of the faces is less successful. In 1877, Burne-Jones also designed the **St Catherine Window** next to the altar, depicting Edith Liddell, sister of Lewis Carroll's Alice, as the saint. Nearby is a monument to Robert Burton (died 1640), author of *The Anatomy of Melancholy*. There is more excellent stained glass around the cathedral, much of it designed by William Morris and Edward Burne-Jones.

Further west, **St Lucy's Chapel** contains a wealth of early 14th-century glass, including a scene showing the martyrdom of St Thomas à Becket, the archbishop of Canterbury brutally murdered by King Henry II's henchmen in 1170. This has survived, despite Henry VIII's instruction that all monuments to Becket be destroyed: here only the saint's head was removed and replaced with plain glass. He keeps company with a number of lewd and grotesque beasts that inhabit the tracery lights.

Exiting the cathedral by the same door, follow the cloisters round to the left, arriving, just before the opening to the Tom Quad, at the foot of the **staircase** to the Hall. Designed by James Wyatt in 1829, the stairs were built under a splendid fan-vaulted ceiling which had been created almost 200 years earlier, in 1640, by Dean Samuel Fell. The best view of the ceiling, and the single slender pillar supporting it, is from the top of the stairs.

Across the landing is the entrance to the **Hall**. With its magnificent hammerbeam roof, this is easily the largest old hall in Oxford, representing the full splendour of the Tudor court. The walls are adorned with portraits of some of the college's alumni, including William Gladstone and Anthony Eden (two of the 13 prime ministers produced by Christ Church) as well as John Locke, the great philosopher, and William Penn, the founder of Pennsylvania. Above the High Table is a portrait of the college's second founder, Henry VIII. The portrait just inside the door is that of Charles Dodgson.

Exit the hall and return to the top of the stairs for a view over the enormous **Tom Quad**, the college's Great Quandrangle. Measuring 264ft by 261ft (roughly 80 metres square), this is by far the largest quadrangle in the city. While considering its size, it is also worth stopping to consider the history of the college and its architecture. Wolsey intended everything about his foundation to be built on the grandest scale. However, all that was completed when he fell from grace in 1529 was the hall, the kitchens behind, and three sides of the Great Quad, including the lower stage of the gate-tower. The college remained in this half-finished state for more than a century. Building work began again around 1640, when Samuel Fell commissioned the splendid fan vault under which we now stand. Shortly afterwards, Charles I made Christ Church his residence and work stopped during the Civil War.

Christ Church is never called Christ Church College. Its members often refer to it as "the House", and – most confusingly – its Fellows are called Students.

BELOW: Tom Quad, Christ Church.

After the monarchy was restored, the autocratic John Fell (Samuel's son) was appointed Dean. He completed the fourth side of the Great Quad, adding the north range, copying Wolsey's work exactly, even right down to the truncated pillars and arches that had been intended to support a vaulted cloister all around the perimeter.

At the western side of the quad and intended to be its focal point, Fell commissioned Christopher Wren to finish the great gate-tower (**Tom Tower**), which he did in adventurous style, adding the bulky octagonal tower with its lead-covered cupola in 1681. Inside the tower, weighing more than seven tons, is the **Great Tom** bell. Recast before being installed, the original bell came from the enormous Osney Abbey to the west of the town (*see page 202*), which was completely destroyed at the Dissolution in 1536.

The bell is named not as some people think after Thomas Wolsey, but after Thomas à Becket, whose martyrdom (*see below*) gave him a considerable cult following. Every night at 9.05pm (Oxford being situated a stubborn five minutes west of Greenwich), Great Tom rings out from Tom Tower, tolling 101 times to signify the number of students admitted to the college at its original foundation. The bell also signalled the hour at which, in theory, all students in Oxford were supposed to be in bed.

The central fountain, dug originally to supply water to the college, is also contemporary with this work. A statue of Mercury was put up in 1695 but was removed in 1817 after being damaged. The current statue, a copy of Giovanni da Bologna's *Mercury*, was donated in 1928 and is sometimes to be seen clothed in sports kit or academic dress when students play their pranks in the relaxed post-exam weeks of summer.

The Great Tom bell was reputedly muffled during World War I for fear that its distinctive tolling would guide German zeppelins over Oxford.

BELOW: the magnificent Tom Tower at Christ Church dominates this part of Oxford.

ST THOMAS À BECKET

The martyred Archbishop of Canterbury, St Thomas à Becket, was born in London around 1118, the son of Norman parents who had settled in England. Despite a modest family background, he studied at Merton Abbey and then Paris before entering the service of Theobold, Archbishop of Canterbury, where he became a trusted assistant. He then studied further at Bologna in Italy and Auxerre in France, specialising in civil and canonical law.

When Henry II came to the throne in 1154, he made Thomas his Chancellor, making him one of the most important men in the kingdom. He accompanied Henry abroad as an advisor on matters of justice, and fought alongside him in battles against the French. This personal bond was broken when Henry made Thomas Archbishop of Canterbury in 1162, for the king had plans to restrict the power of the Church, which Thomas could not support.

Refusing to endorse the Constitutions of Clarendon, aimed at increasing royal and secular power, Thomas resigned and left for exile in France. Attempts to reach a compromise failed, and on 29 December 1170 Thomas à Becket was murdered in Canterbury Cathedral by four of Henry's courtiers. He was canonised in 1173, a powerful symbol of religious conviction and martyrdom.

Follow the eastern range of the quad to the northeastern corner and the **Deanery**. It was here, during the Civil War, that Charles I resided when in the city. The Deanery Garden is just over the other side. The **Fell Tower**, the castellated tower that faces on to the quad, was built between 1876 and 1879, with its statue of John Fell who, for all that he did to improve Christ Church, was a strict disciplinarian and far from popular. The poet Thomas Brown wrote of him: "*I do not love thee, Dr Fell,/The reason why I cannot tell,/But this I know, and know full well,/I do not love thee, Dr Fell.*"

Passing beneath Fell Tower, you pass **Killcanon** on the left, built in 1669 and so called because of the icy winds that blow around the block in winter, and enter **Peckwater Quad**, named after a medieval inn that stood on the site until these grand classical buildings were constructed in 1713. The three enclosed sides of the quad (containing student accommodation) are perfectly proportioned according to all the classical rules. Opposite stands the college **Library**, built in 1716 and originally designed with the ground floor as an open loggia. Its giant Corinthian columns lend weight and splendour to this side of the quadrangle. The library is not open to the public but you can, with discretion, peer through the windows at the ceiling-high bookstacks, leather-bound volumes and fine stucco ceiling.

From Peckwater Quad proceed to Canterbury Quad. On the right is the entrance to the **Picture Gallery** ⓬ (open Tues–Sat 10.30am–1pm and 2–5.30pm, Sun 2–5.30pm; entrance fee), which contains a small but important collection of Old Masters, including works by Tintoretto, Veronese and Van Dyck, as well as a famous Holbein portrait of Henry VIII. Visitors are obliged to leave the college via the Canterbury Quad. ❑

Map on page 150

BELOW:
Peckwater Quad.

NORTHWEST OF THE CENTRE

*After exploring the Ashmolean, you can enter the district
of Jericho to discover the city's publishing heritage
and end with a drink in a pub popular with many authors*

Looking across from the Martyrs' Memorial, the entrance to Beaumont Street is dominated on the left by the famous, yellow-brick **Randolph Hotel** , a splendid Victorian-Gothic edifice dating from 1863. The Randolph is Oxford's most famous hotel. It is a popular venue for conferences, and at the beginning of the academic year in October you can often see nervous Freshers eating there with their parents – a last meal before a new life begins. The Spires Restaurant and Lancaster Room both contain paintings by Sir Osbert Lancaster, commissioned to illustrate Max Beerbohm's 1911 satire on Oxford life, *Zuleika Dobson*. On the Magdalen street side, underneath the hotel, is **Bistro 20** with its continental cuisine.

Ancient collections

Facing all this gothicry is the **Taylor Institute** and, beyond, the Ashmolean Museum. Built from 1841 to 1845 and a rare example in Oxford of neo-Grecian architecture, the forceful design of the two linked buildings is freely based on the Temple of Apollo at Bassae which the architect, Charles Robert Cockerell, had studied. The four statues standing on top of the columns of the Taylor Institute – that is the east wing, facing St Giles – represent France, Italy, Germany and Spain, for the Institution was founded, under the will of Sir Robert Taylor, mainly for the study of the languages of these four countries. The building now houses lecture theatres and the Taylorian Library, devoted to books published in the principal European languages.

Fronting on to Beaumont Street, and surmounted by a statue of Apollo, is the pillared portico of the **Ashmolean Museum** ❷ (open Tues–Sat 10am–5pm, Sun 2–5pm, May–July Wed 8pm; donation). Containing the University of Oxford's collections of art and antiquities, the building was originally known as the University Galleries, housing a sculpture collection donated by Francis Randolph.

The name "Ashmolean" was first applied when extensions were built in 1899 to house the collections of the antiquary and scholar Elias Ashmole. These had hitherto been housed in purpose-built premises on Broad Street (now the Museum of the History of Science, *see page 116*), established by Ashmole in 1683. Regarded as the oldest museum collections in the country, their origins go back to before Ashmole's day, and not to Oxford, but to Lambeth, London. There, in a pub called The Ark, the early 17th-century naturalist and royal gardener John Tradescant displayed his extensive collection of rarities and curiosities either gathered by himself on his trips to Europe or given to him by sea captains. After his death in 1638, Tradescant's son, also called John, infused the

LEFT: Worcester College gardens.
BELOW: the Randoph Hotel, scene of some of the filming for *Shadowlands*.

Powhattan's Mantle, star attraction of the Tradescant Room.

collection with items from the New World, specifically Virginia, to which he travelled on several occasions. Meanwhile, Ashmole had befriended the Tradescants and persuaded them that he would be a suitable curator for their curiosities after their deaths. The younger Tradescant left a contradictory will bequeathing the collection to both Oxford and Cambridge, which his widow and Ashmole challenged. Ashmole won, in time, and in return for an honorary degree, he passed it over to Oxford, along with his own coin collection.

Items from the original "Ark" – or what is left of it after the neglect and sale of many objects in the 18th century – can still be seen in the museum, in the special **Tradescant Room** on the first floor. It is a wonderfully eccentric and eclectic group of objects, including Guy Fawkes' lantern, Oliver Cromwell's death mask and a piece of the stake at which Bishop Latimer was burned, as well as a rhinoceros-horn cup from China, Henry VIII's stirrups and hawking gear, and, as the star attraction, **Powhattan's Mantle**. Powhattan was the king of Virginia, and as any child will tell you, the father of Pocahontas.

Since moving to Beaumont Street, the Ashmolean has developed into one of the world's great museums, hugely enriched by archaeological material, given by such notable excavators as Sir Flinders Petrie, the late 19th-century Egyptologist, and Sir Arthur Evans, who discovered the great palace complex of Knossos on Crete. The Antiquities Department has a fine Egyptian section, and extensive displays covering Ancient Greece (particularly vases), Rome and the Near East, as well as Dark-Age Europe and Anglo-Saxon Britain.

It is in the latter section that the museum's most famous artefact is to be found, namely the **Alfred Jewel**. Found in Somerset in 1693, it is regarded as the finest piece of Saxon art ever discovered. Consisting of an enamel seated

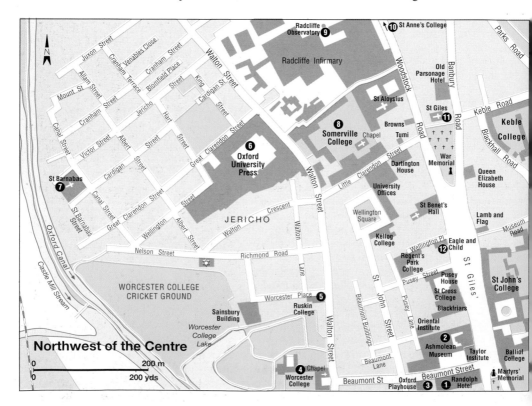

Northwest of the Centre

figure set under a rock crystal in a gold frame bearing the inscription *Aelfred mec heht gewyrcan* ("Alfred had me made"), it isn't in fact an item of personal jewellery but would have been affixed to a pointer for following the text in a manuscript. Such pointers are known to have been given as gifts by Alfred (849–99), along with copies of his translation of Gregory the Great's *Pastoral Care*.

The Department of Eastern Art, which includes some superb examples of Gandharan sculpture, is also impressive, but the other main attraction of the museum is the Department of Western Art on the first floor, which contains a remarkable collection of Italian Renaissance bronzes and paintings. Don't miss the drawings by Michelangelo and Raphael, as well as *The Hunt in the Forest*, painted by the Florentine Paolo Uccello in 1466. There are also more recent works by pre-Raphaelite and Impressionist artists. The Heberden Coin Room, also on the first floor, contains an interesting collection of coins and medals.

Since renovations were carried out in 1995, the public entrance to the museum is no longer through the large blue doors in the centre, but through doors into the west wing. The renovations included the provision of a pleasant café in the vaulted basement, which can also be reached directly from the outside. The museum also puts on a wide range of temporary exhibitions and public lectures.

The Alfred Jewel can be found in the Leeds Room on the first floor (No. 32).

To the theatre

Opposite the Ashmolean and adjacent to the Beaumont Street side of the Randolph is the **Oxford Playhouse ❸** (tel: 01865 798600). Opened in 1923, the original Playhouse, opposite Somerville, was known as the "Red Barn" and in 1938 it moved to the present building on Beaumont Street. It has often struggled with financial problems and in 1987 was forced to close after the imposition of

BELOW: the Ashmolean Museum.

The Oxford Playhouse has been presenting drama for over 75 years.

BELOW: Regency houses on Beaumont Street.

new fire regulations and funding cuts. But in April 1991 the Playhouse reopened and in 1996 underwent a major refurbishment project costing £4 million, £2.5 million of which was provided by the Arts Council Lottery Fund.

Early members of the Playhouse company included Dame Flora Robson and Sir John Gielgud, but perhaps its most celebrated supporters were Richard Burton and Elizabeth Taylor, who in 1966 performed *Doctor Faustus* free of charge, earning the theatre enough extra revenue to afford an extension, the Burton-Taylor Rooms. Burton, who had first acted while in Oxford during World War II, kept a strong allegiance to the city and university and was a generous donor to the Playhouse, and also to St Peter's College and the student newspaper, *Isis*.

Today, the Playhouse offers a broad programme of work that includes drama, dance, music-theatre, opera, popular music and jazz. It has a fledgling youth and education community scheme as well as an attractive bar and coffee shop.

The rest of **Beaumont Street** consists of Regency terraces, several with delicate cast-iron fanlights, verandas and balconies, built between 1822 and 1833. Slightly humbler town houses of the same date line **St John Street** to the right. For anyone wanting to live in Oxford, this is as about as close to the city centre as you can get. Most of the houses serve as college lodgings, or the premises of solicitors, doctors and dentists – but occasionally one does come up for sale.

The western end of Beaumont Street was once occupied by Beaumont Palace, built in the early 12th century by Henry I as his royal residence in Oxford and the birthplace of his sons Richard (the Lion-Heart) and John. Though the palace represented the town's rise in importance during the early Middle Ages, it did not remain here for long; the original door was used by the founders of Merton as their library entrance, where it can still be seen today (*see page 142*).

Wonderful Worcester

At the end of Beaumont Street, cross the road to enter **Worcester College** ❹ (open daily 2–5pm; tel: 01865 278300; free). Worcester is different from most other colleges in that it has no intimate, enclosed quadrangles. But this in no way detracts from the appeal of the place, for as well as some fine architecture, the college has some of the most beautiful gardens.

Founded in the early 18th century, the origins of the college go back to Gloucester Hall, established on the site for Benedictine monks in 1283, but dissolved in about 1539. After the Dissolution, Gloucester continued as an academic hall, despite several Benedictine changes of ownership, but slid into debt and decline. The doorheads of the west range bear the coats of arms, carved in stone, of the principal abbeys connected with the college: Glastonbury, Malmesbury, Canterbury and Pershore.

Revival only came at the end of the 17th century with funds provided by Sir Thomas Cookes, a Worcestershire baronet. The new Worcester College received its statutes in 1714, but the 18th-century building programme was financed by another man, George Clarke, who is remembered by the college as *tantum nos Fundator* ("almost our Founder"). Despite this infusion of money, Worcester was never very wealthy, and the original Gloucester Hall **medieval cottages** owe their survival to the fact that the college could only afford the two neoclassical ranges we see today. Of these, the front or west range is the most interesting, for it contains the **Library** (above the cloister), the **Hall** and the **Chapel** (in the two wings). Designed by Nicholas Hawksmoor, the library was founded on a substantial collection of books and manuscripts donated by George Clarke and includes a large proportion of the surviving drawings of Inigo Jones. The hall and

Map on page 160

Worcester Colleges' medieval cottages.

BELOW:
Worcester College.

chapel were completed by James Wyatt in the 1770s. Both were transformed internally by William Burges, in the latter half of the 19th century. The hall was, controversially, restored to its 18th-century appearance in 1966, but the chapel remains as a splendid example of Burges's highly unusual style. Sadly, the gloom created by the dark stained glass prevents a full appreciation of the lavish interior, with its Roman-style floor mosaics, Raphaelesque frescoes and gilded ceiling. Evangelists fill the niches at each corner of the chapel, and the pew ends are carved with a menagerie of animals and birds.

Worcester is sited on a slope, the land dropping away to the west. A tunnel at the end of the Gloucester Hall cottages leads through to the **gardens**, which are as beautiful as any in Oxford, a fact endorsed by Lewis Carroll in *Alice's Adventures in Wonderland* (1865) when he describes the tunnel "not much larger than a rathole" leading "to the loveliest garden you ever saw".

Landscaped like a small park, the gardens are planted with magnificent trees and shrubs and include a lovely willow-fringed lake, where Alice used to feed the ducks, although in Lewis Carroll's day cows grazed where the college playing fields now are. The lake was reclaimed from the water meadows when the park-like gardens were laid out in the early 19th century, and is now topped up by the overflow from the Oxford Canal, which forms the western boundary of Worcester's grounds. A walk around the lake is highly recommended.

Looking back through the trees there are glimpses of the Palladian facade of the **Provost's House**, while at the northern end of the lake is the **Sainsbury Building**. Regarded as one of the best pieces of modern architecture in Oxford, its carefully juxtaposed roof lines and walls descend to a delightful lakeside terrace. Worcester College's playing fields stretch away to the north.

BELOW:
the 1982 Sainsbury Building at Worcester College.

Map
on page
160

Bohemian Oxford

Exit Worcester and walk north along **Walton Street**. On the corner of Worcester Place stands **Ruskin College ❺**. Not strictly part of the university, this is one
of several institutions founded in memory of the art and later social critic John
Ruskin, for the education of working men and women. The college has strong
links with the trade union movement and the Workers' Educational Association.

Ruskin is appropriately sited on the edge of the former working-class suburb
of **Jericho** (*see below*), occupying the block between Walton Street and the
Oxford Canal. Some say that the name derives from the insubstantial nature of
the jerry-built terraced houses, a few of which date to the 1830s. There was,
however, a pub called the Jericho House here as early as 1688, and the name was
commonly used in the 17th century for any remote place, by analogy with the
biblical town in Palestine.

The area was initially developed to house the increasing numbers of workers
in this part of the city after the arrival of the Oxford Canal in 1790. When the
Oxford University Press moved here from the Clarendon Building in 1830,
further houses were built to accommodate the print workers.

Around the first corner from Ruskin, also on the west side of Walton Street,
the huge, neoclassical **Oxford University Press** building ❻ takes up most of
the block between Walton Crescent and Great Clarendon Street. The south wing
(left) was originally devoted to Bible printing, the north to learned books. If you
want to know more about the history of this world-famous publishing house,
make an appointment to see the OUP Museum (*see page 51*).

It was the print workers who made up the majority of the congregation of the
massive **Church of St Barnabas ❼**, which was built by the canal in 1868.

TIP

Jericho contains
some of Oxford's
most unusual and
atmospheric pubs,
such as the
Bookbinders' Arms –
supposedly the only
pub in Britain of
that name.

BELOW: there are
plenty of individual
shops in Jericho.

LIFE IN JERICHO

Bounded by the canal to the west, Walton Street to
the east, Worcester College to the south and the cemetery of St Sepulchre and the Lucy's Iron Works to the north,
Jericho is one of Oxford's most closely defined communities. It was here that the hero of Thomas Hardy's *Jude the
Obscure* lodged while at Oxford University.

Much of Jericho is terraced housing built by specula-
tors and St John's College for the workers of the university,
OUP, the Foundry and the canal. Jericho developed a reputation for seediness which it retained up to the 1960s when
proposals were made for its demolition. In the event, most
of the housing was saved and Jericho is now inhabited by
a cosmopolitan mix of descendants of the original families, students and young professional people.

For the visitor, the highlights are a number of excellent
cafés, pubs and restaurants, the arthouse Phoenix cinema
and the high Anglican gilt interior of St Barnabas Church.
Along Walton Street are several antique shops, bookshops,
galleries and workshops which contribute to the bohemian
feel of the neighbourhood.

A strong sense of community spirit pervades the area,
with community events, the newspaper and a Residents'
Association supported by locals and newcomers.

The Church of St Barnabas dominates much of Jericho.

You can get to the church and take in some of the atmosphere of old Jericho by taking a stroll down Great Clarendon Street. The church is distinctive for its tall, Italian-Romanesque style tower.

Featured as the cholera-ridden slum of Beersheba in Thomas Hardy's *Jude the Obscure*, Jericho's working-class credentials have long expired, for its prime location at the threshold to the city has made it a desirable area to live, particularly for wealthy students and young professionals. House prices have soared and Walton Street is now lined with craft shops, boutiques, delicatessens and restaurants. Opposite the Press building is the neo-Grecian facade of the old St Paul's Church, built in 1936. It no longer serves as a church today but as **Freuds**, an unusual wine bar and restaurant with live-music programmes specialising in jazz.

If you continue along Walton Street, you will notice away to the north the distinctive octagonal tower of the Radcliffe Observatory (*see page 167*). Passing the **Phoenix Picture House**, which shows foreign and non-maintream films, and Raymond Blanc's brasserie, **Le Petit Blanc** (an affordable version of the great French chef's Le Manoir aux Quat'Saisons), both on the left, you'll get to Walton Well Road, which leads over the canal and railway line to Port Meadow (*see page 204*).

Otherwise, retrace your steps to **Little Clarendon Street**, which links Walton Street with St Giles'. Among various modern administrative buildings of the university are bars, brasseries, cafés, boutiques and gift shops, including **Tumi** selling Latin-American crafts and music.

BELOW: Freuds has a classical dimension.

Little Clarendon Street emerges at the Woodstock Road end of St Giles. Immediately on the left is **Maison Blanc**, a wonderful patisserie, and adjacent to that is **Browns**, a long-established restaurant whose reputation is not only based on good food but also on its child-friendly attitude, popular with families.

Women only

North along Woodstock Road, just after St Aloysius Church is **Somerville College ❽** (open daily 2–5pm; tel: 01865 270600; free). Founded in 1879 specifically for the education of women, it is now mixed. The first "ladies'" college, Lady Margaret Hall, had been established the previous year, but under the aegis of the Anglican Church. A group of breakaway liberal nonconformists founded Somerville, named after the scientist and suffragette Mary Somerville (1780–1872), to take women of all religious persuasions – or none.

Women at Oxford were at first patronised rather than welcomed. They were not allowed to attend lectures; instead, tuition was provided by the AEW, the Association for Promoting the Higher Education of Women. They were not allowed to take degrees until 1920, and Somerville, along with the other four women's halls founded in the late 19th century, was not recognised as a college until 1959. Despite this, its students include an extraordinary number of public figures, not least Indira Gandhi and Margaret Thatcher. Although Mrs Thatcher may have had her differences with the university, she was loyal to Somerville, making a large donation to the £4 million Margaret Thatcher Centre.

The buildings of Somerville are small and homely in scale, some built in the "Queen Anne" style of the late 19th century, others in 1930s neo-Georgian.

Further up Woodstock Road is the **Radcliffe Infirmary**, built from the estates of John Radcliffe, the 18th-century physician, but now surrounded by an accretion of later hospital buildings. The adjacent **Radcliffe Observatory** ❾, completed in 1794, has now been swallowed up by **Green College**, founded in 1979 for graduate medical students. The Observatory, mostly designed by James Wyatt, does not have the expected dome; instead, it is topped by an elongated octagon, carved with personifications of the four winds and modelled on the ancient Greek Tower of the Winds in Athens. Unfortunately there is no public access to the observatory except for one day a year, the college's open day (tel: 01865 274770 for information).

St Anne's College ❿, opposite, traces its origins to the Society of Oxford Home Students, an organisation formed in 1879 to provide higher education for Oxford women – the daughters and wives of dons and students from the local girls' high schools. Because they lived at home, rather than in one of the two women's halls of residence (Somerville and Lady Margaret), they were known as "unattached students", and opponents of women's education were fond of referring to the Society as "Soc. mul. Ox. priv. stud." (abbreviated from the Latin name *Societas mulieram Oxoniae Privatum Studentium*).

The Home Students were taught and supervised in the houses of sympathetic Oxford dons and their friends until, in the 1930s, the numbers of students became so great that more permanent arrangements became necessary, and so the library and lecture rooms were added to the existing Victorian houses on the current site. Designed by Sir Giles Gilbert Scott, son of the Victorian Gothicist Sir George, they were completed in 1937.

During World War II, so many Oxford families were involved in war work that it became increasingly difficult to accommodate students at home and find suitable "hostesses" or chaperones; so hostels were built and by 1942 St Anne's had been transformed into a residential institution like any other, achieving full college status in 1959. A number of buildings were added after the war, notably the **Founder's Gatehouse** (1966), a building in the Modernist idiom reflecting medieval precedents in its polygonal turrets, and the **Dining Hall** (1958–60), with its glass walls and rooftop lantern.

Heading back towards Oxford city centre, the **Church of St Giles** ⓫ sits at the apex of the fork where Woodstock and Banbury roads take their separate ways. The church is largely 13th century and sits in an island of green, facing down the wide, tree-lined thoroughfare, best seen in early September when the traffic is excluded for the annual St Giles' Fair (*see page 169*).

The west (right-hand) side of St Giles' is lined with a pleasing mixture of mainly 17th- and 18th-century buildings, many of them owned by religious bodies who, in this century at least, seem to co-exist in neighbourly harmony. They include the Christian Scientists at Nos. 34–6, **St Benet's Hall**, for Benedictine monks, at No. 38, and the Quakers at No. 43. Beyond

Map on page 160

The inside of Le Petit Blanc was designed by Sir Terence Conran.

BELOW: the Church of St Giles.

Map on page 160

Pusey Street is St Cross College, where theological scholars undergo their training for the Anglican ministry.

Perhaps the most interesting building on this side of St Giles' is the **Eagle and Child** pub ⓬, on the corner of Wellington Place, always very popular among students. From the 1930s to the 1960s it was the meeting place of the informal literary group known as the "Inklings". Led by C. S. Lewis (described by his pupil John Betjeman as "breezy, tweedy, beer-drinking and jolly"), the Inklings included among their fraternity such luminaries as Charles Williams, Nevill Coghill and J. R. R. Tolkien (*see page 117*).

It was here, in these cosy, fireside surroundings, that Tolkien began reading instalments of his saga *The Lord of the Rings* to the assembled company, little realising that it would become such a success that he would be forced, by a torrent of letters, phone calls and visits from fans, to exchange the comforts of Oxford for a life of seclusion in Bournemouth. Eventually, however, after his wife died in 1971, he returned to Oxford's womb, taking rooms in Merton and becoming an Honorary Fellow. He died in 1973 and lies buried in Wolvercote Cemetery, just beyond the ring road to the north of the city.

For two days every September **St Giles** is the scene of St Giles' Fair. Cherished by people of all ages and backgrounds, the origins of this colourful fair date back to a parish wake first recorded in 1624 (*see opposite*). Originating as a toy fair with side shows for children in the 1780s, the fair survived attempts to suppress it in the 19th century because of alleged rowdy and licentious behaviour. Today's fair is no different from any of those that are held up and down the country, except for the poignant contrast between the flashing lights, candy floss and bingo stalls set against the sedate and ancient college buildings. ❏

BELOW: the Eagle and Child pub on St Giles has been an inn since 1650.

St Giles' Fair

The Fair (as it is always called) is one of Oxford's most cherished annual events. Of course, there are those hard-headed citizens who complain that it disrupts trade and traffic, but most people would spring to the defence of an occasion enjoyed by people of every age and type.

St Giles' Fair was originally a parish wake, a religious event dating from 1624. The association with St Giles, the patron saint of beggars and cripples, fixed both the date of the Fair (Monday and Tuesday following the first Sunday in September) and the location, the splendidly wide St Giles Street. By the 18th century, the occasion was known as St Giles' Feast, a time for feasting, sporting events, and the selling of "small wares".

The Fair really came into its own in Victorian times, when "wonders of art and nature" were added. Menageries and freak shows were the earliest sights: an elephant was a regular visitor, as were the Bear Lady and the Double-bodied Hindoo Boy.

New inventions always found their way to the Fair: the photographer with his three-for-a-shilling portraits; the Biograph exhibitions; the miniature railway; the Chairoplane rides. Towards the end of the 19th century, the Fair was a dazzling event, with traction engines called *Alexandra* and *General Buller* providing brilliant illuminations. Taylor's Bioscope Show glittered with 4,000 coloured lights, while the rival establishment, run by Jacob Studt, was approached through Corinthian pillars and graced by troupes of lady dancers.

More surprisingly, females also appeared at the Fair as wrestlers, wearing corsets and black tights. Little wonder, with such attractions on offer, that the Fair became, by 1900, the major holiday not only for Oxford city, but the county beyond. The huge caravan of wagons, caravans and engines gathered in Woodstock Road – then open country – on Sunday, and at 5am on Monday morning, the procession moved into the city.

The Fair had its problems, of course. In 1838, the Mayor of Oxford issued an order excluding gypsies from the site because of pickpocketing. Horseplay was firmly dealt with in 1898, when the Mayor decreed a penalty of two months' imprisonment or a £5 fine for anyone found assaulting another with "a Squirt, Scratch-back, Cracker, Whip, or Brush".

Dramatic events occurred in 1830, after trouble on nearby Otmoor, where the locals were opposing the enclosure by landowners of their common land. Matters came to a head in September, when the militia were called in to stop the systematic destruction by the moormen. About 50 were arrested and taken into Oxford for trial. But the crowds gathered for the Fair were sympathetic to the villagers' cause, the soldiers were pelted with stones, and the prisoners were freed to cries of "Otmoor for Ever".

In many ways, the Fair today looks much as it did in Edwardian times. The traction engines still provide power, and a splendid roundabout always occupies pride of place by the Martyrs' Memorial. But much more elaborate and terrifying rides now take the place of the freaks and theatre shows. ❑

RIGHT: as the saying goes, "a town without a fair is like a body without a heart."

ST JOHN'S AND THE NORTH

Apart from St John's, this area was developed after the great university reforms in the mid-19th century, and includes two remarkable museums

Map on page 174

Starting in St Giles', follow the east side along the long Balliol facade to the point where it meets the considerably more varied frontage of **St John's College** ❶ (open daily 1–5pm; tel: 01865 277300; free).

This college, one of the richest in Oxford, was originally founded by Archbishop Chichele, in 1437, for Cistercian monks and named after St Bernard. After the Dissolution of the Monasteries, it was re-founded, in 1555, by Sir Thomas White, a wealthy member of the Merchant Taylor's Guild. A statue of St Bernard, flanked by the two founders, occupies a niche on the gate-tower. The niche on the inner side contains Eric Gill's splendid *St John the Baptist* (1936), commissioned in belated recognition of the renaming of the college by White, in honour of the patron saint of tailors.

The buildings of the Front Quad survive from the original St Bernard College. The hall, though, was remodelled in the 18th century and given its stone screen, designed by James Gibbs, in 1742. The chapel, on the left, was comprehensively spoiled, internally, in the 19th century. More interesting is the Baylie Chapel to the north, with its plaster fan-vault. This was built in 1662 and houses the monument of Richard Baylie (died 1667), the Royalist President (head) of St John's, who was forcibly ejected from the college by Parliamentary troops during the 17th-century Civil War but was reinstated at the Restoration.

In remaining staunchly loyal to Charles I, Baylie was following the example of his predecessor, Archbishop Laud, who was president from 1611 to 1621 and Chancellor of the University from 1629. During his time as chancellor, Laud drew up a long list of rules governing the behaviour of Oxford scholars, which, for all that Laud was strongly opposed to the Calvinist doctrines of his day, could have been written by a staunch Puritan. Under the Laudian Code, as it is known, professional actors were forbidden to enter the university and scholars were forbidden to hunt, gamble, smoke, drink or wear their hair long or in curls – these rules remained the basis of university discipline until 1854.

Canterbury Quad

It is all the more remarkable, therefore, that Laud also financed the construction of the **Canterbury Quad** at St John's – a group of buildings unmatched in Oxford for their showy exuberance. The passage linking Front Quad and Canterbury Quad is fan- vaulted, a last touch of late Gothic before the Baroque splendours beyond.

We emerge to face a bold, two-storey portal containing a bronze statue of Charles I (by Le Sueur) under the royal coat of arms. To either side, the deli-

PRECEDING PAGES: commuting to work in top gear.
LEFT: an old-style postbox, Park Town.
BELOW: Charles I in Canterbury Quad, St John's College.

cate arcade, carried on slender Tuscan columns, has medallion busts of female figures (by Anthony Gore), representing the Virtues and the Liberal Arts, beneath a running frieze of foliage. Crossing the quad and, turning round, we find that the opposite range is similar but with a statue of Queen Henrietta Maria, wife of Charles I, in the niche. For long the design was attributed to Inigo Jones or Nicholas Stone, two of the greatest architects of their day, but now the credit goes to Adam Browne, a craftsman-architect so obscure that you will search in vain for his name in architectural reference books.

When the quad was completed in 1636, Charles I and his Queen were invited to view the buildings and watch a play in the hall (despite the Laudian Code!). It's said the king's entertainment cost almost more than the buildings.

Posthumous move

The library on the south side of Canterbury Quad (not open) contains memorabilia of both Laud and the monarch, both of whom died on the scaffold – Charles

The Laudian Code forbade almost anything connected with fun, telling students for example, not to "idle and wander about the city or its suburbs, nor in the streets or public market or Carfax".

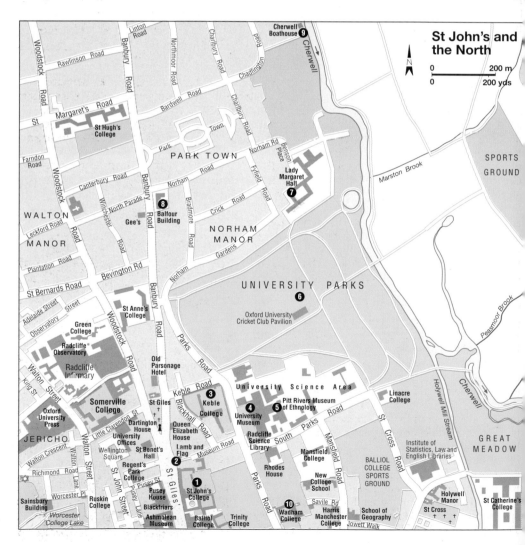

Map on page 174

famously, in 1649 and Laud in 1645, accused by the Long Parliament of high treason. Originally buried in Barking, his bones were quietly re-interred in St John's chapel in 1663.

The east side of Canterbury Quad leads out to the college gardens. Like neighbouring Trinity College (*see page 114*), St John's was built outside the city walls and so the gardens are very spacious. The path around the lawn twists and turns between carefully tended shrubs and groves of trees that were first planted in 1712, providing a wonderful blend of the formal and the naturalistic. Visitors can extend their walk by taking a side path to the north, past rockeries and shady lawns, catching glimpses of more modern college buildings to the north, including "The Beehive", built in 1958, so called because the plan is based on clusters of interlocking octagons, and the Sir Thomas White Building of 1975.

Through to Keble

From St John's turn right, up St Giles', and look for a passageway on the right, by the **Lamb and Flag ❷** – a tavern that opened in 1695 and takes its name from the St John's College coat of arms. The passage takes you, in a matter of a few yards, from medieval Oxford straight into the 19th century, leading as it does to Museum Road, lined with 1870s villas, and out into Parks Road, first laid out in the 1830s.

Directly opposite stands the mighty neo-Gothic facade of the **University Museum** (*see page 176*). Before crossing the road, turn left to arrive at the unmissable bulk of **Keble College ❸** (open daily 2–5pm; tel: 01865 272727; free). At a time when the other Oxford colleges were becoming more liberal and preparing to abolish ancient rules that excluded all non-Anglicans from membership, Keble set out to be assertively different. Committed to turning out clergymen formed in the strict High Church mould, Keble demanded that its students lead an almost monastic life of poverty and obedience.

Fortunately for the students, this objective, the antithesis to intellectual freedom, was soon modified and, while remaining primarily a theological college, Keble adopted more progressive attitudes – accepting, for example, that Darwin's evolutionary theories were not necessarily incompatible with Christian teaching.

The Tractarian founders of the college chose one of their own, William Butterfield, as the architect, who proceeded to produce a riot of Victorian Gothic on a scale hitherto unseen. Contentious from the very start, Keble continues to attract its fair share of criticism. It was built not of Oxford stone, but brick, and in addition to the dominant red, Butterfield used different colours to create his hallmark polychromatic patterning.

Nowhere are the aspirations of the college's creators more evident than in the enormous **Chapel**. But the interior here could only appeal to connoisseurs of kitsch, for the stained glass is lifeless and the mosaics of biblical scenes around the walls (inspired by Giotto's great fresco cycle at Assisi!) are sickly sweet, like illustrations from a child's *Life of Jesus*.

A small side chapel to the south was added in 1892, specifically to house Holman Hunt's famous painting *The Light of the World*. Butterfield refused to allow

Arcade detail in St John's Canterbury Quad

BELOW: Keble College: a memorial to John Keble, founder of the Oxford Movement.

the picture to be hung in the main chapel on the grounds that it is "a place of worship, not a gallery". Holman Hunt, on the other hand, was so angry when he learned that the college was charging visitors to see the picture that he painted another and gave it to St Paul's Cathedral in London. The side chapel also contains a painting by William Keys, *The Dead Christ Mourned by His Mother*.

Brick remains the preferred building material at Keble. Though much derided by Keble critics, the new Arco building along Keble Road, both blends in with its brick surroundings and sets new dynamic accents of its own.

Dinosaurs and dodos

Opposite Keble is another assertive Victorian building, a cross between a French château and London's St Pancras railway station, that houses the **University Museum ❹** (open daily noon–5pm; free). This, however, is in an entirely different class, a delightful and innovative building that often induces a smile for the ingenious, half-humorous, half-serious details.

The museum began in 1855 at a time when Oxford was beginning to teach experimental science. Unlike the old humanities, which could be taught in a room, or even while strolling around the river meadows, science teaching required laboratories, and the block of land to the east of Parks Road was set aside for this purpose.

The museum was the first building to be erected, together with the Inorganic Chemistry Laboratory alongside – curiously enough designed to resemble the medieval Abbot's Kitchen at Glastonbury Abbey. The aim of the museum was didactic and all-embracing: to tell the history of life on earth. Its construction was supported by numerous progressive thinkers of the age, including John Ruskin.

BELOW:
the delightfully
eccentric
University Museum.

Such an objective was bound to be controversial in an age that still clung to biblical ideas of Creation – and when the building was completed in 1860, it was inaugurated by the now-famous debate between the Bishop of Oxford, Samuel Wilberforce and Professor Thomas Huxley on Darwin's evolutionary theories.

The Bishop, according to contemporary accounts, thought that he had won the day when he asked Huxley "was it through his grandfather or his grandmother that he claimed his descent from a monkey?" At least one lady fainted and the meeting degenerated into a near-riot when Huxley said that he was "not ashamed to have a monkey for his ancestor, but he would be ashamed to be connected with a man who used great gifts to obscure the truth".

Map on page 174

Casts of megalosaurus footprints have been set into the lawn in front of the University Museum – exact replicas of those unearthed at Audley Quarry to the north of Oxford.

Controversies of a different nature surrounded the building itself. Critics called the design "indecent" and "detestable", because to them the Gothic architectural style should be reserved for religious buildings, not one devoted to a secular purpose. The Dublin firm of builders employed to erect the museum hired as stonemasons two brothers who have passed into Oxford legend. The brothers O'Shea, who carved all the animals and birds of the corbels and window surrounds, were not only renowned for their fondness for drink but also for their irascibility. Dons who continually interfered with the brothers' work, objecting to the subjects portrayed, were likely to find themselves featured in unflattering caricature in stone. Sadly, the brothers were ordered to destroy this work.

The interior of the museum is lit by a glass roof, supported by slender columns and a wrought-iron vault that makes you feel as if you are inside the rib cage of one of the great dinosaurs displayed on the floor below. Slender iron columns, ornamented with representations of trees and shrubs, divide the hall into three bays; the arcade columns around the perimeter of the main hall are each hewn from a different British rock, all clearly labelled.

BELOW: the O'Shea brothers at work on the University Museum in 1906.

Statues of eminent scientists line the walls, looking down on cases of stuffed animals and skeletons of creatures living and extinct. At the centre of the hall are the Oxford dinosaurs – not reactionary dons, but fossil skeletons found in the Jurassic rocks of the Oxford area as the city began to expand in the 19th century. The focal point is the fine skeleton of an iguanodon.

Apart from the dinosaurs, a famous attraction of the museum is the painting by John Savery of the Dodo in the northwest corner of the building (*see page 178*). The bird in question, described as an over-sized flightless dove with a hooked beak, was brought to England in 1638 and formed part of the Tradescant and subsequently Ashmolean collections. This same painting inspired Lewis Carroll's famous character in *Alice in Wonderland*.

It is also worth visiting the upper gallery for its collections of insects, butterflies and birds. There are great views across the main hall; notice the scale model of the sun, moon and earth attached to the balustrade.

More discoveries

If you're impressed by the University Museum, then you'll be staggered by what lies through the doors to the rear. The **Pitt Rivers Museum of Ethnology** ❺ (open Mon–Sat 1–4.30pm; free) was built in 1885 to house the collection of Lieutenant-General Augustus

John Savery's painting of the famously extinct Dodo, which hangs in the University Museum.

BELOW: the interior of the University Museum.

Henry Lane Fox Pitt-Rivers (1827–1900), built up during his service in exotic lands with the Grenadier Guards.

Pitt-Rivers pioneered a sociological approach in archaeology and ethnology and emphasised the instructional value of common artefacts. His original collection consisted of some 15,000 objects, but since then the number has swelled to well over a million, of which some 400,000 are on permanent display. The museum is literally packed with case after case of splendid objects from all corners of the earth – scarey demons, potent fertility figures, colourful totem poles and exotic masks – as well as practical objects such as boats, tents, saddles and snowshoes.

A remarkable theme of the museum is the continuity and similarities that exist between cultures; illuminating parallels are drawn between the use of magical charms among the tribes of Asia and similar practices among Christians in "civilised" Europe. To help achieve this, and in accordance with Pitt-Rivers' wishes, the objects are displayed not by region but by type, so model Chinese junks are to be found next to African dug-out canoes, and so on. Visitors will be intrigued by a cabinet containing the shrunken heads of Ecuadorian Indians, complete with detailed instructions on head shrinking. Attendants will point out all kinds of other ghoulish delights, many of them – including a giant toad – hidden in drawers. Children will be fascinated by the witch-in-a-bottle.

Flanking the south side of the lawn in front of the museum is the **Radcliffe Science Library**, the science department of the Bodleian, which receives free copies of all British scientific publications (including popular and children's publications). Access to the library – an unmatched resource for any kind of scientific research – is possible with a Bodleian Library reader's ticket.

DEAD AS A DODO

John Savery's remarkable painting of the dodo in the University Museum is now considered to be something of an exaggeration, for experts agree that the ill-fated bird was not nearly as grotesque as the depiction suggests. What is beyond dispute, however, is that the dodo was the unfortunate victim not only of hungry sailors, who were easily able to capture the flightless creature, but of evolution itself.

First sighted around 1600 on the Indian Ocean island of Mauritius, the dodo (*Raphus cucullatus*), a close relative of the pigeon, was a large bird with a heavy, ungainly body and short, useless wings. Because it could not escape, it rapidly fell prey to the Dutch sailors who first visited the area and to imported cats, rats and pigs which destroyed its nests.

The destruction of the island's forest – and hence the dodo's food supply – was another factor in its rapid extinction. The last living bird was sighted in 1681. Today, scientists believe that the dodo actually evolved from a bird capable of flight into a flightless one. Having discovered in Mauritius a habitat with plenty of food and no natural predators, the dodo did not need to fly and over the generations lost the ability to do so.

Map on page 174

Just to the north of the museum, bright summer days in particular attract locals and visitors alike to the huge expanse of the **University Parks** ⑥. Dotted with magnificent trees and shrubs and bordered on its eastern side by the River Cherwell, the park is a wonderful place for a stroll. It is also the home of the **Oxford University Cricket Club**, and this is one of only two places in England where first-class matches can be watched free of charge. If you're not there for the Australians or the Pakistanis, there may be a county fixture going on.

Detour to North Oxford

The University Museum was part of the 19th-century expansion of the university, particularly in the field of science. Since that time, the area around it has developed into the University Science Area, consisting of a not always harmonious jumble of buildings ranging from 1930s functionalism (clearly visible in the Inorganic Chemistry faculty building from University Parks) to 1960s concrete and glass structures, each housing different faculties, ranging from Mathematics to Applied Physics to Microbiology.

As the university grew beyond its old medieval core, new accommodation was required for increasing numbers of professors and their families, as well as wealthy merchants and traders, and this demand helped spawn the development of the affluent district now known as North Oxford, which begins just north of the University Parks and extends out along the Banbury and Woodstock roads.

Just to the north of University Parks, **Norham Gardens** was laid out from 1860, and although Italianate villas feature in early plans, neo-Gothic was all the rage by the time the estate came to be developed. Built of brick, with high gables, ornate stone dressings sculpted with fruits and flowers and the occasional

The Oxford University Cricket Club has produced several world-class players during its history, not least Colin Cowdrey (Brasenose) and Imran Khan (Keble).

BELOW: cricket in University Parks.

turret, these houses were praised by Ruskin as "human and progressive", but were ridiculed by others, as were their inhabitants: the Rev. W. Tuckwell disapproved of the fact that professors, tutors and fellows now lived family lives in the "interminable streets of villadom", rather than residing in college "celibate and pastoral".

At the end of Norham Gardens (also reached via an alley from University Parks) is **Lady Margaret Hall** ❼ (check at the porter's lodge for visits), founded in 1878 as a women's hall of residence (it is now mixed) and itself occupying one of the newly built villas. Strong connections with the Church of England distinguished this college, named after Lady Margaret Beaufort, the scholarly mother of Henry VII, from its contemporary, Somerville.

The original villa, Old Hall, is the undistinguished yellow-grey brick building to the right of the entrance. Better by far is the Queen Anne-style red-brick extension, designed by Basil Champneys and similar to the splendid work he did at Newnham College, Cambridge.

For the chapel, yet another style was employed – Byzantine – with an external octagon that forms a dome inside. It was designed by Sir Giles Gilbert Scott in 1931. The beautiful triptych was painted by Burne-Jones around 1863. The Hall is also blessed with gardens that stretch to the River Cherwell, where remnants of old water meadows are carpeted with daffodils, cowslips, fritillaries and primroses in spring.

Head back to Banbury Road and go north. At No. 60 is the **Balfour Building** ❽, which houses an annex of the Pitt Rivers Museum and is also well worth visiting (same opening times as the Pitt Rivers Museum). The annex contains a fascinating **Hunters and Gatherers** section, describing the past and present from

The novel The House in Norham Gardens, *by Penelope Lively, gives an atmospheric account of a childhood spent in a Gothic-Victorian villa.*

BELOW: Regency-style crescent in Park Town.

Map on page 174

prehistoric axe-heads to Eskimos and Bushmen, as well as the **Musical Instruments Collection**, with specimens from all over the world, again, like the main Pitt Rivers Museum, arranged according to type. Headsets are provided so that you can listen to the various types of music as you walk through the gallery. Concerts are held here in summer.

On the opposite side of the road is the glass-covered conservatory of **Gee's** restaurant, and immediately north of that is **North Parade**, which offers a variety of good restaurants, and has a definite "villagey" atmosphere in comparison to all the grand neo-Gothic residences round about. There are two good pubs in North Parade, the Gardeners' Arms and the Rose and Crown. The latter was built in 1867 on the site of a small market garden, evidence of the area's semi-rural character at the time.

Further north, entered from the east side of Banbury Road, is the elegant residential enclave known as **Park Town**, interesting from an architectural point of view because its houses are much admired examples of late Regency style – so late (built from 1853 to 1855) that they might almost be called neo-Regency. Built around crescents, these stucco-fronted houses, with attractive iron railings, remind us more of Cheltenham than of Oxford.

The next street on the right beyond Park Town is Bardwell Road. Just around the corner beyond the famous Dragon School, where Bardwell Road merges with Chadlington Road, a path on the right leads down to the River Cherwell and the **Cherwell Boathouse** ❾. This is a popular base for punting (*see page 205*) as well as home to the Cherwell Boathouse restaurant, a small, intimate and elegant place, with river views, good food and local artists' work permanently displayed on the walls.

BELOW: colourful North Parade.

NORTH AND SOUTH PARADES

One of Oxford's many eccentricities in the realm of street names is the strange fact that North Parade lies to the south of South Parade.

Officially called North Parade Avenue (although the Avenue part is never used), its name is widely believed to hark back to the English Civil War of 1642–51 when Oxford was periodically besieged by Paliamentarians. North Parade, it is said, was the north patrolling ground of the defending Royalists, while South Parade (a mile or so further north along Banbury Road), was the south patrolling ground of the Parliamentarians. Christopher Hibbert's *Encyclopedia of Oxford*, however, dismisses this as a myth, even if it offers no other explanation.

There is also a sort of etiquette attached to certain street names, which can cause confusion among the uninitiated. The High Street, for example, is widely abbreviated to "the High", while very few people add "Street" to "Cornmarket". Pronunciation is also more a matter of usage than logic. Cherwell is pronounced "charwell", while Magdalen should sound like "maudlin". Visitors should also be careful not to confuse Magdalen Street (in the centre of town, between Cornmarket and St Giles') with Magdalen Road, a suburban thoroughfare linking Cowley Road with Iffley Road.

Map on page 174

One of Dorothy Wadham's ingenious design ideas was to situate the college library over the kitchens – so as to keep the books dry!

BELOW: Wadham College Hall.

The heart of Oxford is easily reached again by returning down Parks Road towards Broad Street, stopping first to admire the 18th-century gates, on the right, that separate the road from the long vista of Trinity College Gardens.

An unchanging vista

Directly opposite is **Wadham College ⑩** (open only to visitors booked on a tour at the Oxford Information Centre; tel: 01865 277900; entrance fee) regarded as the youngest of the "old" (pre-Victorian) foundations. Nicholas Wadham, a retiring and obscure Somerset landowner, left his considerable wealth for the foundation of a college at his death in 1609. Wadham's widow, Dorothy, proved an energetic executor, despite being over 75 years old, and by 1613, less than five years later, the college was virtually complete. Thus Wadham is the only ancient college to have been built at one go, and it has scarcely changed since. The buildings are strictly symmetrical and were designed by the West Country builder William Arnold, who borrowed motifs from other Oxford Jacobean-Gothic buildings, but put them together in a highly accomplished manner. The Front Quad is entered through the fan-vaulted gate-tower. Directly opposite, the fine portal is similar to the exactly contemporary Tower of the Five Orders in the Old Schools Quadrangle (*see page 93*): here, though, the statue of James I is joined by the founder and foundress.

The chapel is entered by the passageway on the far left (northeast) corner of the quad, and has some of Oxford's finest 17th-century stained glass. The east window, depicting the Passion and Resurrection, is the only one in Oxford painted by Bernard van Linge (dated 1622), brother of the more prolific Abraham, whose work is found in several college chapels. The other significant object is the fine screen of 1613, with its strapwork, slender columns and cresting.

To the left of the chapel is the **Fellows' Garden**, filled with rare and ancient trees, including a striking copper beech, planted in 1796. The garden completely surrounds the chapel, and the **Cloister Garden**, to the rear, contains a modernistic bronze statue of Sir Maurice Bowra by John Doubleday. Bowra, a literary scholar who presided over Wadham as Warden from 1938 to 1970, was renowned for his ascerbic and often bawdy wit. ("Awful shit, never met him" is one of his renowned judgements. Of the Master of Balliol, he once remarked: "He has been ill but unfortunately is getting better. Otherwise deaths have been poor for the time of year.")

Famous alumni include the architect Christopher Wren and chemist Robert Boyle, who, having finished their studies, went on to pursue their careers in London and to found the Royal Society.

The southeast side of Wadham's Front Quad is an exact match of the northeast, with the hall a mirror of the chapel but with a splendid hammerbeam roof. The garden of the adjacent Back Quad contains a giant lime tree of considerable, though unknown, age. The heady scent of its summer flowers is not only irresistible to bees but spreads to fill the air as far as the city centre, which, for all that it seems a long way off in Wadham's quiet precincts, is only a few steps away. ❏

A Cyclist's City

Each working day about 26,000 trips are made in and out of Oxford's central area by bicycle, and an estimated 20,000 bikes can be on the streets at any one time. Not surprisingly, mishaps occur — though the number has been falling, from 200 reported accidents in 1984 to 130 by 1997.

Cycling has always played an important part in Oxford's transport system. William Morris, the car magnate, began his career building and racing bicycles, and in 1922 Morrell's Brewery produced a *Hunting and Cycling Road Map of Oxford and District*, over-printed with a list of hotels and inns repre-senting distances from Oxford.

Theft was not so common then. Today bikes are taken from all over the city, with a few noto-rious areas, including the railway station. Else-where in the city, Oxford City Council (one of the first local authorities to provide for the needs of the urban cyclist) has installed over 350 "Sheffield" stands. These tough steel hoops are impossible to break, and together with the increased use of U-bolt steel locks, they have helped bring about a decline in the number of thefts (now around 2,500 as against 4,500 in 1992).

To counter theft, the Police Cycle Depart-ment, attached to the Central Police Station, keeps records of all bikes and can produce serial numbers, colours, decoration, modifi-cations and accessories for almost every model. Bikes are kept in two cycle stores: one for the "found" and "miscellaneous" and the other for "crime" bikes (pending court cases). The cleverly designed store holds 200–300 cycles. The "found" bikes are kept for at least six weeks. Unclaimed cycles are auctioned; the average price is £10.

Cyclists are recommended to have a Green Card – a record issued by the Cycle Depart-ment on which an owner can list the bicycle's frame size, type, number and distinguishing marks. The police ask the city's cycle dealers to accept secondhand cycles only if a Green Card is presented. A useful free service by the Cycle Department is postcoding bicycles (any Saturday morning between 9 and 11am).

Not least because of car congestion, Oxford City Council is committed to making travel by bicycle safer and easier, and has produced a comprehensive *Cycling Guide*. Three signed routes use minor roads and purpose-built tracks free of motorised traffic. The North and South Oxford routes provide quiet alternatives to main roads into the city and the Donnington route links Cowley Road and Iffley Road.

Almost all cycle lanes are advisory, which means that motorists should avoid driving in them, although it is not illegal to do so. Cycle lanes provide a reminder to motorists to look out for cyclists and to give them space. Cyclists are allowed to use all bus lanes.

The junction with Parks Road and Broad Street has one of the highest cycle flows in the country. To ease congestion, the Advanced Stop Line, the first to be introduced in Great Britain, allows cyclists to wait at the traffic lights in front of motor vehicles.

Racing is popular and there are three local clubs for national and international races. The Oxford University Cycling Club is Britain's oldest surviving cycling club. ❑

RIGHT: simply the best way to get around.

WEST TO THE CANAL

*In medieval times the western part of the city was crowded
with wharves unloading cargo from the Upper Thames.
Today it gives an insight into Oxford's industrial past*

This route includes a journey into Oxford's industrial past. When the canal arrived from the Midlands in 1790, the area around Castle Mill Stream became a bustling inland port. Activity declined with the arrival of the railway in 1844, but the brewing industry was to continue until the closure of Morrell's Brewery in 1998.

From Carfax walk along **Queen Street**, lined by chain stores and every bit as busy as Cornmarket Street, but perhaps more chaotic with buses nudging nose to tail through the crowds of shoppers. In the summer, some light relief is provided by **Bonn Square ❶**, named after Oxford's twin city in Germany, and a popular meeting place; it is also site of a memorial to men of the Oxfordshire Regiment who died in various campaigns on India's northwest frontier. There is often live music in the form of buskers playing on or near the square.

A welcome bequest

On the opposite side of Queen Street is the sprawling Westgate Shopping Centre, one of numerous ugly modern buildings erected in this part of the city centre during the 1970s.

Continue on into **New Road**, whose construction across the castle bailey in 1769 marked the beginning of local road improvements which were formalised by the creation of the Paving Commission two years later. On the left you'll see an imposing, fortress-like building. Formerly the prison entrance, this is now part of **County Hall**. Down the hill on the right is the unmistakable sturdy tower of **Nuffield College ❷**.

The site and funds for the college were donated to the university in 1937 by Lord Nuffield, alias William Morris, who began life repairing bicycles in the High Street (*see page 106*), progressed to designing the "Bullnose" Morris in Longwall Street and ended up by establishing the first ever mass production line for cheap cars at Cowley (whose successor, Rover, continues to thrive, albeit under BMW ownership). His manufacturing goals achieved, Nuffield was determined to use part of his vast fortune for good causes, including hospitals and charities. As far as the university was concerned, he had originally envisaged establishing a college specialising in the practical skills of engineering and accountancy, but was persuaded instead to fund a post-graduate college devoted to the study of social, economic and political problems.

Formal agreement was reached in 1937, but progress was slow because Nuffield disliked the original "un-English" designs for the college, and, by the time new designs were completed, war had been declared. In the event, work did not begin until 1949, and this

LEFT: May Day entertainment.
BELOW: Nuffield College.

Lutyens-inspired, Cotswold-style college, very much a product of 1930s architectural thinking, was not completed until 1960. Nuffield had devoted the best part of his wealth to the project, but still referred to it as "that bloody Kremlin, where left-wingers study at my expense". Committed to providing a bridge between the academic and the non-academic worlds, Nuffield College has been the source of some major research developments in British social science.

Attractive to some, plain ugly to others, the Stalinesque **tower** houses the library, which contains 70,000 books on its 10 floors. It was intended to be part of a large college chapel, but this plan was altered as a consequence of the delays and financial problems surrounding the whole project. Except for the tower, Nuffield is much like a Cotswold country house on a large scale, with two courtyards in the pattern of traditional colleges, linked by steps, surrounding lily ponds and rose beds. The college is built on the site of New Road wharves' terminus of the Oxford Canal, once used to unload coals from the Midlands to warm many a cosy set of college rooms; some irony that the last vestiges of the canal trade should have been levelled by the pioneer of cheap motoring. The chapel of Nuffield, scaled down from its original grand proportions because of escalating costs, is now no more than a room on the top floor of "L" staircase, entered from the lower quad. John Piper, the artist, designed the glass and simple wooden box pews, modelled on those of Ivychurch in the Romney Marshes.

From castles to caskets

The green mound on the other side of the road is what remains of the **Castle ❸** (closed to the public), built by Robert d'Oilly, Oxford's Norman governor, in 1071. The mound was originally topped with a wooden keep (later rebuilt in

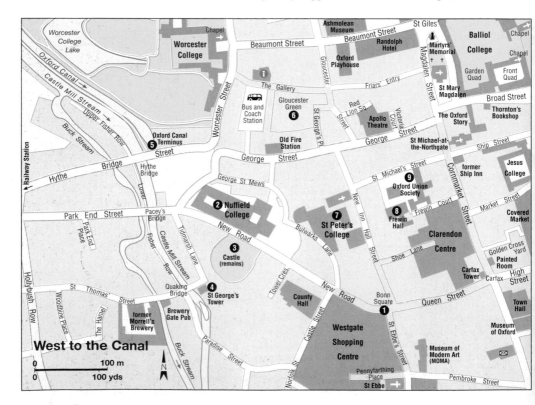

stone), and the outer bailey was surrounded by a moat with water from one of the branckes of the Thames used to power the castle mills – hence Castle Mill Stream. Many historic figures are associated with the castle. In 1142, Matilda (the Empress Maud) was holed up here for three months while battling to gain the English throne after the death of her father, Henry I, in 1135. She escaped in the depths of winter down the frozen Thames, camouflaged against the snow in nothing but a white sheet. She never became queen. From the mid-12th century, the castle was used to house prisoners, and although the fortifications were torn down after the Civil War, it remained the site of a prison. The present forbidding structure was built in the 19th century. The last public execution took place here in 1863; the last prisoner moved out in 1993. There are plans to transform the prison into a museum and open the mound to the public. A museum, hotel and shopping complex are expected to open in 2002.

Continue along New Road until the next turning on the left, into Tidmarsh Lane. At the very end, the view is dominated by **St George's Tower ❹**, which Robert d'Oilly built at the southern side of the castle bailey in 1074, above the chapel of St George which he founded within the walls. It was the Secular Canons of St George who established here what is regarded as the first learning establishment in Oxford.

Follow the road round to the right, across Quaking Bridge and into St Thomas Street. On the opposite side of the road stands the former **Morrell's Brewery** which closed in 1998. An independent, family-run concern that had belonged to the Morrell family since 1792, this was the last brewery in Oxford. At one time no fewer than 14 breweries thrived in this part of the city, drawing their water from wells deep beneath the Thames and using the river and the canal for

Map on page 186

Quaking Bridge, perhaps so named because it was originally built of wobbling timber, dates back to the 13th century, but was replaced by the current iron construction in 1835.

BELOW: swanning around on Fisher Row.

transport. The first brewery here in Tidmarsh Lane was established in 1452 by the monks of neighbouring Osney Abbey (*see page 202*). The Morrell's premises have been sold, but the adjoining **Brewery Gate** pub remains open.

Canalside

Return to the Quaking Bridge. On the corner of **Lower Fisher Row** is the house lived in by Edward Tawney, who ran the Brewery prior to its takeover by the Morrell family in 1792. Follow the attractive Fisher Row which leads north along the Castle Mill Stream. The original fishermen's and canal bargees' cottages have gone, but it remains a pretty spot, overhung by a pendulous willow and often frequented by swans.

Emerging at the end, cross Park End Street to Hythe Bridge Street and the present-day terminus of the **Oxford Canal ❺** on **Upper Fisher Row**, where a sign headed **Oxford Canal Walk** indicates the distances to towns further up the waterway. While visitors might find the 83 miles (134 km) to Coventry somewhat ambitious, a short walk along the canal towpath, lined with colourful narrowboats, is worthwhile. The canal runs along the back of Worcester College (*see page 163*), past the district of Jericho and then Lucy's Ironworks, where steps up to the bridge provide access to Port Meadow (*see page 204*).

To the west along Hythe Bridge Street and Park End Street is **Oxford railway station**. The original station was deliberately kept well out of the centre of Oxford because, among other reasons, the railway was thought likely to corrupt young students – making it easy for them to travel to places of ill-repute, such as Ascot racecourse. The existing station lies on the Great Western Railway line to London. Another line, closed in 1967, terminated at the junction of Park

TIP

It is perfectly possible to cycle along the canal towpath (as long as it's not too muddy). You can get to places like Port Meadow much more quickly and easily escape Oxford altogether. An excursion to the pleasant village of Thrupp, 6 miles (10km) up the canal (*see page 245*) is recommended.

BELOW: Oxford Canal has some beautiful scenery.

End Road and Hythe Bridge Street: part of the old station, painted red, white and blue, stood on the site until 1999, when it was demolished to make room for a new road scheme and the construction of the new Saïd Business School, built by the university from funds donated by various businesses and benefactors, notably Wafic Saïd. The demolition of the old railway station created considerable controversy, especially when environmental activists occupied the site in an attempt to save a row of trees. The listed building was eventually dismantled and carted off to the nearby Quainton Railway Centre.

Beyond the railway line lies the district of **Osney** (*see page 202*).

Map on page 186

Shopping

To the east, Hythe Bridge Street leads back towards the city centre. Opposite, fronting on to Worcester Street, is an adventurous brick building, with three lead-covered angle towers enclosing Gloucester Green, which is entered a little further up Worcester Street, on the right. Opened in 1989, **Gloucester Green ❻**, is a large pedestrianised shopping square. It has been a welcome addition to the Oxford townscape, tidying up an area that had served as a windswept and litter-strewn bus station ever since 1932, when the cattle market on the site was closed down. The present bus station has been integrated into the scheme.

Before you get into the main square, look out for the Old School House, which now houses the city's Tourist Information Centre, where leaflets can be obtained as well as bookings made for guided walking tours. Continue under the arch into the square itself, which is surrounded by a variety of shops and eating places and is the scene every Wednesday of an **open-air market**, with stalls selling everything from pots and pans to brooms and doorknobs. Every Thursday there's a popular **fleamarket.**

Of the pubs that once served the thirsty cattle drovers, only the **Welsh Pony**, in George Street, now survives, albeit transformed into a fashionable continental-style café-bar. Further up, the **Old Fire Station** has been redeveloped to house a theatre as well as a bar/restaurant which is transformed into a disco in the evenings. Opposite, the delicate neo-Jacobean Social Studies Faculty was originally built in 1880 as the City of Oxford High School, and numbered T. E. Lawrence among its pupils. George Street is now lined with pubs and restaurants, ranging from the more traditional inn (The Grapes) to the esoteric (Mongolian Wok Bar). Some of the most popular are the Wig and Pen and Cock and Camel, whose strange names seem to verge on pastiche.

Along New Inn Hall Street

Proceed up George Street to **New Inn Hall Street** on the right, past the cinema. This street marks the eastern boundary of the medieval city, and was once just inside the walls. The original New Inn Hall has gone but **St Peter's College ❼**, halfway up on the right, now occupies part of the site. St Peter's was founded in 1929, and did not achieve college status until 1961, but the buildings are much older. The college is entered through **Linton House**, built in 1797 as the headquarters of the Oxford Canal Company which then moved,

A wall mural in Gloucester Green typifies its fun nature.

BELOW: at the Wednesday market in Gloucester Green.

Map on page 186

in 1828, to the neo-classical **Canal House**, which now serves as the Master's Lodge. The college chapel is the former church of St Peter-le-Bailey, which was built in 1874 to the design of Basil Champneys on the site of the original Norman church.

Opposite St Peter's, **Frewin Hall** ❽ is an attractive house, set well back from the street, dating to the 16th and 18th centuries, and converted into student accommodation in the 1970s. Next to the entrance, a plaque indicates a house that was the first Methodist meeting house in Oxford, used for the first time in 1783, eight years before the death of John Wesley, who had founded the Oxford Movement while at Lincoln College.

Frewin Hall itself backs on to the red-brick Gothic premises of the **Oxford Union Society** ❾ (closed to the public), built in 1857 as a permanent home for the debating club that was founded in 1823. Harold Macmillan, Britain's prime minister from 1957 until 1963 and later Chancellor of the University, called it "an unrivalled training ground for debates in the Parliamentary style". The list of past Union Society presidents reads like a *Who's Who* of the political and journalistic world – and not merely of Great Britain, since Benazir Bhutto, president in 1977, went on to become prime minister of Pakistan.

The Union Society fronts on to St Michael's Street, with the Saxon tower of **St Michael's Church** framed at the Cornmarket end (*see page 120*). St Michael's Street is comparatively peaceful compared to the main arteries of central Oxford. Visit the delightful Nosebag restaurant, or try the excellent Three Goats' Heads pub, serving traditional and contemporary food.

To complete the route, return to Carfax either via Cornmarket or back along New Inn Hall Street and Queen Street. ❑

BELOW:
the view along St Michael's Street to New Inn Hall Street.
RIGHT: detail of a facade in St Michael's Street.

The Oxford Union

Again and again in its history, the young speakers who catch the president's eye have gone on to catch the eye of the country, even the eye of the world," wrote political journalist David Walter in his book *The Oxford Union*. It's a fair claim: the Oxford Union Society, founded in 1823, is the most famous student-run body in Britain, possibly in the world, and seven of its officers have become prime ministers.

Like most such student organisations, the Oxford Union runs discos and jazz evenings and operates a cheap bar. But what sets it apart are its weekly showpiece debates. Modelled on Westminster's parliamentary procedure, these constitute nothing less than a top-notch political training ground. They give students a chance not only to hear leading public figures defend their views but also to hone their own debating skills in preparation for the anticipated day when they themselves will be leading public figures.

Richard Nixon and Jimmy Carter have both spoken here. British cabinet ministers regularly make the 50-mile (80-km) trek from London. Preachers, playwrights and popular comedians have all pitted their wits against the difficult acoustics and an unusually discerning and frequently rowdy audience. Even Hitler was given false hope in 1935 when the Oxford Union carried the controversial motion that "This House would not fight for King and Country". (Oddly, he failed to appreciate that what people say they would do in certain circumstances often bears little relation to their actual behaviour.)

The Union's training for the rough and tumble of real politics is ruthlessly practical. To become president of the Union a student must clamber up the proverbial greasy pole by winning various elections, perhaps becoming initially a committee member and later secretary, treasurer or librarian. Just to make things a bit more interesting, the Society's celebrated Rule 33 forbids a candidate from informing anyone, except "close personal friends", that he or she is running for office.

RIGHT: the Oxford Union is as strong today as it has ever been.

This awkward handicap spurs candidates to find ingenious ways of circumventing the rule. They are thus liable to buy drinks for total strangers, casually letting slip in the conversation the fact that they just might be standing for election this term. This practice, known as "hacking", is scorned by the non-political students.

Once elected, the president assumes significant responsibilities. Four speakers have to be found for each of the eight debates held every term, and the Union, which has a staff of 30 and a turnover of around £500,000 a year, has to be managed efficiently and profitably.

It is no small task. In the mid-1980s, the Union's fine Victorian buildings, including a library with pre-Raphaelite murals, were in serious disrepair and bankruptcy seemed a possibility. But sponsorship of debates and events and a Japanese bank donation of £1 million helped towards restoration. The resulting new-found vitality boosted university membership to 7,000 and there are now around 65,000 members worldwide. Dues are £120 for lifetime membership – good value. ❑

THE CANAL – OXFORD'S GREEN CORRIDOR

Neglected for much of its 200-year history, the Oxford Canal might easily have been lost forever after World War II. Now it enjoys renewed esteem

When the Oxford Canal was completed in 1790, it had a huge and immediate impact. After centuries of academic and religious privilege, Oxford suddenly found itself confronted by a rapidly changing industrial world.

Those who welcomed this workmanlike intruder were not disappointed. Investors soon saw the demand for their principal product of coal turned into massive profits.

Within a decade the Canal Company expanded its original city centre wharves just south of Hythe Bridge Street to encompass the site now occupied by Nuffield College. The labour for this work came from the conveniently located Oxford Castle Gaol, whose governor, Daniel Harris, also found time to grace Oxford's waterways with his skills as an engineer, surveyor and architect.

BUOYANT TIMES TO BENIGN NEGLECT

Until the mid-19th century Oxford treated the canal as an honoured guest. When the railway arrived in the 1840s, however, a decline set in, and although it took another century before the Company conceded the struggle to carry freight in any volume, the canal suffered a kind of benign neglect from there on. The Company withdrew from the city centre in the 1930s, and the entire canal could easily have been lost forever, but it survived thanks to the efforts of enthusiasts who foresaw the waterway's leisure potential.

Apart from a foundry in Jericho, the canal has always defied the industrial stereotype. In 1898 it was described as "an arcadian scene of pastoral beauty". Hints of its rural nature are still evident. The towpath provides a refuge from modern city life. And with so much activity – hire boats, private craft, Oxford's floating restaurant, the occasional cargo vessel – it's an experience not to be forgotten.

▷ **NARROW ESCAPE**
The freedom to move your home and vary your views is appealing. At under 7 ft (22 metres) wide, though, there's little room for materialism.

▽ **POST MODERN**
The origins of traditional canal art are obscure, but the style endures. The post-box indicates a permanence the old boaters could never have imagined.

◁ PASSAGE OF TIME
◁ PASSAGE OF TIME
The continuity of two centuries is maintained as a distinctive narrowboat passes through history along the Thames.

△ CHILD LABOUR
Children were once essential crew for the working boatman. Nowadays a boating holiday provides kids with exercise, fun and an appreciation of both history and nature.

△ FAMILY BUSINESS
A rare day off for this boatman and his family, pictured around 1900. The last horse-drawn cargo boat on the canal ceased trading in the 1950s.

◁ INCOME STREAM
People are the 21st-century cargo, sustaining the original commercial intent of the Canal. Oxford's busy hire fleet and floating restaurant operate from Jericho.

WHAT LIFE'S LIKE ON THE CANAL

A step along the Oxford Canal towpath from Hythe Bridge Street brings an instant sense of relief. The noise, pollution and traffic are forgotten as you enter a calmer, gentler world of boats, anglers and swans.

It's the boats which make the scene really special, and in Oxford there is an unusually high number which are year-round homes. Distributed along the 3 miles (5 km) of canal between Wolvercote and the city, they form a single linear community, united by shared dependence on and responsibility for the same stretch of water, and by an unspoken awareness of common chores and comforts, pleasures and problems.

The canal residents have had to struggle to gain acceptance, perhaps a throwback to the prejudices against working boatmen. Today they provide interest in a quiet part of the city.

They are not alone. Dotted around Britain's (2,000 miles/3,200 km) of inland waterways are other pockets of residential boats. The national Residential Boat Owners' Association (RBOA) give these "floating voters" a collective voice.

RIVERS, LOCKS, MEADOWS AND ABBEYS

The rivers Thames and Cherwell and their surrounding meadows provide a playground not only for energetic oarsman, but also for walkers, picnickers and punters

Map on page 198

For many towns and cities built by a river, the water is simply an obstruction to be bridged, or a convenient sewer. For Oxford, the rivers **Thames** and **Cherwell** (pronounced "charwell") have historically played a vital role in the development of the city. Early signs of human habitation are to be found on Port Meadow, while the Thames and its various arms were also the site of some of the earliest monastic foundations in Oxford, which spawned the development of the university. They include Osney Abbey (now a Victorian terraced-house community) to the west, and Godstow Abbey, beyond Port Meadow to the northwest of the city.

In more recent times, philosophers have resolved complex syllogisms while walking the riverbanks, in true Platonic fashion. Poets, painters and storytellers – notably Lewis Carroll – have been inspired by the calm, scenic beauty of the meadows, and, in our own age, ecologists have come to realise that the meadows, regularly flooded but never ploughed or fertilised (except by cows), are a haven for rare plants and insects.

PRECEDING PAGES: a Thames narrowboat. **LEFT:** strong-arm tactics. **BELOW:** view across Christ Church Meadows.

Christ Church Meadow and beyond

Less sensitive souls have often mooted plans to tame or use these "wastelands": a four-lane highway, crossing Christ Church and providing an inner-city relief road, was first proposed in 1933 and revived in 1968. W.H. Auden penned a poem in protest at the proposals ("may the Meadows be only frequented by scholars and couples and cows"). The combined efforts of Oxford's townspeople and the academic population brought a halt to these plans, proving with what affection everyone in the city holds their river landscape.

Christ Church Meadow ❶ borders the River Thames to the south of the city. It is not actually possible to walk on the meadow itself because it is fenced off to contain its herd of fine cattle. However, a walk around it is highly worthwhile, not only for giving the feeling of country so close to the city, but also for the magnificent views of the spires and towers of the colleges to the north.

There are several ways of reaching the meadow: either through the War Memorial Gardens past the Meadow Buildings of Christ Church (*see page 153*); from Merton Lane through to Merton Grove and on to the Broad Walk (*see page 143*); or via the turnstile gate behind the Head of the River pub (*see page 153*).

Approaching from the north, joining the Broad Walk just opposite the Meadow Buildings is the **New Walk ❷**, which leads along the west side of Christ

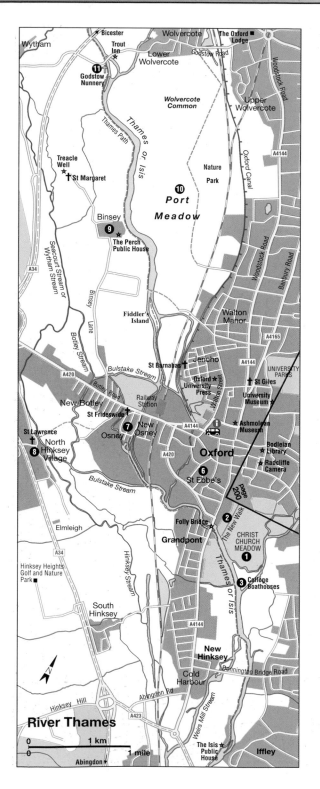

Church Meadow towards the river. The New Walk is lined with tall trees planted by the head of Christ Church, Dean Liddell, in 1872, turning a muddy pathway into an avenue. The Dean's daughter, Alice, came this way with Lewis Carroll in July 1862, on the way to a boat trip during which he began to tell the stories that resulted in *Alice's Adventures in Wonderland*.

The New Walk leads to a wide, straight stretch of the Thames – also called the Isis within Oxford, a Latin name first coined in 1535 by John Leland, who seems not to have been at all happy with the pre-Roman Celtic name (from tam, meaning "broad" and wys, meaning "water"). Moored on the other side of the river you will see a variety of cruise boats run by Salters Bros, which ply the river between Oxford, Dorchester and Abingdon. If you want to explore the rivers yourself, there are punts, rowing boats, pedalboats and motorboats for hire next to the Head of the River pub (reached by turning right and through the turnstile gate – *see page 153*).

To continue the walk, head downstream (southeast) along the river. During term-time you will probably see rowing crews training along this stretch of the river. Activity gets particularly frenetic during the Trinity term in May, when it is the scene of Eights Week (*see page 137*) – also a lively social event, with partisan crowds either celebrating or drowning their disappointment in wine, depending on the performance of their college eights.

College members and their guests watch the races from the verandahs of the bankside **College Boathouses** ❸, situated beyond the arched bridge at the confluence of the Thames and an arm of the Cherwell. The best way to see the excitement of Eights Week races is the stand on the towpath downriver from the boathouses, near Donnington Bridge. From there you can see the races start and most of the "bumps" take place.

Until the turn of the century, ornate floating barges were used instead – the last of these, Keble College barge, remained in use until 1958 and part of it is now displayed in the Museum of Oxford (*see page 149*). In his satirical novel, *Zuleika Dobson*, Max Beerbohm has the entire student population of Oxford commit mass suicide by leaping from their barges into the river, all hopelessly in love with Zuleika – not, perhaps, so far from the truth as one might think, since romantic emotions still run high as the summer term draws to a close and final-year students either cement or break their Oxford liaisons on these banks.

The path stops just beyond the boathouses, so if you want to see any more of the Thames, go back along the path, through the turnstile, and cross Folly Bridge to the south bank of the river. It is possible, from here, to follow the Thames path for some 2 miles (3 km) down to the lock at **Iffley** (*see page 208*).

The Cherwell

Returning to the Thames at Christ Church Meadow, there are further possibilities for walkers. Just before the arched bridge that leads to the boathouses, take the leftward path that follows the bank of the River Cherwell from its confluence with the Thames. The Cherwell, which rises in Northamptonshire, is a narrow and shallow river, used for punting rather than races, with many a tree-hung peaceful backwater, rich in bird and plant life.

From the area around the confluence, the **views** across Christ Church Meadow, with the spires of Oxford in the background, are magnificent, particularly the towers of Christ Church, Merton and Magdalen. After a short stretch, the River Cherwell divides – the right hand (southernmost) branch is the **New Cut ❹**, dug during the Civil War in the 1640s as part of the city defences, intended to halt

Maps
on pages
198 & 200

Ruskin believed that physical work brought with it a sense of dignity, preferring it to sporting activities. "Even digging rightly done," he wrote, "is at least as much an art as the mere muscular act of rowing."

BELOW: limbering up on the Ergonometer.

Parliamentary troops approaching from the London side. The Cherwell path eventually returns to meet Broad Walk, on the left, and Rose Lane to the right, which leads to the **Botanic Garden** (*see page 143*). At the other side of Magdalen Bridge, visitors to Magdalen College can contine the water walks theme by exploring the Cherwell along Addison's Walk (*see page 133*).

If you want to see more of the Cherwell, you don't have to reach it via Magdalen College. Exit the Botanic Garden and walk down to the Plain (*see page 135*). The road to the left, off The Plain, forms the main street of the suburb of **St Clement's**. A few 17th-century, timber-framed buildings survive from the time when St Clement's was a village, but most now date to the early 19th century, when speculative developers laid out a network of new streets. The area now has many characterful pubs and shops selling everything from near-antiques to theatrical costumes.

Where St Clement's Street divides, take the left-hand fork into Marston Road and look for the lane that leads to the river, opposite the government buildings. This path leads to **Mesopotamia Walk** ❺; the name derives from the Greek, meaning "between the rivers", as in the ancient kingdom that lay between the Tigris and Euphrates. Here the path follows a narrow strip of land between two branches of the Cherwell, a popular stretch of the water for punting and picnics. The path crosses a number of bridges, before reaching a weir where punters have to disembark and manhandle their boats over the metal rollers to one side.

From the weir, a path to the left crosses a concrete bridge to merge with South Parks Road and Linacre College. On the right we meet again the huge expanse of **University Parks** (*see page 179*), with its magnificent trees and shrubs and lovely walks by the river. Here it is possible to continue north

Nearby is Parson's Pleasure, a bathing spot used by generations of students and dons. Nudity is almost de rigueur and passing women in punts and boats are expected to avert their eyes.

BELOW: a casual stroll along Mesopotamia Walk.

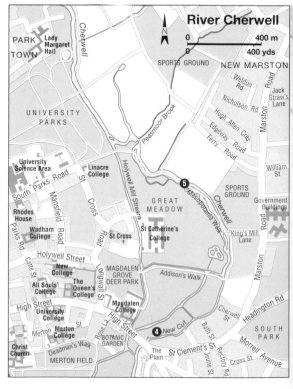

along the banks of the River Cherwell, over bridges and across fields towards the northern edge of the city.

Maps on pages 198 & 200

Out West

From Folly Bridge, the path along the Thames also leads west. You get on to it via a small opening just to the south of the bridge. On the other side note the grand, Venetian-style residence, with its crenellation and white statues, backing on to the river. Built in 1849 by a wealthy eccentric, Joshua Caudwell, Caudwell's Castle was supposedly once a brothel, but is now divided into (expensive) private flats.

The north side of the river at this point is occupied by recent residential developments with attractive terraces and walkways along the river. These mark the southern boundary of St Ebbe's. Once a working-class suburb of Oxford, **St Ebbe's ❻** was chosen as the site for the town's new gasworks in 1818, and the arrival of the railway in Oxford in 1844 further stimulated speculative building. Not much of the original St Ebbe's remains today, most of its Victorian houses having been pulled down in the 1960s and the population rehoused at the purpose-built Blackbird Leys estate in east Oxford.

The Venetian-style Caudwell's Castle on Folly Bridge.

If you continue along the south bank of the river, you soon leave the residential district of Grandpont behind and once more enter a riverscape flanked by green, with the occasional used or disused bridge as a reminder of past industrial progress. Grandpont nature park is just a step away from the river, a popular recreation area for local residents. Note the wooden sculpture of a giant hand emerging from the grass.

Continue beyond the railway bridge to a long, straight section of the river, beyond which lies Osney Lock and the suburb of **Osney ❼**. Also reached from

BELOW: the Head of the River pub.

Botley Road over a bridge built in 1888, the main part of Osney is an island surrounded by arms of the River Thames. The district has nicely preserved 1850s terraces and characterful waterside pubs, and in summer the river is usually busy with narrowboats and cruisers.

It may seem difficult to imagine today, but back in the Middle Ages the whole island was occupied by one of the largest Augustinian monasteries in England. Founded in 1129, but completely destroyed at the Dissolution in 1536, **Osney Abbey** was among the first major centres of learning in Oxford. Once the third-largest church in England, Osney Abbey housed Great Tom, the huge bell that chimes in Christ Church's Tom Tower (*see page 156*). Nowadays, only the remnants of a 15th-century outbuilding can be glimpsed through the gates of the Osney Marina at the end of Mill Street (second left after the railway bridge heading out of town).

From Ferry Hinksey Road there is an attractive short walk over the meadows, via a bridge over the Thames to the village of **North Hinksey** ❽. This village, with its thatched cottages, riding stables, Norman church of St Lawrence and pub, still manages to retain a rural feel. John Ruskin is commemorated on one of the picturesque cottages. In 1874, Ruskin organised teams of undergraduates to work on road improvements in the village – with the intention of convincing his students (who included Oscar Wilde) of the "pleasures of useful muscular work".

Alice again

Back in Osney, the church of St Frideswide on Botley Road contains a door panel, with a relief of the saint praying by the Thames, carved by Alice Liddell, herself a pupil of Ruskin's, in 1890. Other reminders of the saint as well as the

BELOW LEFT:
the Church of
St Lawrence,
North Hinksey.
BELOW RIGHT:
narrowboat
berthed at Osney.

heroine of *Alice's Adventures in Wonderland* can be seen in the remote church of St Margaret in **Binsey** ➒. The church is reached down Binsey Lane on the other side of Botley Road, and, once past the messy builders' yards, the suburbs give way to a patchwork of small fields surrounded by high hedges and tall trees. Binsey itself is a tiny farming hamlet but with a renowned pub, **The Perch**, beside the Thames, a favourite lunchtime retreat for weekend walkers, with a good playground for children.

Beyond the village, a single-track road leads to the little late-Norman church. Just beyond the west end is the **Treacle Well** that features in the story told by Lewis Carroll's Dormouse at the Mad Hatter's Tea Party. In Middle English "triacle" meant any liquid with healing or medicinal powers – only later did it come to mean a syrup.

This well is said to have sprung up at the command of St Frideswide. The king of Wessex, her enforced and self-appointed suitor, was struck blind by thunder when he tried to carry the saint away forcibly. Frideswide agreed to cure him on condition that he leave her in peace; the well appeared miraculously and its waters restored the king's sight.

Hundreds of pilgrims used to visit the church. Few come now and the rustic nave, lit only by oil lamps, has been colonised by bats. The simple wooden pulpit has a carving of St Margaret trampling on a dragon set into the front. If you look inside, you will find another relief of St Margaret on the inner face – not by Eric Gill, though it has wrongly been attributed to him – with clearly delineated breasts. Regarded as too sensual for public display, she is condemned to face the feet of the incumbent preacher rather than risk arousing the passions of the congregation.

Map on page 198

Peeping into the Treacle Well at Binsey.

BELOW:
Port Meadow.

A PARADISE FOR BIRDS

The wide expanse of Port Meadow, usually flooded for several months each year, is something of a haven for a surprising cross-section of bird species.

The best months for bird-watching are *those between November and March when heavy rains and cold drive walkers and their dogs off the Meadow. The presence of standing water encourages the annual arrival of large numbers of dabbling ducks – wigeon, teal and pintail – as well as flocks of late-migrating birds such as golden plovers and lapwings in autumn. If you are lucky, you could see a flock of up to 2,000 lapwings in the area.

A rarer sight is the snipe, with its distinctive long bill used for probing for worms, and once a popular gamebird because of its weaving flight. Other passing waders include the godwit, with its upturned bill, and the ruff, so named after the male's ring of feathers around the neck in the mating season.

According to the Oxford Ornithological Society, the Meadow is best approached over the bridge from Walton Well Road for the most interesting views of birdlife. On the east side, in Burgess Field, the experienced ornithologist may also catch a glimpse of reed buntings, stonechats and the short-eared owl.

Map
on page
198

Binsey inspired one of Gerard Manley Hopkins' most celebrated poems, "Binsey Poplars", which laments the cutting down of the poem's trees and, metaphorically, the loss of the poet's innocence.

BELOW: the Trout Inn, often seen in episodes of TV's *Inspector Morse.*

Binsey seems remote from all the bustle of central Oxford, even though the nearest suburbs are only half a mile (1 km) away. It sits just to the west of the Thames, while to the east, sandwiched between the river and the city, is the great expanse of **Port Meadow ⑩**. Used continuously for grazing ever since its first mention in the *Domesday Book* (1087), the meadow is a rare piece of Old England; it has never once been ploughed over, and today, except for during the winter months, visitors are still invariably outnumbered by horses and cattle.

In winter, when the flooded meadow freezes over, skaters come out to test the strength of the ice. The birdlife is rich at all times of the year, and in summer you can often make out the outlines of Iron Age farming enclosures and hut circles, delineated by the buttercups that grow taller over buried features such as ditches and foundation trenches.

A pleasant walk crosses the meadow and the bridge over the Thames, and follows the west bank of the river past Binsey to Godstow, where a 15th-century bridge leads to the scant remains of the medieval **Godstow Nunnery ⑪**. Founded in 1138 by Benedictine monks, the nunnery is now a romantic ruin and it was here that Rosamund Clifford, mistress of King Henry II, was buried in 1175. According to legend, "fair Rosamund" was murdered by the jealous Queen Eleanor, but the truth is probably less melodramatic, since she seems to have retired to the nunnery when Henry grew bored with her. Nearby, the **Trout Inn**, originally a fisherman's cottage, was rebuilt in 1737, and is famous for the peacocks that wander around the attractive riverside garden. It is a popular place on long summer evenings, but nice also in winter with its roaring log fires.

For the route back, it is possible to take the Godstow Road until it meets the Oxford Canal, and follow the towpath all the way to its end at Hythe Bridge.❑

Messing about on the rivers

Punts, as much a feature of Oxford as bicycles and spires, have come to embody the timeless romance of the privileged university world. Yet long before the first student ever skipped lectures in favour of punting up the slow-flowing Cherwell, the punt played a vital part in the lives of watermen up and down the Thames. River dredging, fishing, ferrying, transporting and delivering were all duties once carried out by this humble craft.

Decline in river transport in the mid-19th century could have led to the disappearance of the punt altogether. Fortunately, the Victorians, recognising the delights of punting, claimed it as their leisure craft. Punts were modified from broad pontoons that could carry cattle to the slender "saloon" comprising two back rests for passengers – a design still in use today.

Increased use of power craft on rivers has resulted in a sharp decrease in punting and it has survived as a feature almost unique to Oxford and Cambridge. As a Thames craft, the punt was not introduced to Cambridge until the early Edwardian era, when it was imported from Oxford. The Oxford tradition is to punt from the slope, stern first, whereas in Cambridge, punting from the deck end is the norm.

Some Oxford colleges have their own punting fleets and most have private hire arrangements. Punts can be hired in the summer from 10am to sunset from three points: Folly Bridge, Magdalen Bridge and the Cherwell Boathouse. They cost £10 to £12 an hour (US$16–$19) and can take up to six people, but their use is restricted to swimmers. Paddles are provided in case poles get stuck in the mud. Rowing boats can also be hired.

Newcomers might find that the Cherwell provides fewer hazards than the Thames and is notable for its absence of rowing crews and powerboats. It is navigable by punt up to Islip. The Thames will be congested with university rowers below Iffley Lock.

Numerically, rowing is by far the most popular sport among students and a large proportion of rowers are women. The Participants range from non-competitive water-lovers who are *exploring the river to the elite university team. Each college has its own rowing society and the societies are brought together under the umbrella of Oxford University Boating Club (OUBC), founded in 1939.

From early morning until dusk throughout the year, Eights, Fours and Sculls can be seen accompanied by coaches who cycle or run along the towpath, megaphone in hand. On the stretch of river beyond Christ Church Meadow are the college and OUBC boathouses. Just before Iffley Lock is the Isis Tavern, watering hole for many a rower and home to much boating regalia. The two main events in the rowing calendar are Torpids and Eights Week (*see page 137*).

By far the most glamorous event in rowing is the inter-Varsity race, first staged in 1829. Oxford "dark blues" take on Cambridge "light blues" in the annual Putney-to-Mortlake race. The prestigious Blue is awarded in rowing and other sports to those competing in a university team against Cambridge. ❑

RIGHT: punting is a big part of life in summer.

OXFORD'S OUTSKIRTS

Map on page 208

*Beyond Oxford's suburbs, which include Cowley, the birthplace
of Morris Motors, there are some stunning views
of the "City of Dreaming Spires"*

Large houses line the complex of narrow lanes that lead to **Boars Hill ❶**,
and such was the pressure of development that the Oxford Preservation
Trust purchased the remaining land in 1928 to ensure that the views
would not be destroyed.

One Boars Hill resident, Sir Arthur Evans, famous for his archaeological dis-
coveries at Knossos, worked with the Trust to build an artificial mound at the
summit of the hill. Evans' intention was partly to provide work for the local
unemployed during a period of economic depression, and partly to create a
vantage point from where to admire the views, famously immortalised in
Matthew Arnold's poem *Thyrsis*, where he describes the winter scene:

> *Humid the air! leafless, yet soft as spring,*
> *The tender purple spray on copse and briers!*
> *And that sweet city with her dreaming spires,*
> *She needs not June for beauty's heightening.*

The tumulus that Evans built, known as **Jarn Mound ❷**, rises to 50 ft
(15 metres), and the summit is 530 ft (162 metres) above sea level. It was completed in 1931 and the surrounding area planted with trees to create a wild garden. Now it is overgrown with bracken and scrub, and the topograph on the
summit has gone, the column on which it stood bro-
ken. Even so, the views are unchanged: to the northeast
the ancient buildings of Oxford appear, framed
between ancient trees that seem deliberately planted
to hide the modern suburbs – if you go at dusk, the
setting sun adds its own rich colouring to the scene.

Turn round and you see another extensive view,
stretching southwest over the Vale of the White Horse
to the Berkshire Downs.

LEFT: beakhead
carvings at the
entrance to the
church of St Mary
the Virgin, Iffley.
BELOW: Iffley Lock.

Happy Valley

Heading clockwise around the ring road, Chilswell
Valley, better known as **Happy Valley ❸**, is reached
by turning off the southern by-pass (A34) at a well-
signposted garden centre and following a footpath to
Chilswell Farm. The view from this southern hillside
is almost as perfect a picture of the celebrated dreaming spires as you will find, remarkably unobstructed
by power lines and other modern-day eyesores. What
is striking is how small Oxford seems from this van-
tage-point, its towers and steeples encircled by hills.

From the same exit from the ring road you can also
visit the Hinksey Heights Golf and Nature Park,
where the view is, if anything, even more beautiful.
Here the golf club welcomes visitors (as long as they
keep off the golf course itself) and you can use the
bar and restaurant. A well-marked trail takes you
through woods and over streams until you come to a

fishing lake, stocked with six types of coarse fish (day angling permits available for £5 from the golf club). The surrounding countryside is inhabited not just by golfers, but also by foxes, badgers and deer as well as a wide range of birdlife.

Iffley and Cowley

From this point, it is 2 miles (3 km) by the thundering ring road to **Iffley ❹**, a village on the southern edge of the city worth seeking out simply for its **parish church of St Mary the Virgin**. In the whole of England there is scarcely a more complete example of the late 12th-century Romanesque style. The rose window of the west end is later (inserted in 1856), but most of the remaining doorways, windows and arches – covered in sawtooth ornament and carved with beakheads, the signs of the zodiac, fighting horsemen and symbols of the Evangelists – date from around 1180.

After Iffley comes the extensive suburb of **Cowley ❺**, dubbed "Motopolis" by John Betjeman who hated this industrial town on the doorstep of his beloved Oxford because it was devoted to producing the motor car that "roars down the lanes with its cargo of cads, poisons the air, deafens the ears and deadens the senses".

Cowley was responsible for a massive 43 percent increase in the population of Oxford between 1921 and 1939, as the success of the Morris motor attracted labourers from the depression-hit Midlands and South Wales. They were accommodated in what John Betjeman called "strips of shoddy houses... indistinguishable from Swindon, Neasden or Tooting Bec".

A small, historical gem is to be found hidden away from the suburban grime of Cowley Road, however. Up a small pathway opposite the Bingo Hall is St

TIP

The Isis pub on the towpath near Iffley is well worth a visit, especially in summer when its shaded riverside garden is most attractive.

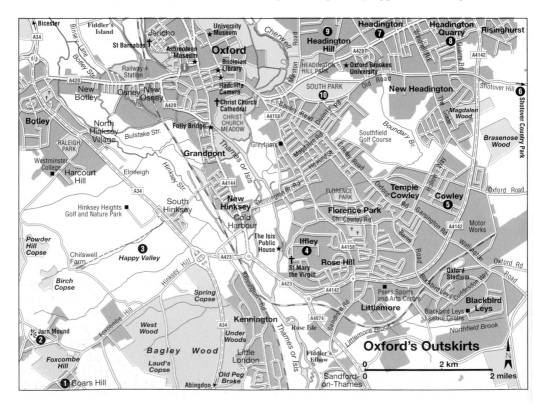

Oxford's Outskirts

Map on page 208

Bartholomew's Chapel, flanked by a row of almshouses. Founded in 1126, the chapel was connected to a leprosy hospital, situated at a suitable distance from the medieval city. The buildings are still there in a special Conservation Area, a world away from the main road just a few hundred yards away.

Passing through Cowley, (for there is nothing really for the visitor there), Rover Group, the successor to the Morris Motor Works and now owned by Germany's BMW, lies either side of the eastern by-pass, with the woodland of Shotover Country Park rising behind.

A walk on the wild side

The eastern and southern perimeter of the city, delineated by the busy ring road, offers some spectacular views of Oxford from surrounding hills as well as some interesting nature walks.

To reach **Shotover Country Park** ❻ by car, it is best to drive along Old Road from Headington, cross the ring road and climb up through a wooded residential area. The park itself comprises 250 acres (100 hectares) of mixed natural habitat, including grassland, heath, wetland and woodland. Recognised by English Nature as a Site of Special Scientific Interest, it also provides good views over the eastern part of Oxford.

Walks are clearly laid out and the area is a favourite with dog owners and mountain-bike enthusiasts. You may notice some conspicuous hollows in the ground; these are what is left of what used to be a yellow ochre mining works. The area was also once the haunt of highwaymen, as the old London road passed over the hill, and carriages containing the well-to-do were an irresistible temptation for Oxford's equivalents of Dick Turpin.

BELOW: the views of Oxford from Boars Hill are stunning.

Map
on page
208

Headington Hill Hall was once the family home of discredited publishing tycoon Robert Maxwell. It comes complete with helicopter pad and gold bathrooms.

BELOW: the controversial shark.
RIGHT:
Magdalen Bridge.

News and views

Headington ❼ consists of several distinct "villages". **Headington Quarry ❽**, as its name suggests, originally supplied the limestone and roof tiles from which much of medieval Oxford was built. The current suburb developed around the quarrymen's cottages, some of which still remain, dating from the 17th and 18th centuries. This village is home to one of England's best-known teams of Morris dancers, the Quarrymen.

Old Headington lies on the opposite side of the London Road, and was once the resort of undergraduates seeking illicit pleasures in alehouses, beyond the jurisdiction of the Proctors or Bulldogs. In the 18th and 19th centuries, wealthy tradesmen built large houses on the leafy hillside. One of them, Bury Knowle House, is now the Headington Library and occupies attractively landscaped grounds. Just to the north, restored 17th-century cottages surround St Andrew's Church, which has a Norman chancel arch and 15th-century chancel roof.

Headington Hill ❾, which plunges steeply into central Oxford, was built up mainly in the 19th century. Oxford United's football ground is on the right, off Sandfield Road, and further down is Headington Hill Hall, once part of Robert Maxwell's publishing empire, Pergamon Press, but now owned by Oxford Brookes University.

At the bottom of Headington Hill is the lower part of **South Park ❿**, a large expanse of green stretching sharply upwards. There is usually a bonfire and fireworks in November. From the top of the park, where there are playing fields and a children's playground, you can look down on to the surprisingly compact city centre, picking out the major landmarks such as Magdalen Tower and the domed top of Tom Tower. The view is particularly lovely at dawn or sunset. ❑

SHARK!

The very ordinary suburb of Headington is not renowned for its avant-garde architecture, so there was much consternation one morning in August 1986 when the residents of New High Street awoke to find a 25-ft (8-metre) fibreglass shark plunging through the roof of one of its houses. The fishy installation was the handiwork of a local sculptor, John Buckley, who was also responsible for two other Oxford landmarks (both now gone): the kicking can-can legs on the Not the Moulin Rouge cinema and the giant Al Jolson-style hands on the Penultimate Picture Palace – both establishments belonging to the shark's proud owner US-born entrepreneur and radio presenter Bill Heine.

At first, neighbours were incensed by the sculpture which Heine claimed symbolised the arbitrary horror of the nuclear age. The City Council tried to force him to remove the shark, claiming that it infringed planning permission regulations, but the eye-catching symbol stayed put fighting off all opposition until it became accepted as part of the landscape. Eventually, the shark's aesthetic merits were recognised with an award from the Southern Arts Council. You can see the tail protruding from the roof from the London Road, but it's worth taking a detour down New High Street to get a better view.

THE SHAKESPEARE
BIRTHPLACE TRUST

MARY ARDEN'S H

ENTRANCE FO
VISITORS THRO
CAR PARK

TRIPS OUT OF OXFORD

*Within easy reach of Oxford are the lovely Cotswolds, riverside
towns, Stratford-upon-Avon, Warwick and stately homes*

Drive for just a few miles outside Oxford and you will be immersed in countryside that you didn't realise was so close to the busy city. To help you explore its beauties, the following chapters are divided into routes, beginning with the road to Stratford-upon-Avon. First on the route is Woodstock, famous for the splendid Blenheim Palace and its associations with Winston Churchill, and a charming market town. The road on from Woodstock leads to the pretty villages of Great Tew and Hook Norton before reaching the ancient Rollright Stones. The final stretch to Stratford offers some more delightful villages with names like Compton Wynyates and Clifford Chambers.

Stratford-upon-Avon is a shrine to the playright William Shakespeare, and visitors from all over the world come to see what all the fuss is about. The tour around the town takes in all the important sights, such as his birthplace, his home at New Place, his school, the Guild Hall, and his burial place, Holy Trinity Church. There are other sights as well, such as the Garrick Inn and Harvard House, both 16th-century, the canal and beautiful Bancroft Gardens.

From Stratford you can detour to Warwick, dominated by its Castle, a very popular attraction, packed with history. Other highlights of the town are St Mary's Church and a Doll Museum.

From Warwick we return to Stratford and head back to Oxford along country roads which meander through the villages of Wellesbourne, Kineton and Radway, famous for its magnificent Radway Grange. Upton House is a 17th-century showpiece for impressive works of art by European Masters. Banbury is next, famous for its nursery rhyme about the Cross. The route ends along the Oxford Canal, taking in Aynho and Upper and Lower Heyford.

The north Cotswolds is filled with typical Cotswold towns, such as Chipping Norton, Moreton-in-Marsh, Chipping Camden, Broadway, Bourton-on-the-Water and Stow-on-the-Wold, as well as some famous and charming houses, like Sezincote and Snowshill Manor.

West now to follow the Thames on its twisting path to some of the area's most beautiful scenery at Lechlade, and on to Regency Cirencester and Cheltenham, and Bibury, England's most beautiful village.

The final route is along the lower Thames past medieval Abingdon and 7th-century Dorchester to commuter-land at Goring and Streatley, the regatta-centre of Henley-on-Thames, and back to Oxford via the famous houses of Cliveden and Hughenden Manor and a duck decoy at Boarstall. ❑

PRECEDING PAGES: Blenheim Palace's impressive facade; Mary Arden's house at Wilmcote.
LEFT: quiet times by the Thames.

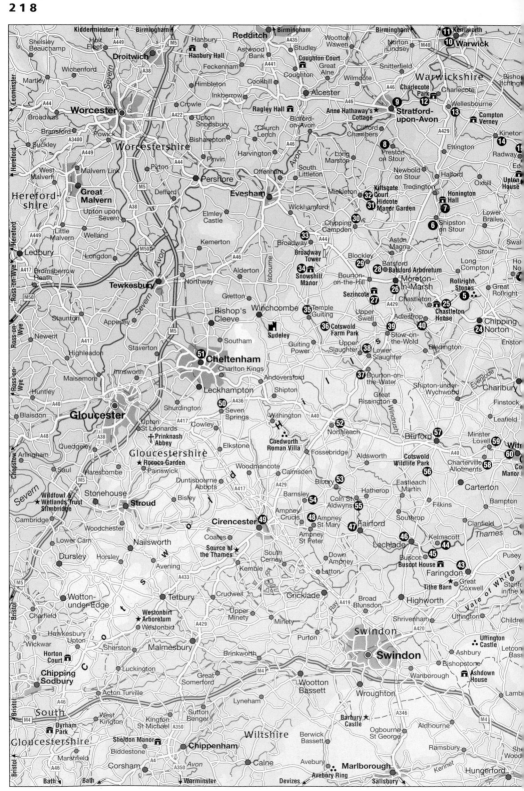

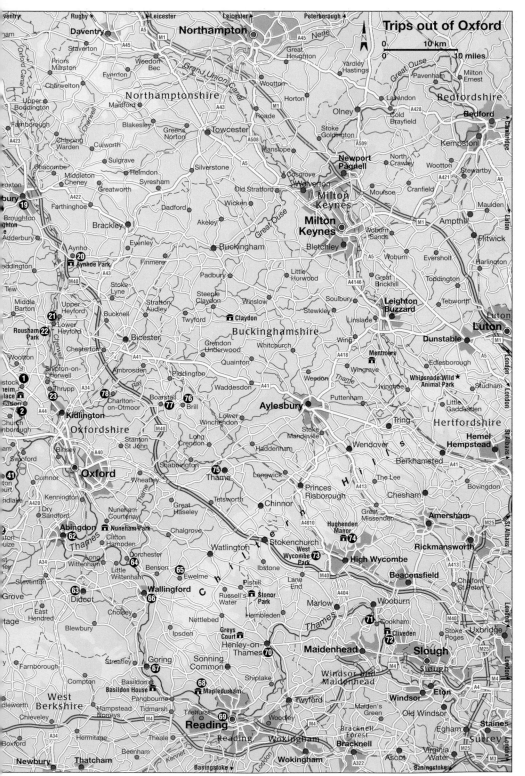

Map
on pages
218–9

Stratford-
upon-Avon
Oxford
London

THE ROAD TO STRATFORD

*It would be a shame to rush to charming
Stratford-upon-Avon along the busy main highways,
missing out the memorable sights along the route*

Stratford-upon-Avon lies about 60 miles (100 km) northwest of Oxford and exerts a magnetic attraction, having acquired international status as the most important literary shrine in England. Its environs are fascinating, too.

Woodstock and Blenheim

Leaving Oxford on the A44, it is only a matter of minutes before you reach the handsome market town of **Woodstock ❶**. The main street (Park Street) lies off the main road and is flanked by fine Georgian-fronted houses and a collection of pubs, cafés and boutiques.

The town derived much of its former prosperity from glove-making, and while all the factories in Woodstock itself are now closed, gloves are still made in surrounding villages and sold at the Woodstock Glove Shop, next to the town hall. Also in Park Street, the Oxfordshire County Museum in Fletcher's House provides an overview of the region's archaeology, agriculture and domestic life, and the gardens to the rear are used to display contemporary sculpture. Opposite, the church of St Mary Magdalene was lavishly restored in 1878, but the best part is the 18th-century tower, carved with swags of flowers around the clock and parapet.

BELOW:
the floral fountain
at Woodstock.
RIGHT:
Blenheim Palace.

At the far end of Park Street, a triumphal arch announces the entrance to **Blenheim Palace** (house: March–Oct daily 10.30am–5.30pm; park: all year daily 9am–4.45pm). There is still half a mile (1 km) to go before you reach this monumental building, for it lies at the heart of a vast estate, covering 2,700 acres (1,100 hectares) – the palace alone occupies an area of 7 acres (2.8 hectares). Not for nothing is it called a palace, rather than a mere manor, although that is what it was originally.

Take a trip on the steam train through Blenheim's grounds.

Royal blood

Woodstock was, as far back as records go, a royal manor, frequented by a succession of monarchs for deer hunting, when the land was still part of the great forest of Wychwood. Henry II installed his mistress, Fair Rosamund Clifford, at Woodstock, until Queen Eleanor discovered her hunting lodge hideaway. By the 16th century the original royal palace was decayed, and the last remaining buildings were demolished after the Civil War.

In 1705, Queen Anne gave both the manor and the funds to build the palace to John Churchill, 1st Duke of Marlborough and forefather of Winston Churchill. This was his reward for defeating the French army at Blenheim, on the Danube, the previous year, a major victory that temporarily thwarted Louis XIV's desire to dominate Europe.

The Queen made it quite clear that the palace was to be no mere private house, but a national monument, a symbol of Britain's supremacy – by implication, a building to outshine even Louis XIV's own splendid palace at Versailles. Consequently, the best architects of the day were consulted. Christopher Wren was the obvious candidate, and many of his masons, men who had worked on St Paul's, were employed on the project. But Wren was rejected in favour of John Vanbrugh, whose designs for Castle Howard were greatly admired by Churchill. Vanbrugh is therefore credited as the architect of this baroque masterpiece, but his assistant, Nicholas Hawksmoor, ought to share the credit – for it was he who supervised much of the work.

BELOW: Blenheim Palace is steeped in the spirit of Winston Churchill.

In the event, it is remarkable that the building was completed at all, let alone on such an heroic scale. Parliament quibbled about the cost, funds ran out, and the Duchess of Marlborough constantly opposed the grandiose scheme, declaring "I mortally hate all gardens and architecture", and insisting that all she wanted was "a clean, sweet house and garden, be it ever so small". The Duke ended up bearing a great deal of the cost himself, and such was the enmity between architect and client that Vanbrugh never saw the finished building; when he tried to visit in 1725, the Duchess refused him entrance.

A true folly

Even when completed, Blenheim continued to be controversial: Horace Walpole called it "execrable" and Alexander Pope, ever with an eye to practicalities, quipped "'tis very fine; but where d'ye sleep and where d'ye dine?" Yet now Blenheim excites the imagination and invites superlatives. The skyline, with its bizarre chimneys, its pinnacles resembling stacks of cannon balls and its ducal coronets, creates a wonderful silhouette, viewed across the lakes and avenues of the park, landscaped by "Capability" Brown.

Symbols of soldiery

Everywhere you look there are symbols of military prowess – over the main entrance, Britannia stands supreme in armour above the Marlborough coat of arms. Chained slaves writhe on the upper pediment, and the gates to the side wings have carvings of the cock of France being savaged by the British lion.

Inside, the gilded state rooms are rich in furniture and portraits of the Marlboroughs. Tapestries, woven in Brussels, celebrate the 1st Duke's victories. In the magnificent saloon, life-size *trompe l'oeil* figures, representing the peoples of the four continents and painted by Louis Laguerre in 1719–20, lean over balconies as spectators to the state banquets that still are, on occasion, held in this huge, unheated room (for the sake of symmetry, there are no fireplaces).

Despite its scale and discomforts, Blenheim also serves as a home, and the small room where Sir Winston Churchill was born in 1874 attracts as much attention as the state apartments. Like his ancestor, the 1st Duke, Sir Winston is remembered as a great war leader. Unlike the 1st Duke, who is commemorated by a monument of exaggerated proportions in the palace chapel, Sir Winston is buried in a simple grave in the parish church of **Bladon ❷**, on the southern periphery of the estate.

Rescued village

Some 6 miles (10 km) further north, the B4022 meets the A44, just outside Enstone, and the right turn leads to the picturesque village of **Great Tew ❸**.

BELOW: Winston Churchill's grave in Bladon churchyard.

WINSTON CHURCHILL

Sir Winston Churchill was born on 30 November 1874 in a simple room to the west of the Great Hall. Once used by the 1st Duke's domestic chaplain, Dean Jones, the room now forms the core of a permanent exhibition of Churchilliana, including manuscripts, paintings and personal belongings. Visitors can also see letters written by Sir Winston, mostly to his father, Lord Randolph Churchill, as well as a piece of shrapnel that narrowly missed him in World War I.

Recalling his earliest association with Blenheim Palace, Sir Winston was once asked whether just before his birth, his mother, Lady Randolph, was attending a ball in the Long Library or was out with a shooting party in the park. He replied with customary dry wit: "Although present on that occasion, I have no clear recollection of the events leading up to it."

Blenheim continued to play an important part in Winston's life, and it was there that he proposed to his future wife, Clementine, in the Temple of Diana. The house also acted as inspiration for several of his paintings, including the depiction of the Great Hall that can be seen in the collection. From the saloon you can see the tower of Bladon Church, where Winston and Clementine are buried.

Dubbed "the place where time stood still", this estate village contains scarcely a modern building, simply because the late landlord permitted no new development; indeed, as the number of labourers employed on the estate steadily declined, the stone and thatch cottages were simply left to rot. One visitor, in 1972, described the derelict houses surrounding the green as "one of the most depressing sights in the whole country".

Now, thanks to new ownership, the cottages have been fully restored to their appearance in the early 19th century, when, as part of a model farm, the village was carefully landscaped. Quite a number of the cottages were given Gothic embellishments at the time, though many date to the 16th century. Set back behind colourful gardens, they present the kind of picture that calendar and chocolate-box manufacturers find irresistible.

The church of St Michael lies south of the village, just within the grounds of the park, and the churchyard is entered through a 17th-century stone gateway. Inside is a noteworthy monument to Mary Anne Boulton (died 1829) by Francis Chantrey. The Boultons, descendants of Matthew Boulton, the Birmingham engineer who made his fortune manufacturing steam engines as a partner of James Watt, acquired the estate in 1815 and gave the 17th-century house its current neo-Gothic appearance.

The B4022 continues north for just over a mile (2 km) to the A361. If you turn left, and then right via Swerford, a pretty village on the River Swere, you will reach **Hook Norton** ❹. Real-ale lovers will know this as the source of "Hooky", a beer made by traditional methods in the red-brick Victorian brewery at the west end of the village. This prominent building is surrounded by cottages built of the local orange-coloured ironstone – as is the church of St Peter, commanding the

Map
on pages
218–9

The village of Hook Norton is famous for its traditional May Day celebrations, including not only the locally brewed beer but also music and Morris dancing.

BELOW: the pretty, restored village of Great Tew.

hilltop at the centre of the village. The lively Norman font inside is carved with a charmingly rustic Adam, with his hammer and spade, and a flirtatious Eve, holding her apple, as well as signs of the zodiac.

Legendary stones

Three miles (5 km) west of Hook Norton, through the village of **Great Rollright** and across the A3400, you will find the remains of a prehistoric stone circle. Standing on the high ridge of the northern Cotswolds, the **Rollright Stones ❺** form a henge 100 ft (60 metres) in diameter. They date to around 3500 BC. The stones of the circle itself are known as the King's Men, while the solitary stone on the opposite side of the road is the King and the five further east, once the burial chamber of a long barrow, are the Whispering Knights.

The names refer to a legend, first recorded in 1586, that the stones represent petrified men who will one day wake to rule the land. They were tricked, according to the story, by a local witch who promised their leader that he would be king of England if he could see Long Compton, the village in the valley below, from this spot. This simple task proved impossible – some say that the witch conjured up a mist – and so she transformed them with the words: *Thou and thy men hoar stones shall be/And I myself an elder tree.*

Other legends about the stones abound – to their detriment, since they have often been chipped away by visitors (including Civil War soldiers on their way to battle) believing in their magical properties.

The Rollright Stones are too close to the busy A3400 to make a good resting spot, but an ideal place for a peaceful picnic is along the unclassified road back to the main road, across and left towards the Sibfords. This high road, with fine

BELOW:
the Rollright Stones are said to have magical properties.

views all round, forms the county boundary between Oxford and Warwick for much of its length, and drops, after 4 miles (7 km), into the Stour Valley at **Traitor's Ford**. Nobody seems to remember now who the traitor was; but the ford, with its clear stream and woodland either side, makes a perfect spot for relaxing on a hot summer's day.

From the ford, an ancient track, **Ditchedge Lane**, leads directly to **Compton Wynyates**, accessible only to walkers – motorists have to take the longer route through Sibford Gower. Compton Wynyates, a romantic Tudor mansion of rose-coloured brick, is no longer open to the public; but you can glimpse it, nestling into the wooded hillside, from the road to the west.

Windmill Hill, rising beyond to the north, is crowned by a stone tower mill, complete with its sails, while on **Compton Pike**, to the south, is a pyramidal structure, dating to the 16th century, built to be lit in the event of an invasion.

Some 5 miles (8 km) west is **Shipston on Stour ❻**. The name (originally Sheepston) is a reminder that the town was once host to one of England's largest sheep markets. It is home to many handsome former coaching inns.

Odd quirk

Two miles (3 km) north, **Honington Hall ❼** (open June–Aug, Wed and Bank Holiday Mondays 2.30–5pm) is a 17th-century brick house that could pass for the ordinary domestic manor of some country squire, but for the odd quirk of a series of busts all around the facades, depicting 12 Caesars. Even more extra-ordinary is the sumptuous plasterwork inside.

The house was built in 1685 by Sir Henry Parker who, having made a fortune as a London merchant, had the village church remodelled in a style that resembles Wren's elegant City of London churches. The monument to Parker and his son Hugh is the best of several splendid pieces of carving, in both marble and stone, to be found within.

From Honington, continue up the A3400 to New-bold-on-Stour and then, if you want to avoid the main road, take the minor road left that runs parallel to the pretty, winding River Stour. At **Preston on Stour ❽** you will find another stylish 18th-century church, this time in the Gothic style, and an east window made up of 17th-century glass from diverse sources, all illustrating the theme of death. The village has several ornate 16th- and 17th-century timber-framed houses and even the red-brick Alscot housing estate, an early example of its kind, dating to 1852, has a certain undeniable charm.

At **Clifford Chambers** attractive cottages line the single street that leads to the manor house, restored – or rather rebuilt – by Sir Edwin Lutyens in 1919. Here, too, is the first of many buildings associated with Shakespeare, for the 16th-century timber-framed rectory was the home of one John Shakespeare during the 1570s. Since William's father was called John, biographers have speculated, lacking any records for the dramatist's early years, whether this might have been his childhood home.

From Clifford Chambers continue on the B4632 and A3400 for a short while to **Stratford-upon-Avon ❾**.❏

Map on pages 218–9

BELOW: on the lookout for a good catch.

STRATFORD-UPON-AVON

Map on page 230

Basking in Shakespeare's enduring fame, Stratford remains one of England's most crowded tourist destinations. To go or not to go? That is the question

Stratford-upon-Avon is an extraordinary phenomenon. People from all over the world, many of whom cannot quote a single line from William Shakespeare's work, consider a trip to Britain incomplete unless they visit Stratford. If any of them are puzzled or disappointed by what they find, it seems that they never pass the message around.

Part of the lure is that so few details of Shakespeare's life can be authenticated. It is known that his father, John, was a successful glove-maker and wool merchant, and that his mother, Mary Arden, was the daughter of a well-to-do farmer. William went to school in Stratford, and married Anne Hathaway in 1582; they had three children. Most of his professional career in the theatre, however, was centred in London, though he spent the last five years of his life (1611–16) in Stratford. The rest is largely speculation.

The Shakespeare industry dates to the mid-19th century, when a pub called the Swan and Maidenhead, in Henley Street, came on the market. This had long been considered Shakespeare's birthplace, and in 1847 a public appeal was launched to buy the building as a national monument. A trust was formed and, between 1857 and 1864, the property was restored to its "original" appearance, a process that involved virtually rebuilding the house that is seen today.

PRECEDING PAGES: Anne Hathaway's Cottage. **LEFT:** Holy Trinity Church. **BELOW:** Shakespeare's Birthplace.

Shakespeare's Birthplace Ⓐ (open Mar–Oct, Mon–Fri 9am–5pm, Sun 9.30am–5pm; winter to 4pm) is the starting point for a tour of Stratford. The rooms are furnished as far as possible in late 16th-century style, as well as having small-scale displays on aspects of family history and William's work. The room in which Shakespeare is supposed to have been born, on 23 April 1564, is lit by a window inscribed with the signatures of illustrious guests such as Sir Walter Scott, Thomas Carlyle and Isaac Watts.

You can, however, learn much more about Shakespeare at the **Shakespeare Centre** Ⓑ just along the street (opening times as above). Here is an excellent exhibition entitled "William Shakespeare – His Life and Background", which gives a concise and visually appealing account of the context of the playwright's life in Stratford, then London, and finally Stratford again. There are displays on the town of Stratford itself and on the countryside which inspired so much of Shakespeare's imagery. As well as original documents and copies of such items as his marriage licence bond, there are portraits, furniture, a wonderful model of the Globe Theatre in London, and a reconstruction of "Shakespeare's Study", the kind of room he may well have worked in.

Beyond the Shakespeare Centre, the pretty garden has been planted with many of the trees, shrubs and flowers mentioned in his plays.

The American Fountain is an exuberantly ornate clock tower and fountain.

A short distance away, at 19 Greenhill Street, old and valuable children's toys are on display in Giles Brandreth's excellent **Teddy Bear Museum** **C** (daily 9.30am–6pm, closes 5pm Jan and Feb) – a good place to take children when they are bored by their parents' preoccupation with stuffy old poets.

This museum faces on to the broad expanse of Rother Street, a car park for most of the week but the venue on Friday for the town market. The **American Fountain** was given to Stratford on the occasion of Queen Victoria's 1887 Jubilee by the Philadelphia newspaperman George C. Childs.

Wood Street, to the left, leads to the town centre and has a sprinkling of those heavily timbered properties that we associate with the ancient heart of England, when the extensive Forest of Arden, which once covered the country north of Stratford, provided a ready supply of materials.

The **High Street** has some of the town's most ornate buildings, many of them stripped of 18th-century brick and stucco facades early in this century to reveal the original timber framing.

Overlooking the little paved open space at the first crossroads, the **Garrick Inn** and **Harvard House** **D** make an eccentric and flamboyant pair of buildings. Both date to about 1596, built just after a fire destroyed much of the town. Harvard House is elaborately carved with flowers and grotesque heads, and was the home of Katherine Rogers. She married Robert Harvard of Southwark, and their son, John Harvard, died in Massachusetts in 1638, a year after he emigrated to the New World. He bequeathed much of his estate to Harvard College, which now owns this house and uses it to display material relating to the Harvard family. The house (open May–Sept daily 10am–4pm) also contains the Neish Collection of pewter, with pieces ranging from Roman times to the 19th century.

BELOW: detail of Harvard House.

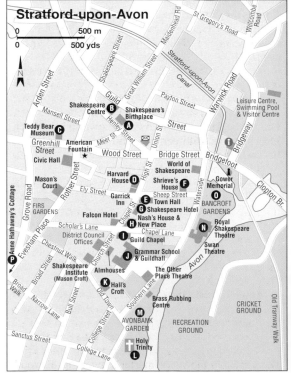

Map on page 230

Originally called the Reindeer, the Garrick Inn was renamed after the great 18th-century Shakespearian actor David Garrick. He was greatly influential in the revival of interest in Shakespeare's dramatic works and helped to organise the first festival in his honour, the Garrick Jubilee, in 1769. The festival was a great social occasion, patronised by royalty – hence the bold slogan "God save the King" painted in the same year across the Chapel Street facade of the **Town Hall Ⓔ**, a solid neo-Palladian building marking the end of High Street, completed in 1768. The statue of Shakespeare, on the Sheep Street frontage of the Town Hall, was presented by Garrick. Opposite the Town Hall, there is a mosaic portrait of the Bard over the doorway of the Victorian red-brick **Old Bank**.

The mosaic of Shakespeare over the Old Bank doorway.

In Sheep Street you will find numerous souvenir shops and restaurants not only flanking the street but also running up the alleys behind. The **Shrieve's House Ⓕ** (40 Sheep Street) is an interesting example of a 16th-century merchant's house, with a cart entrance and long, cobbled back yard, lined with buildings that would have been used as workshop and warehouse space – now converted to shops.

Chapel Street continues the timber-framed theme, first with the magnificent many-bayed and gabled **Shakespeare Hotel Ⓖ**, and then, at the corner of Scholars Lane, the **Falcon Hotel**, the lower two storeys of which date from around 1500. Opposite is another property of the Birthplace Trust, **Nash's House Ⓗ** and the **Site of New Place** (open Mar–Oct, Mon–Fri 9am–5pm, Sun 9.30am –5pm; winter to 4pm). The former belonged to Thomas Nash, who married Shakespeare's granddaughter, Elizabeth Hall. It is now a museum of material relating to the history of Stratford. **New Place** was one of the town's largest houses, and Shakespeare was wealthy enough to purchase it in 1597. He later retired to the house and died there on his 52nd birthday, in 1616.

BELOW: the Site of New Place with the Guild Chapel.

Irascible cleric

A later owner, Rev. Francis Gastrell, had little respect for the poet's memory. He was so annoyed by the constant stream of visitors wanting to see the mulberry tree in the garden, planted by Shakespeare, that he cut it down. In 1759 he demolished the house itself, rather than pay rates. Sensibly, no attempt has been made to reconstruct it. Instead, the foundations are exposed and paths thread through delightful gardens. The Knot Garden is planted with flowers known to have been grown in the 16th century, and the Great Garden beyond, originally the orchard and kitchen garden to New Place, has box and yew hedges.

The **Guild Chapel Ⓘ** opposite served as the chapel of the Guild of the Holy Cross, a body of local worthies who regulated trade in the town, fixing prices, collecting levies and allocating funds to charitable purposes. A wealthy member, Sir Hugh Clopton, later Lord Mayor of London, paid for the rebuilding of the nave in 1496. Just visible on the chancel wall is a *Last Judgement* painting.

Adjoining the chapel is the 15th-century former **Guildhall Ⓙ**, part of which was used as the town Grammar School. It is conjectured, reasonably enough, that Shakespeare was a pupil here. The delightfully named "Pedagogue's House" in the courtyard behind was probably the schoolmaster's dwelling. Beyond,

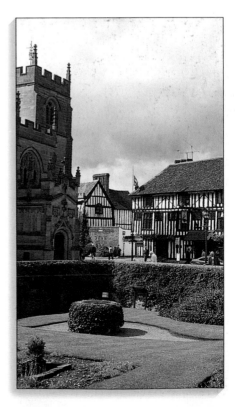

15th-century almshouses, still used as such, stretch for a distance of 50 metres, an impressive range with massive studs and a jettied-out upper storey.

Further down Church Street the character of the buildings begins to change, as timber gives way to the brick of elegant townhouses. **Mason Croft**, an early 18th-century building, was the last home of Marie Corelli (1855–1924) – real name Mary Mackay – the prolific novelist who, despite critical derision, was as popular in her heyday as Shakespeare was in his. The house is now an international centre for Shakespearian research, owned by Birmingham University.

Turning left, into Old Town, you reach **Hall's Croft** **K** (open Mar–Oct, Mon–Fri 9am–5pm, Sun 9.30am–5pm; winter to 4pm). Of all the buildings associated with Shakespeare, this is the least altered and most atmospheric. It dates to the late 16th century and was the home of Dr John Hall, husband of Shakespeare's daughter Susanna. One room is equipped as an apothecary's dispensary, and the walled garden has ancient mulberry trees and perennial borders.

Further down, an avenue of lime trees leads to **Holy Trinity Church** **L**, idyllically sited by the River Avon and a fine example of a 13th-century church. You have to pay to visit the most interesting part of the church – the chancel – where Shakespeare's monument is the chief attraction.

The poet's son-in-law, Dr John Hall, took a wax impression of Shakespeare's face at his death, and this was used by the Dutch mason Gerard Jansenni, or Johnson, as the basis for the painted alabaster bust of Shakespeare. It is thus the best likeness we have of the poet; other portraits, based on this, have tried to make him look less self-satisfied.

BELOW: the Bancroft Gardens and Gower Memorial.

The nearby tomb slab, covering Shakespeare's grave, is famously inscribed: *Good Frend For Jesus Sake Forbeare/To Digg the Dust Enclosed Heare:/Blese Be Ye Man (that) Spares Thes Stones/And Curst Be He (that) Moves My Bones.* These words have often been interpreted as implying that the grave contains evidence of the "true" authorship of Shakespeare's works – for, despite substantial evidence to the contrary, many people still believe that Shakespeare was only a front for some other writer. All requests to investigate the tomb have been refused.

Burial places

Other Shakespeare family tombs are found nearby: namely, those of his wife Anne (*née* Hathaway), his daughter Susanna, and those of Thomas Nash and Dr John Hall. The 16th-century misericords should not be missed; they date from around 1500 and provide an amusing commentary on contemporary domestic life.

Just north of Holy Trinity churchyard, back in Old Town, a gate on the right leads to the **Avonbank Garden** **M**, with its 19th-century summerhouse (now a brass-rubbing centre) and paths that follow the River Avon to the **Royal Shakespeare Theatre** complex **N**. The first part of the complex to come into view is the **Swan Theatre**, with a curved end and sweeping lead-covered roof, like some romantic mid-European castle. Partly used as a museum, displaying costumes, props and theatrical mementoes, this incorporates all that remains of the original theatre, built in 1879 but damaged by fire in 1926.

The rest of the theatre was designed by Elizabeth Scott and completed in 1932. A radical building in its own time – shaped like a stack of bricks and almost windowless – it now seems an embarrassing mistake. Yet it serves its purpose well, and the remodelled interior is nightly packed with visitors.

In front of the theatre, the **Bancroft Gardens** surround a large canal basin, marking the point where the Stratford Canal joins the River Avon. The 1888 **Gower Memorial** has the alert figure of Shakespeare seated on a plinth, surrounded by statues of Hamlet, Prince Hal, Falstaff and Lady Macbeth. The **nine-arched bridge** was built in 1823 for the tramway whose horse-drawn carriages and goods wagons once rattled their way between Stratford and Shipston-on-Stour. It was converted to pedestrian use in 1918 and is a good place from where to get a grandstand prospect of activities on the river. Further north, the **Clopton Bridge** was built in the late 15th century.

The **Stratford Canal**, completed in 1816, runs north to the Grand Union. As an alternative to travelling by car, you can follow the canal towpath for 3 miles (5 km) through the town and out, past a long flight of locks, to the hamlet of **Wilmcote**. Here, the Shakespeare Birthplace Trust has restored the 16th-century home of Mary Arden as a museum of country life in Tudor Warwickshire.

For the return journey you could perhaps visit **Anne Hathaway's Cottage**  (open Mar–Oct, Mon–Fri 9am–5pm, Sun 9.30am–5pm; winter to 4pm) in the suburb of **Shottery**. This 15th-century thatched farmhouse was once the home of Shakespeare's wife, and stands in a delightful cottage garden. Furnished with Hathaway family heirlooms, pride of place is given to the famous bed that Shakespeare bequeathed to his wife – the only thing he left her in his will, fuelling speculation that their marriage might not have been a happy one. ❑

Map on page 230

A sightseeing bus tour is a good way to get your bearings.

BELOW: the nine-arched bridge over the Avon.

PLEASE
DO NOT TOUCH
THE TOMBS

WARWICK

The city of Warwick is best known for its magnificent castle, but there are many other sights here, including the glorious Beauchamp Chapel, which was built for earls but is fit for kings

One of the most delightful old towns of the English Midlands with a wealth of late medieval and Georgian buildings, **Warwick** ⑩ is built on a rise above the Avon. From much of the surrounding countryside, the town seems to be dominated by the majestic tower of St Mary's Church, but it is above all the great castle – often described as England's finest medieval stronghold – on its rocky bluff overlooking the river that draws visitors here in great numbers.

Warwick's origins go back to Saxon times, when, in the second decade of the 10th century, Ethelfleda, the Queen of Mercia and a daughter of King Alfred, laid out a settlement and built a fortification. This first stronghold almost certainly underlies the base of the great motte built on the orders of William the Conqueror which forms part of the defences of the present castle and which is known as Ethelfleda's Mound. The town seems to have flourished under the protection of the castle and its lords, great magnates with a major influence on the course of English history. But in 1694 a great fire consumed much of the area within the old walls. Rebuilding took place in a harmonious style, with use of brick and of the local attractive but rather soft sandstone making an agreeable contrast with the surviving timber-framed buildings.

LEFT: the Beauchamp Chapel.
BELOW: crest at Lord Leycester's Hospital.

Contrasting styles

The basic layout of the town is that of a cross formed by High Street, Church Street, Jury Street and Castle Street. Their meeting point is marked by substantial edifices all dating from the time of the town's rebuilding, including the **Court House** Ⓐ of 1725 whose ground floor is occupied by the Tourist Information Centre and which also houses the Town Museum and the Warwickshire Yeomanry Museum.

Lined with dignified Georgian buildings, the High Street leads to the 12th-century **West Gate** with its massive archway partly cut into the living rock. Above it is St James' Chapel and the beautiful timber-framed almshouses of **Lord Leycester's Hospital** Ⓑ (open summer, Tues–Sat and Bank Holiday Mondays 10am–5.30pm, winter 10am–4pm). The institution was founded in 1571 by Robert Dudley, Earl of Leicester, supposedly the lover of Queen Elizabeth I, as a home for old soldiers, and it is still the home of a community of ex-servicemen. An archway leads to a quadrangle, where steps lead up to the gallery and the magnificent mid-15th century **Guildhall**, off which is the Chaplains' Dining Hall, housing the Museum of the Queen's Own Hussars. Equally striking, entered at ground level, is the Great Hall with its sturdy roof structure. **St James' Chapel** is approached via steps and a passageway between buttresses, high above the traffic and giving a good view of the timber-framed

Tools of the trade in the Master's Garden.

houses opposite. Lit by a 15th-century candelabrum, the chapel was begun in the 14th century and is full of atmosphere. A passageway leads to the rear of the hospital and into the restored **Master's Garden**, set within old walls.

Modern life in Warwick centres on the area around the Market Place with its fine stone-built **Market Hall C** of 1670. The building, its arches now blocked in with windows, is now the home of the **Warwickshire Museum** (open Mon–Sat 10am–5pm, summer Sundays 2–5pm). The museum, whose entrance is guarded by one of the many bears seen around the town, has displays on local natural history as well as a model of the town as it was before the great fire and the striking mid-16th century **Sheldon tapestry map** of Warwickshire.

Final resting place

The tower of **St Mary's Church D** rises above Church Street. The tower, 174ft (53 metres) high, can be climbed, the reward being a superb view of the town and castle in their green Warwickshire setting. The church is the glory of the town, despite the rebuilding of nave and tower after the fire. Spared by the fire were the Norman crypt with its massive columns, the Dean's Chapel with lovely fan vaulting, the 14th-century chancel, and the **Beauchamp Chapel**. Completed in 1464, the sumptuous chapel is one of the most evocative burial places in England, with the tombs of Richard Beauchamp, Ambrose Dudley and Robert Dudley, Earl of Leicester and founder of the hospital named after him.

BELOW:
the Market Hall.

The gilded **brass effigy of Richard Beauchamp**, Earl of Warwick, was made some 15 years after his death in 1439 and is rightly famous. The great magnate lies with his head resting on a helmet, his hands raised in supplication. At his feet are a bear and a griffin; around the tomb are figures of weepers and angels.

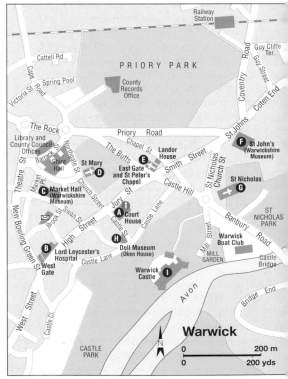

Follow Church Street back to its junction with High Street and Jury Street. The latter leads to the charming 15th-century **East Gate** Ⓔ topped by a chapel dedicated to St Peter and now only used by pedestrians. Beyond is Smith Street, at the far end of which is **St John's** Ⓕ, a fine early 17th-century stone building which is now part of the **Warwickshire Museum** (open Good Friday–late Sept, Fri, weekends and Bank Holidays 10am–1pm, 2–4pm) and includes reconstructions of a Victorian classroom and kitchen. The **Museum of the Royal Warwickshire Regiment** shares the building.

St Nicholas' Church Ⓖ overlooks **Castle Bridge**. This handsome 100-ft (30-metre) single-span structure was built in 1793 to replace the medieval bridge. Now a cul-de-sac, **Mill Street** completely escaped the effects of the fire and contains a fine array of timber-framed houses. From the **Mill Garden** at the far end is a fine view of the castle's Caesar's Tower high above.

The castle can be approached via its Stable Block at the foot of Castle Street. One of the prettiest of the town's streets, Castle Street also has one of the prettiest houses in Warwick, a timber-framed early Elizabethan building named after its owner, Thomas Oken, a prosperous mercer and benefactor of the town. His home is now the delightful **Doll Museum** Ⓗ (open Easter–late Sept, Mon–Sat 10am–5pm, Sun 1–5pm, winter Saturdays until dusk), inhabited not only by dolls but also by other toys and games.

The Castle

Warwick Castle Ⓘ (open April–Oct 10am–6pm, Nov–March 10am–5pm) was once described as "the most perfect piece of castellated antiquity in the kingdom". The natural potential of the site – on a sandstone spur above the Avon –

The Warwickshire Regiment's most famous soldier was Field Marshal Bernard Montgomery, hero of El Alamein; his famous beret is a prize exhibit in the museum.

BELOW: preparing for battle – part of the castle's Kingmaker exhibition.

THE EARLS OF WARWICK

Richard Beauchamp, the 5th Earl of Warwick, resides in the Beauchamp Chapel in St Mary's Church. His tomb is one of the finest medieval monuments in England, a glittering memorial to the knightly hero who loyally served three English kings – Henry IV, Henry V and Henry VI – both as soldier and diplomat. Less nobly, it was also Richard Beauchamp who, as governor of France, presided over the trial and execution of Joan of Arc, in 1431.

The Earls of Warwick were a powerful lot, and the most powerful of all was Richard Neville, the "Kingmaker". He had obtained the title by virtue of his marriage to the daughter of the Earl of Warwick and when he himself inherited, he had so much land and wealth that he was able to hold the balance between the Yorkist and Lancastrian factions during the first half of the Wars of the Roses (1455–85). First he supported the Yorkists, establishing the Duke of York as Edward IV; then, having grown too big for his boots and been driven into exile by Edward, he returned under the banner of Henry VI. Edward was now forced to leave the country, but he came back to reclaim his throne and at the Battle of Barnet in 1471, this "impudent and shameless Warwick… proud setter up and puller down of kings" *(Shakespeare, Henry VI Part 3)* finally met his end.

Map on facing page

Guests at the Royal Weekend Party of 1898 – one of many attractions in the castle.

BELOW: Warwick Castle reflected in the Avon.

has been fully exploited by successive owners and builders and there are few views more emblematic of England's historic heritage than that of Warwick's walls and towers rising above luxuriant parkland and reflected in the river. The castle's history stretches over a period of more than 1,000 years, beginning with the fortification built by Ethelfleda. It was only two years after the Conquest, in 1068, that King William ordered the castle to be re-founded, a standard Norman motte and bailey construction which was succeeded in the 12th and 13th centuries by a more permanent stone structure. Much of the fabric of this castle was replaced in the mid-14th century by Thomas Beauchamp, Earl of Warwick, who built Caesar's Tower and the clock tower, while his son, another Thomas, was responsible for Guy's Tower. The greatest of the castle's lords, Richard Neville, known to history as Warwick the Kingmaker (*see page 237*) devoted little time to architecture, but his successor, the Duke of Clarence, found time to build the north gate and start work on the Clarence Tower before being accused of high treason and meeting a horrible end, according to some sources and to Shakespeare, by being "drowned in a butt of Malmsey". For a while, the castle was in the hands of his brother, King Richard III.

Eventually it became the property of the Greville family. The Grevilles, who became Earls of Warwick in 1759, were responsible for the conversion of the medieval fortress into a princely palace. Walls and towers remain as reminders of medieval might, and basements, dungeons and undercroft preserve their ancient character, but the habitable part of the castle consists of a sumptuous series of state rooms of Jacobean and later date. In the 18th century, the grounds were re-landscaped by Capability Brown and extended north towards the new bridge across the Avon. Today, the castle is operated by Madame Tussaud's. The famous waxworks has further enhanced its appeal to visitors, particularly by animating the interior with a series of convincing historical tableaux.

From the **Stable Block** entrance, a curving pathway makes a dramatic approach to the **gatehouse and barbican** with **Guy's Tower** rising up splendidly on the right to a height of 128ft (40 metres). Once within the great circuit of walls, the visitor has various choices. Beneath **Caesar's Tower** are the **Armoury**, **Torture Chamber** and **Dungeon**. Further underground chambers and passageways of the medieval castle house the highly entertaining tableaux entitled "Kingmaker". This is a convincing evocation of the preparations which preceded the Battle of Barnet in 1471 (*see page 237*). As well as armourers and others at work, there are children larking about, a horse giving off a powerful stable smell, and living costumed figures barely distinguishable from their waxwork counterparts.

A very different epoch is evoked in the tableaux of the **Royal Weekend Party of 1898**. Towards the end of the 19th century, Warwick had become a great centre of social life, largely due to the influence of the Countess of Warwick, born Frances but universally known as Daisy. Among the guests populating some of the former private apartments are the young Winston Churchill, Field Marshal Lord Roberts, the future George V lighting a cigarette, and Edward Prince of Wales, a frequent visitor and rumoured lover of Daisy

The Chapel, Great Hall and State Rooms are reached by stairs. The early 17th-century **Chapel** has medieval stained glass and superbly carved wooden panels. The 18th-century Dining Room boasts splendidly framed royal portraits, including a famous study of Charles I on horseback. The **Great Hall** exudes the atmosphere of the Middle Ages with its displays of arms and armour. The **State Rooms** compete with each other in magnificence: the Red Drawing Room has bold red lacquer panelling; the Cedar Drawing Room a superb plaster ceiling; the Green Drawing Room mementoes of the Civil War; the Queen Anne Bedroom a bed intended for that royal personage but never used; while the Blue Boudoir has a portrait after Holbein of Henry V.

Next to the so-called **Ghost Tower** the great **mound** rises to a surprising height. Topped by mock fortifications, it offers a magnificent prospect over the castle grounds, the river, and the lush countryside beyond.

Kenilworth

If Warwick is one of England's finest castles, then **Kenilworth ⑪**, barely 4 miles (6 km) to the north of Warwick (open April–Oct 10am–6pm, Nov–March 10am–5pm), must surely rank as one of its finest castle ruins. Kenilworth, too, occupies an important place in the history of the nation, with some famous names among its past residents. The castle was deliberately destroyed after the Civil War, but the original Norman keep still stands, as does the shell of the Great Hall, built by John of Gaunt, and the grand apartments constructed during the tenure of Robert Dudley, Earl of Leicester. The castle's natural defences were strengthened by flooding the surrounding marshland. The lake is no longer there, but Kenilworth remains an evocative place. ❑

**Maps:
City 236
Area 218**

TIP

Another attraction of the castle is the walk along the ramparts, but you need to be fit to cope with all the steps – particularly in Guy's Tower.

BELOW: the Norman keep at Kenilworth.

STRATFORD TO OXFORD

*The journey back to Oxford is equally rewarding,
taking in manor houses, Banbury Cross and
a different perspective on Oxford Canal*

Map
on pages
218–9

Leaving Stratford by the B4086, you follow the River Avon for just over 3 miles (5 km), through cow-filled pastures, to **Charlecote Park** ⓬ (open April–Oct, Fri–Tues 11am–6pm, house closed 1–2pm). Here, according to one of the many unsubstantiated stories about Shakespeare, young William is said to have been caught and prosecuted for poaching deer by the owner, Sir Thomas Lucy. In revenge, Shakespeare based the character of Justice Shallow (*Henry VI, Part Two* and *The Merry Wives of Windsor*) on him. Shallow is described as having a coat of arms incorporating "a dozen white luces", in which he takes inordinate pride. Sir Thomas does indeed have "luces" (a pun on Lucy, and an archaic word for freshwater pike) in his coat of arms, and these can be seen in the church of St Leonard, just inside the grounds of the park.

St Leonard's was completely rebuilt from 1851 to 1853 by Mary Elizabeth Lucy, who described its predecessor as "a wretched old church". The family monuments, however, were left alone. Shakespeare's Sir Thomas (died 1600) is the armoured figure in alabaster lying recumbent by his wife on a tomb chest. His son, also Sir Thomas (died 1605), is depicted with his widow and children. Best of all is the fine sculpture of the scholarly grandson, another Sir Thomas (died 1640), reclining beneath a pile of books.

It was the first Sir Thomas who, inheriting the Warwickshire estate in 1552, rebuilt the manor house. The result, despite 19th-century additions, is still recognisably Elizabethan, including the mellow brick gatehouse, the porch and much of the stable and brewhouse block. Before entering the house, it is a good idea to see the introductory video, shown in a room of the stable yard, which is based on the memoirs of Mary Elizabeth Lucy, the 19th-century mistress of the house who did so much to give the interior its present mid-Victorian appearance.

Red and fallow deer still roam in the park, which was landscaped by "Capability" Brown, making full use of the setting of the house, situated on the banks of the rivers Avon and Dene.

Scenic villages

The B4086 continues east through **Wellesbourne** ⓭, a traffic-torn village where a body of farmworkers, led by Joseph Arch, met in 1872 to form what became the National Agricultural Labourers' Union, demanding a minimum wage of sixpence a day.

Two miles (3 km) on, the road crosses a bridge over the lakes fronting **Compton Verney** mansion, built about 1714 in a wooded valley.

Kineton ⓮ is next, a village of grey and brown lias stone cottages, with the wooded motte of a 12th-century castle by the bank of the River Dene.

LEFT: thatch and sandstone in Wellesbourne.
BELOW: guardian of Charlecote Park.

Radway church has a monument to Captain Kingswell, who fell at the Battle of Edge Hill.

BELOW: Edgehill Tower, modelled on Warwick Castle.

Four miles (6 km) on, before the road begins to climb steeply up **Edge Hill**, take the minor road right to **Radway** ⓯. Leave the car to follow a 2-mile (3-km) walk of this historically important and beautiful part of Warwickshire.

Radway village, with its thatched sandstone cottages, lies on a series of terraces beneath Edge Hill. From the road that leads northeast out of the village, to the right of Grafton Cottage, a steep path climbs up to woods on the brow of the hill. From the path there are views of **Radway Grange**, an Elizabethan house transformed by the squire and amateur architect Sanderson Miller. Miller was a pioneer of the Gothic-Revival style, refronting the east front of the manor with ogee-arched windows around 1745 – some three or four years before Horace Walpole made the style fashionable by rebuilding Strawberry Hill in Richmond.

The footpath turns right, through the woods that skirt Miller's estate, and into the village of **Edgehill** ⓰. Here Edgehill Tower, now the Castle Inn, is another Sanderson Miller work (1746–50). Miller built it as a place to entertain his friends, including the writer Henry Fielding whose *Tom Jones*, regarded as the first English novel, was read for his approval before it was published.

The tower is also of great historical importance, for it marks the spot where Charles I planted the Royal Standard on 23 October 1642, at the start of the first major battle of the Civil War. The actual battle site, where the king's army, led by Prince Rupert, met the Parliamentarians under the Earl of Essex – both sides suffering heavy casualties but neither able to claim victory – lies in the plain below. Owned by the Ministry of Defence, it cannot be visited, but there are clear views from the path that leads back to Radway. The village church contains Sanderson Miller's monument, and an effigy of the Royalist Captain Kingswell, one of many who died in the inconclusive Battle of Edge Hill.

Map on pages 218–9

Pomp and majesty

Two miles (3 km) south of Edgehill, by the A422, is splendid **Upton House** ⑰ with its impressive art collection and delightful sloping gardens (open March–Oct, Sat–Wed 2–6pm, *see below*).

Four miles (7 km) further along the A422, just before the village of **Wroxton**, you can detour south to **Broughton** ⑱ to visit the picturesque manor house – called a "castle" on the strength of its wide defensive moat. Despite 16th-century remodelling, Broughton Castle (2–5pm Wed and Sun, mid-May–mid-Sept; plus 2–5pm Wed, Thur and Sun, Jul and Aug) is one of the most complete medieval houses surviving in the country, dating to around 1300. All the Elizabethan owners did was to add the magnificent oak panelling, fireplaces and plasterwork, adding comfort and luxury to the spartan rooms, and employing craftsmen who worked in the latest Flemish, French and Italian Renaissance styles.

An important series of monuments in the next-door church commemorates the various owners, including Sir Thomas Wykeham (died 1470), a forceful figure, realistically carved, and members of the Fiennes family, ancestors of the late 17th-century traveller and writer Celia Fiennes.

From Broughton, it is a short distance to the market town of **Banbury** ⑲, on a major road junction marked by a cross celebrated in the nursery rhyme *Ride a cock-horse to Banbury Cross/To see a fine lady on a white horse;/With rings on her fingers and bells on her toes,/She shall have music wherever she goes.* The rhyme probably refers to a visit made by Queen Elizabeth I, and the present cross, erected in 1859, commemorates the marriage of Queen Victoria's daughter to the Crown Prince of Prussia. The ponderous figures of Queen Victoria, Edward VII and George V were added in 1914.

UPTON HOUSE

Externally, the measured, stately facade of Upton House dates to the reign of William and Mary, having been refronted in 1695. Internally, the house is neo-Georgian however, and was remodelled in 1927 to house an outstanding collection of paintings accumulated by the 2nd Lord Bearstead. The collection comprises representative works by many of the best-known European Masters, including Bosch, the Breughels, Holbein, Rembrandt, Constable, Hogarth and Stubbs.

The son of the founder of the Shell oil company, Lord Bearstead was also a collector of fine porcelain, and the house contains an impressive array of 18th-century Chelsea figures and Sèvres tableware set among the well-preserved décor of the 1920s and 1930s. A collection of artwork used by Shell for advertising is also on show.

Outside, this National Trust property is surrounded by extensive gardens, with large lawns descending to pools in the valley. You can walk down to the pools beside cleverly crafted trickling waterfalls. The terraces are full of colourful herbaceous borders, and there is a large kitchen garden. In late summer visitors can appreciate the National Collection of asters (Michaelmas daisies), which are at their most spectacular in September and October.

BELOW: the gardens at Upton House are well worth a visit.

The original cross, standing on the site of the town's medieval horse fair, was destroyed by the townspeople, as was the old church – for Banbury was a hotbed of zealous Puritanism, satirised in another 17th-century rhyme: *To Banbury came I, O profane one,/And there I saw a Puritan one/Hanging of his cat on Monday/For killing a mouse on Sunday.*

The church was rebuilt in a severe classical style between 1790 and 1822 and described at the time as "more like a gaol than a Christian temple". A painting of Christ in Majesty, imitating mosaic work, was commissioned in 1876 in an attempt to brighten the interior.

Banbury's history is told in the town's excellent small **museum**, at 8 Horsefair, opposite the cross. A new phase in Banbury's history was ushered in by the completion in 1992 of the M40 motorway linking London and the West Midlands. When construction work was in progress, the locals were sharply divided on the issues involved; running as it does right past the town, the motorway was bound to have a major impact on economic development.

Canalside life

Future plans include the creation of new facilities for canal cruisers, gently chugging up and down the **Oxford Canal** that passes through the eastern edge of Banbury. The canal was planned by the pioneering engineer James Brindley, and completed in 1790. Faced with undulating countryside, Brindley designed a route that follows the natural contours, thus minimising the number of locks required. Consequently, the canal meanders through Oxfordshire, making hairpin bends to pass round hills, and, for the southern part of its route, following the contorted River Cherwell, used to top up the water level in the canal.

BELOW:
Banbury Cross.

The whole course of the canal, from its junction with the Grand Union at Napton, almost to the heart of Oxford, is outstandingly beautiful, and deservedly popular with narrowboat enthusiasts – most of whom hire a boat for the week, but some of whom live permanently on the canal, making a living wherever they can from casual work, boat restoration or handicrafts.

The southern stretch, from Banbury to Oxford, is arguably the most beautiful, for the meadows between the canal and the River Cherwell often flood, and the resulting wetlands are a rich haven for rare flora and fauna.

Just off the canal route, there are many other attractions. At **Aynho** ⑳, 6 miles (10 km) south of Banbury, the church of St Michael, rebuilt from 1723 to 1725, looks more like a country house than a place of worship. The interior retains its 18th-century box pews, gallery and pulpit.

Aynhoe Park (the spelling differs) bears the unmistakable stamp of "Capability" Brown's naturalistic landscaping, and the house, largely rebuilt after Royalist troops set fire to it in 1645, is the work of several idiosyncratic architects, most notably Sir John Soane. Further south, **Upper** and **Lower Heyford** ㉑ are both attractive villages, and much more peaceful now that the huge US airbase on the hilltop above Upper Heyford has ceased operations. The stretch of canal between the two villages is outstanding.

Map on pages 218–9

Here the canal and the **Cherwell** are separated by no more than a narrow bank. The Cherwell in summer becomes little more than a flower-filled ditch, and yet you will sometimes see huge basking perch here, so large that the water scarcely covers them. Crayfish live in the stones and brick of the canalside wall and bridges, and the water margins are thick with reedmace, meadowsweet, water forget-me-not and yellow flag. At Lower Heyford, the 14th-century church, old manor, farm and rectory form an attractive waterside group close to the original hay ford, after which the village is named.

Less than a mile (about 1 km) south, **Rousham Park 22** (Gardens daily 10am–4.30pm all year, House 2–4.30pm Wed, Sun and bank holidays Apr–Sept) is, in the words of Horace Walpole, a place "to enjoy philosophic retirement". William Kent, a pioneer of the Romantic style in landscaping, transformed this naturally beautiful site on the banks of the Cherwell into a picturesque garden, complete with ruined follies and the cascades of Venus's Vale. Longhorn cattle, placid animals despite their ferocious-looking horns, graze in the fields beyond the sweeping lawns, and the walled gardens incorporate a 17th-century pigeon-house, complete with revolving ladder for taking the eggs from the tiers of nesting holes.

Further south, the busy roads leading out of Oxford begin to impinge. From the church at **Shipton-on-Cherwell**, known as the bargees' church, you look across the canal and river to **Hampton Gay**, once a substantial village, now no more than a church surrounded by the grassy humps of medieval house platforms, for the parish was depopulated by the Black Death in the 1340s.

At **Thrupp 23**, the canal widens, and the basin, with its canal workers' cottages and The Boat inn, is used as a last mooring point before the final chug into Oxford itself. ❑

In 1646, there was a contest at Aynho Church between two candidates for the post of rector. Each had to preach a sermon. On winning, Robert Wylde wittily replied with a pun on the village name: "I got the Ay and he the No!"

BELOW: tranquillity on the Oxford Canal.

NORTH COTSWOLDS

*The remarkable beauty of the Cotswolds owes much
to the distinctive architecture of entire golden
villages that are built of Cotswold stone*

Map
on pages
218–9

Oxford

London

The **Cotswolds** form a prominent range of hills to the west of Oxford. The limestone of these hills, formed on the bed of the shallow Midland Sea, has long provided a first-class building material, that is soft enough to carve when newly dug, but rapidly hardens to provide a durable stone.

The limestone lies close to the surface; the soils of the Cotswolds are shallow, not easy to cultivate but ideal pasture for grazing sheep. Until this century, wool was the area's staple product, a source of great wealth for those who controlled the land – initially the great monastic estates of Gloucester, Tewkesbury, Evesham, Winchcombe and Malmesbury; later the landowners who acquired monastic lands after the Dissolution. In addition, a new breed of middle-class merchants accumulated great fortunes from the 14th century onwards by acting as middle men between the wool producers and the weaving towns of the Low Countries, Italy and Spain.

Quiet opulence

This former affluence is visible everywhere in the Cotswold landscape, characterised by opulent manor houses, cathedral-like barns and ornate parish churches built to splendid proportions by wool-rich men who counted on their salvation in return for generous endowments.

Chipping Norton ㉔, 12 miles (20 km) northwest of Oxford, is a prime example: a typical Cotswold town on the northwest limits of the limestone belt. Market Square was once the venue for an important sheep fair. Gabled almshouses – typical of Cotswold vernacular architecture, with their stone-mullioned windows and drip mouldings to channel rain away from the face of the buildings – line the path to St Mary's Church. This has a hexagonal porch, with leering devils carved on the bosses inside, and the soaring nave was rebuilt around 1485 by the wool merchant John Ashfield. To the north of the church are the extensive remains of a Norman motte and bailey castle.

Chipping Norton also has an imposing tweed mill, visible on the right as you leave the town on the A44 Evesham road. Bliss Valley Mill, with its domed tower, was designed in 1872 by the Lancashire mill architect George Woodhouse, to look like a country house – which is what it has ended up as, for after the mill closed in 1980 it was converted into luxury apartments.

Four miles (7 km) on, a minor road leads left to **Chastleton House** ㉕, built around 1605 by another wool merchant, Walter Jones. Shortly afterwards, the family fortunes declined and the house escaped later improvements, surviving as an example of Jacobean domestic architecture. At the top of the house, a long gallery runs the length of the building. Originally

LEFT: Cotswold
country pursuits.
BELOW:
vintage exhibit in
Chipping Campden.

intended for indoor games, such as bowls, like many of the rooms, it is lavishly plastered with bold Flemish-style friezes and ceilings.

Moreton-in-Marsh ㉖ comes next, a busy town on the junction of the Roman Foss Way and the later Oxford to Worcester road. Numerous former coaching inns still do a brisk trade serving cream teas to passing motorists, but there is a cluster of characterful shops at the northern end of the High Street. Where the Oxford road joins the High Street there is a 16th-century curfew tower; the bell in the tower continued to be rung until 1860, reminding householders to "cover their fires" (the derivation of "curfew") before retiring to bed – for many a town (most notably London in 1666) was destroyed when stray sparks triggered a conflagration.

Two miles (3 km) out of Moreton, the A44 climbs steeply up the Cotswold scarp, through the pretty but traffic-torn village of **Bourton-on-the-Hill**, and towards the summit a left turn leads to **Sezincote** ㉗ (Garden 2–6pm Thur, Fri and bank holidays Jan–Nov, House 2.30–6pm Thur, Fri, May–Jul and Sept). Here you will find one of the most curious and delightful houses ever built in the English countryside: an Indian palace made of golden limestone, tucked into the valley of the River Evenlode, which is channelled into a series of canals representing, in Moghul fashion, the rivers of life. Begun in 1805, Sezincote was built for Charles Cockerell who, on retiring from service with the East India Company, wanted to create a rajah's palace, complete with onion domes and peacock-tail windows.

The Prince Regent, on seeing it in 1807, loved it so much that he ordered existing plans for Brighton Pavilion to be scrapped, and new ones drawn up "more like Sezincote". External appearances, though, are deceptive, for guided tours reveal that the interior is elegantly European in the classical tradition.

BELOW: Sezincote: the external appearance can be deceptive.

More Oriental influence

Another expatriate returning home created **Batsford Arboretum** , on the opposite side of the A44. Lord Redesdale, a retired Tokyo diplomat, built his manor house in neo-Elizabethan style in 1888, but he planted the surrounding path with oriental species and decorated it with Japanese temples and statues of the Buddha. The arboretum is very colourful in spring, when the cherry trees blossom, and in autumn, when the Japanese maples turn a fiery crimson.

The village of **Blockley** ㉙, 2 miles (3 km) west, brings us back to the traditional Cotswolds. Formerly an estate belonging to the bishops of Worcester, the surrounding hillsides once supported vast flocks of sheep, and flourishing villages round about were deliberately destroyed to create further grazing. But Blockley survived, and today's village consists of elegant townhouses occupying the heights and smaller rows of cottages squeezed into narrow terraces all the way down the valley side. At the bottom only one mill survives (now a private house) of the six that produced silk to supply the ribbon makers of Coventry.

Blockley's church contains several imposing Renaissance and baroque monuments to the owners of **Northwick Park**. This 17th-century mansion, now converted to apartments, lies just north of Blockley, and the road that skirts the western perimeter of the estate provides a splendid view of nearby **Chipping Campden** ㉚.

There is a wealth of colourful plants at Batsford Arboretum.

Campden is arguably the Cotswold's most beautiful market town. Certainly, it is the best preserved, thanks to the work of the Campden Trust, established in 1929 to restore and maintain town properties using traditional materials. One of the founders of the Trust, F.L. Griggs, designed many of the attractive wrought-iron signs that hang from shops in the High Street, where the buildings read like a history of Cotswold vernacular architecture in microcosm.

BELOW: there's still work for thatchers in the Cotswolds.

Attractive shopfronts add to the charm of Chipping Campden.

Early in the 20th century Campden was "invaded" by craftsmen from the Mile End Road in east London, where C. R. Ashbee, inspired by the example of William Morris, had founded his Guild of Handicrafts, devoted to reviving skills lost to industrial processes. Descendants of George Hart, one of the original 50 craftsmen who came with Ashbee in 1902, still make handcrafted silverware in the Old Silk Mill in Sheep Street.

Two other men have left a lasting mark on Campden. The fine Market Hall, jutting out into the High Street, was given by the local squire, Sir Baptist Hicks, in 1627. Further north, opposite Church Street, is Campden's oldest house, built around 1380, with an ornate two-storeyed bay window, by William Grevel. Needless to say, both men made their money from wool, Sir Hicks at a time when the Cotswolds cloth trade was beginning to decline, faced by competition from abroad. Even so, he was able to endow the almshouses in Church Street, built in 1612 in the shape of the letter "I" to honour James I, and also to build a mansion alongside the church. This was destroyed in the Civil War – some say by Hicks himself, to prevent it from falling into Parliamentary hands, others say by drunken Cromwellian troops. Enough survives, though, including the gate houses and two garden pavilions, to indicate what a fanciful building it was.

The church itself is attributed to the earlier man, William Grevel, described on his memorial brass as "the flower of the wool merchants of all England". He left money for the church to be rebuilt and the work, completed some 100 years after his death, is a splendid example of the Perpendicular style at its best.

A mile (2 km) northwest of Campden, over the summit of Dover's Hill, is a natural amphitheatre on the Cotswold scarp. Worth visiting for the panoramic views over the **Vale of Evesham**, this is also the venue for the "**Cotswold Olympicks**", held every Friday following the Spring Bank Holiday, followed by the Scuttlebrook Wake Fair on the next day. The "Olympicks", which features shin-kicking and stick-fighting among its bizarre events, was founded by the eccentric local lawyer Robert Dover in 1612, and, after crowds of "beer-swilling Birmingham yahoos" got the games prohibited in 1852, they were revived in 1951.

BELOW: the gazebo at Hidcote Manor Garden.

Gardeners' delight

Two miles (3.5 km) north of Campden are two of England's finest gardens, standing on opposite sides of the same road above **Mickleton**.

Hidcote Manor Garden ③, for all its maturity, was begun only in 1948 (open April–end of Oct daily except Tues and Fri 11am–6pm, then June and July Tues). All that existed before was a few walls and 11 acres (4.5 hectares) of windswept Cotswold upland. Major Lawrence Johnson transformed this into one of the most influential gardens of our age, "a cottage garden on the most glorified scale", according to the writer Vita Sackville-West. Its structure is relatively formal, based on the concept of a series of rooms, walled with yew and planted thematically – yet the underlying discipline is hardly evident as climbers tumble from one room to the next, and happy combinations of self-seeded flowers are left to do as they will. Visitors can also enjoy the fine views.

Map on pages 218–9

Kiftsgate Court ㉜ (open Apr–Oct daily) is equally renowned in gardening circles for its prolific rambling rose, *Rosa filipes* "Kiftsgate". Having colonised several trees, it must surely be England's largest climbing rose, and is delightful in early summer, cascading down in showers of white blooms. The rest of the garden is full of unusual plants, and the views from the swimming-pool terrace look over wooded slopes to the Vale of Evesham.

Golden houses

From Mickleton, the B4632 southwest follows the Vale, with the steep-faced Cotswold scarp rising to the left, all the way into **Broadway ㉝**. Packed with tourists throughout the summer, this town of ancient golden houses nevertheless merits a visit. Those who cannot afford lunch at the Lygon Arms, renowned for its cuisine, can at least admire its handsome Renaissance doorway, dated 1620, and the cordon-trained fruit trees growing the full height of the facade. Many another ancient and wisteria-clad townhouse in Broadway now serves as a teashop, boutique or art gallery, and the renowned furniture maker Gordon Russell has his showroom and factory at the bottom end of the High Street.

Have a seat at Kiftsgate Court while admiring the rambling roses.

If you want to escape the crowds, you can follow the Cotswold Way long-distance footpath from the centre of the town, up the steep sides of **Broadway Hill**, to the **Tower** at the summit. This folly was built in 1800 and stands 65 ft (20 metres) tall on top of a 1,024-ft (412-metre) hill, giving extensive views which, on a clear day, extend to the cities of Worcester and Warwick. William Morris used the tower as a holiday retreat, and there are displays there about his life and work, and about the Cotswold wool industry.

BELOW: impressive Broadway Tower.

Less than a mile (about 1 km) to the northeast, along the ridge of the hill, is another picturesque folly, built in the 18th century as a "gaze-about house", now part of The Fish Inn.

At the western end of Broadway, a narrow road signposted to Snowshill Manor passes the Norman **church of St Eadburga**, standing next door to the Court House, whose ancient topiary yews spill from the garden into the churchyard.

Two miles (3 km) on is **Snowshill Manor ㉞**, a popular National Trust property best avoided at weekends because of the volume of visitors (daily except Tues 2–5pm Apr and Oct, 2–6pm May–Sept). The former owner, Charles Paget Wade, led a solitary life here between 1919 and 1951, carefully restoring the Tudor house that had once belonged to Catherine Parr, the last of Henry VIII's six wives. Wade filled his house to the rafters with a magpie collection of extraordinary diversity: everything from bicycles to Samurai armour. Perhaps his best achievement was the terraced garden, which was created by clearing away unsightly 19th-century buildings, and brims with colourful flowers.

Cotswold heritage

From Snowshill, a high and narrow lane crosses the heights of the Cotswold uplands, attractive in summer, but bleak and chill in winter, through Taddington and into the beautiful wooded Windrush Valley. **Temple Guiting ㉟** (pronounced "guyting") was once a prop-

The Cotswolds have two animal sanctuaries: Cotswold Farm Park and Cotswold Wildlife Park.

erty of the crusading Knights Templar, and the Windrush, much diminished in size since the stream has been tapped to provide drinking water, used to drive the hammers of fulling mills, used in wool processing.

This industry continued into the 18th century: the tomb of John Mowse (died 1787) in St Mary's Church records that he was a wool dyer, who employed a great number of the poor of the parish in the various parts of his trade. He may also have contributed to the rebuilding of the church, with its fine wooden furnishings and George II coat of arms, unusually made out of plaster. Two miles (3 km) southeast is **Cotswold Farm Park** ➌ (*see below*).

Six miles (10 km) downstream, the River Windrush flows through the centre of **Bourton-on-the-Water** ➐, crossed by a series of elegant 18th-century stone bridges. Bourton is a village to avoid if you do not like people, for the combined attractions of the Model Village – a one-ninth scale replica of Bourton itself, made in 1937 – a Motor Museum, Model Railway and Birdland all make this one of the most-visited tourist attractions of the region.

The Slaughters

This same fate has overtaken the nearby hamlets of **Lower** and **Upper Slaughter** ➑, so named because of the sloughs, or marshes, that once bordered the River Eye flowing through the two villages. Simple clapper bridges, made of huge planks of limestone, cross the stream as it flows between carefully tended banks and in front of the mill in Lower Slaughter, a much-photographed building.

Similar in character, but far more peaceful, is the little hamlet of **Upper Swell**, with its 18th-century bridge, watermill and mill pool fed by the River Dikler. Occasionally in summer the **Abbotswood** estate, south of Swell, is open

BELOW:
Lower Slaughter.

COTSWOLD FARM PARK

Cotswold Farm Park is headquarters of the Rare Breeds Survival Trust. Here the Henson family keeps a flock of the traditional breed of Cotswold sheep upon which the medieval prosperity of the region was based. Nicknamed "Cotswold lions" because of their distinctive long, curly fleece, these big-limbed animals are descended from sheep introduced by the Romans.

The foundation, in 1892, of the Cotswold Sheep Society by another local farmer saved the breed from extinction, but even now they are regarded as rare – like the Gloucester Old Spot pigs and Old Gloucester cows that are also protected and displayed at the Farm Park.

Gloucester Old Spot pigs were once the cottager's breed *par excellence*, but tend to be too fatty for today's tastes for lean pork and bacon. Old Gloucester cows, with their distinctive white tails, were a triple-purpose breed. Not only did their milk create the famous Double Gloucester cheese and the oxen top-grade beef, but they were also well suited to ploughing.

Another 40 or more rare breeds can also be seen at Cotswold Farm Park, including goats, rabbits, ponies and huge shire horses (open April–Oct, tel: 01451-850307). Most are placid, so the park is suitable for children.

under the National Gardens Scheme. Well worth visiting, Abbotswood is one of the finest works of Sir Edwin Lutyens, who designed the garden, with its pools and water channels, as well as the striking house, in 1902.

Antiques and Austen

Stow-on-the-Wold ⑳, a mile (2 km) east, sits on the summit of an 800-ft (240-metre) hill and has the reputation for being a chilly place: "Stow-on-the-Wold, where the wind blows cold" is an ancient taunt. The great Stow Horse Fair is now held at **Andoversford** (near Cheltenham), moved because of the nuisance caused by gypsy horse breeders converging on the town. Stow prefers more genteel visitors and caters for them with numerous antique shops, tea rooms and a museum of antique dolls in Sheep Street.

Stow's church, to the west of the grassed-over Market Square, was so ill-treated by Royalist prisoners, captured in the Battle of Stow, one of the fiercest of the Civil War in the 1640s, that it had to be extensively repaired. From this time dates the curious Gothic north porch, flanked by two twisted and ancient yews.

Before returning to Oxford along the A44, lovers of literature might like to make a final stop at **Adlestrop ⑳** – for two reasons. First, Jane Austen was a frequent visitor to Adlestrop House, formerly the rectory, where her uncle was the incumbent. The house – private but visible from the churchyard – has an 18th-century Gothic facade and was the model for her descriptions of North-anger Abbey in the eponymous novel. The other reason is the station; it is now closed but the original sign fills the village bus shelter. Below it, a bench bears a brass plate inscribed with the words of Edward Thomas's brief poem, evoking all the pleasures of a summer Cotswold day: "Yes, I remember Adlestrop". ❏

The Stow Horse Fair at Andoversford is held in mid-May, mid-July and mid-October. It is well worth a visit.

BELOW: the stocks at Stow-on-the-Wold.

THE UPPER THAMES

The River Thames can be followed from Oxford all the way to its source near Cirencester. Along the route are attractive houses, villages and churches

Map on pages 218–9

Walkers can follow the River Thames from Oxford to Cirencester along the newly designated **Thames Long Distance Footpath**. You can also hire a motor cruiser and take to the water, at least as far as Lechlade, the river's highest navigable point. By car you will miss out on some of the river's tranquillity but you can easily divert to see the sights along its course.

To Stanton Harcourt and Kingston Bagpuize

Heading out of Oxford on the B4044, you cross the river 6 miles (10 km) west at **Swinford Toll Bridge**, an elegant stone bridge built in 1769 to replace a dangerous ford. In Eynsham, turn south towards **Stanton Harcourt** ❹. Here you will find a fascinating medieval manor house complex surrounding the parish church. The gatehouse was built in 1540 and enlarged in 1953 to form the house of the present owners. Much of the original manor house was demolished in 1735 and the stone reused to build a new Harcourt family seat at Nuneham Courtenay.

Pope's Tower, however, remains. It is named after the poet Alexander Pope who resided here in 1717 while working on his translation of Homer's *Iliad*. A window pane records his stay and is scratched with the words "In the year 1718, I Alexander Pope finished here the fifth volume of Homer".

The Great Kitchen also survives, built in 1380 and reroofed in 1485. The octagonal timber roof is very beautiful – "like the web of a giant spider" according to one architectural historian – yet Pope recorded that local people felt differently: "They believe witches keep their Sabbath here, and that once a year the Devil treats them with an infernal vision, viz. a toasted tiger stuffed with tenpenny nails."

Less likely a setting for such horrors is difficult to imagine. The old walls and fish ponds of the manor have been transformed into a pleasing formal garden, and the nearby church of St Michael contains many fine monuments to the Harcourt family.

Three miles (5 km) south, through Standlake, the minor road meets the A415, which crosses the confluence of the River Windrush with the Thames by means of a 15th-century bridge – replacing one of the first bridges to be built across the Thames in 1280.

At **Kingston Bagpuize** (pronounced "bagpews") ❷, 2 miles (3 km) south, Lady Tweedsmuir often conducts visitors personally around her home, Kingston House, built in the reign of Charles II, and – unusually in this region of stone – out of the then fashionable red brick. The house has a magnificent cantilevered staircase and a Georgian summerhouse in beautiful gardens.

At **Pusey House**, 4 miles (6 km) west, the garden is considered one of England's finest but is no longer open to the public. Designed in 1934, long herbaceous

PRECEDING PAGES: a typical day in busy Bibury. **LEFT:** 15th-century stained glass in Fairford Church. **BELOW:** Thames lock-keeper.

borders, packed with plants, lead to a lake where water-loving plants surround a Chinese Chippendale-style bridge. Banks of shrubs and mature trees frame distant views of the Berkshire Downs.

Market towns and manor houses

At **Faringdon** ❹❸, 5 miles (8 km) west, the 17th-century Town Hall, supported on stout limestone columns to provide a market below, stands on an island in the centre of Market Place surrounded by Georgian inns and townhouses. To the southwest, **Great Coxwell** is one of England's earliest and finest medieval barns.

William Morris knew this corner of Oxfordshire intimately. He purchased the Thames-side manor at **Kelmscott** ❹❹ (open April–Sept Wed 11am–1pm and 2–5pm), 3 miles (5 km) northwest of Faringdon, in 1871 and lived there until his death in 1896. The manor is furnished with his own textiles, wallpapers and a portrait of his wife Jane, painted by Rossetti. Morris is buried in St George's churchyard nearby.

Buscot Park ❹❺ (Apr–Sept, 2–6pm Wed–Fri plus 2–6pm every second and fourth full weekends in the month) on the other side of the river, also has preRaphaelite connections, for the walls of the parlour are used to display Burne-Jones's rich series of paintings based on the story of Sleeping Beauty, executed in 1890. The same artist designed the Good Shepherd window in the village church, some 2 miles (3 km) west of Buscot House itself.

From the nearby Buscot Lock, you can walk along the Thames to **Lechlade** ❹❻, just over a mile (2 km) away. Walking is by far the best way to approach the town for, as you reach St John's Bridge, there is a splendid view of the elegant church and spire, rising above the surrounding water meadows.

William Morris described Great Coxwell barn "as noble as a cathedral", and the great timber roof, supported on stone columns, dates to the late 13th century, when Cistercian monks built it to store their tithes.

BELOW: peace and quiet at Lechlade.

Map on pages 218–9

St John's Lock marks the highest navigable point of the river and the nearby marina is always busy with holidaymakers in summer. By the side of the lock is a friendly reclining stone figure known affectionately as "Old Father Thames" – though he in fact represents Neptune. He was carved by the Italian artist Rafaelle Monti for the 1851 Great Exhibition and resided at Crystal Palace until 1958, when he was moved to the source of the Thames near Coates. He was transferred to this more public spot in 1974 because of repeated vandalism.

As you cross the meadows to Lechlade Church, you follow in the footsteps of the poet Shelley who stayed here in 1815 after rowing upriver from Windsor. He composed his *Stanzas in a Summer Evening Churchyard* while sitting beside the church, having dined on "three well-peppered mutton chops" at the New Inn.

Beautiful as it is, the church is scarcely a rival for the magnificent building at nearby **Fairford** ⓐ, built from 1490 by father and son wool merchants called Tames. The magnificent and near-complete set of 15th-century stained glass was produced in the workshops of Barnard Flower, Master Glass Painter to Henry VII and also responsible for the windows of King's College Chapel, Cambridge. Based on woodcuts in the *Biblia Pauperum* (*Poor Man's Bible*), one of the earliest printed books, the windows provide a wonderful vision of pre-Reformation religious beliefs; in particular, the enthralling west window depicts in vivid detail the torments of the Damned in Hell.

The richly carved choir screen, featuring the pomegranate emblem of Catherine of Aragon, widow of Prince Arthur and then first wife of his brother, Henry VIII, dates to around 1501. It is carved with scenes from fable and popular sermons, while outside, jesters and grotesque beasts tumble around the parapet.

Away from the river

East and south of Fairford, the River Thames gets lost, almost, among acres of gravel workings and the waterparks – providing facilities for fishermen and weekend sailors – created out of the flooded pits left after the gravel has been extracted.

Four miles (7 km) southwest of Fairford, the church at **Down Ampney** has a display of Vaughan Williams memorabilia; the composer was born in 1872 in the nearby Old Vicarage. The other **Ampneys**, strung out along the Ampney Brook to the north, all have Saxon churches. Best of all is the little church of **Ampney St Mary** ⓑ, standing alone in fields south of the A417, as the original village was abandoned in 1348 because of the Black Death.

Three miles (5 km) west is **Cirencester** ⓒ, the "Capital of the Cotswolds". In Roman times it was Britain's second-biggest city, and the award-winning **Corinium Museum** in Park Street (open daily 10am–5pm, Sun from 2pm, Nov–Mar closed Mon) shows the wealth of material that has been uncovered in the town, including accomplished mosaics and tableaux illustrating daily life in the Roman city.

Cirencester's wide Market Place, lined with pastel-painted Regency and Victorian shops, is fronted with one of the Cotswolds' largest and finest wool churches – graced by a richly embellished 15th-century tower, and entered through an imposing fan-vaulted porch

BELOW: Cirencester's fine townhouses.

whose upper room once served as the town hall. From the tower there are panoramic views over the town and the chestnut-lined avenues of **Cirencester Park**, laid out by the 1st Earl Bathurst with the help of his friend, Alexander Pope. Most of the park is open to the public.

Beginnings

To find the **source of the Thames**, you have to leave Cirencester on the A433 Foss Way and look for a layby after the Coates turning and before the railway bridge. Towards Cirencester, 100 metres back from the layby, a path to the north leads across fields to the source, at the edge of the woods surrounding Trewsbury House.

There is a rival "source" of the Thames, and a more spectacular one than this muddy patch, at **Seven Springs** ⑤⓪, 12 miles (20 km) north of Cirencester, just off the A436 to the left of the junction with the A435. Local people unsuccessfully petitioned Parliament in 1937 for this to be recognised as the true source. It does, however, mark the beginning of the Churn, a pretty river that makes the drive to Seven Springs along the A435 especially attractive.

Almost every village along the route will demand your attention – for all of them have Saxon or early Norman churches. If you have time to visit only one, make it St John's at **Elkstone**, the most complete 12th-century Romanesque church in the region, covered in bold carvings of dragons and beakheads.

Cheltenham and beyond

From Seven Springs the A435 drops over the Cotswold scarp to the town of **Cheltenham** ⑤① in the Vale below. With its elegant Regency and neo-Grecian

TIP

Detailed directions are necessary to reach the source of the Thames because the spring is elusive – and it's often totally dry during the summer.

BELOW:
Sudeley Castle's gatehouse garden.

SUDELEY CASTLE

Sudeley Castle, "a place of muche nobility", is 900 years old and set in 1,500 acres (600 hectares) of landscaped park and gardens. It is one of England's finest stately homes and a place with strong royal connections.

Sudeley was once the home of Catherine Parr, the sixth, and surviving, wife of King Henry VIII. She moved there with her new (and fourth) husband Thomas Seymour, having scandalously remarried only a month after the king's death in 1547. Even more scandalous was the fact that she and Seymour had been lovers before she married Henry four years earlier. Reunited, Catherine and Seymour set up home in Sudeley Castle, employing a vast retinue of maids, ladies in waiting and 120 gentlemen of the household. A contemporary poem remarked that "her house was termed a second court, of right/Because there flocked there still nobility."

The happiness and ostentation were short-lived, however, as Catherine died soon after giving birth to their child aged only 36. She was buried in the Chapel of St Mary. Seymour, it seems, did not mourn for long, though soon pursuing Princess Elizabeth, who at the age of 15 rebuffed him. She later visited Sudeley as Queen, notably in 1592 to celebrate the anniversary of the Spanish Armada's defeat buildings, this town was no more than a village until medicinal springs were discovered in the 18th century and, after George III's visit in 1788, it was adopted as a summer resort by the wealthy. Later it became a place of retirement for colonial civil servants and army officers (contemptuously described by William Cobbett as "East India plunderers, West India floggers and English tax dodgers").

Today it is noted for its smart shops, annual arts festivals and horse racing. In March, during Gold Cup week, the top event of the National Hunt calendar, the town is transformed into an outpost of Ireland. Northeast of Cheltenham, just outside Winchcombe, is the delightful **Sudeley Castle** (*see page 260*).

To avoid the busy main road back to Oxford, take the A40, but turn right 3 miles (5 km) east of Cheltenham at Dowdeswell and follow the road to **Withington**. This pretty village has one of the Cotswolds' most characterful pubs, The Mill, and the road westward, with views of the wooded Coln Valley, leads to **Chedworth Roman Villa** (open Mar–Sept Tues–Sun 10am–5pm, Nov/Dec to 4pm). The villa enjoys an idyllic setting, in a sheltered combe, and dates originally to around AD180. Centrally heated dining rooms and sauna baths were provided as a retreat from the cold English winter. One lively mosaic floor portrays winter as a shepherd in woollen cloak and hood.

At **Northleach** 52 you can hear tape-recordings of more recent shepherds, talking in the rich Cotswold accent about their work – just one of the features that makes the **Cotswold Countryside Collection**, housed in an 18th-century prison, a rewarding museum (Apr–Oct, 10am–5pm Mon–Sat, 2–5pm Sun).

Northleach parish church continues the rural theme, as wool merchants paid for its construction, and many of those who donated funds are commemorated by an outstanding series of memorial brasses: look particularly for the Scors-Fortey brass of 1450 – the border is engraved with charming vignettes, including a snail, a pig, a hedgehog and a crab. Note, too, that the inscription gives the year of Thomas Fortey's death as MCCCC47, the last two figures being an early example of the use of Arabic, rather than Roman, numerals; this indicates that Cotswold wool merchants had contacts with their Moorish counterparts in Spain.

A real beauty

A detour south to **Bibury** 53 will again avoid the congested A40, and Bibury is certainly worth a visit, despite the crowds of tourists who come to see the village regarded as the most beautiful in England. From the Saxon church at the east end you can follow the trout-filled River Coln, past Arlington Row, a group of 17th-century weavers' cottages, to **Arlington Mill**, a museum that contains a representative collection of furniture made by members of the Cotswold Arts and Crafts movement in the early 1900s.

At **Barnsley** 54, 3 miles (5 km) southwest, Rosemary Verey's outstanding and influential garden, created in the grounds of the former rectory, has become almost a pilgrimage centre for those who know and love her gardening books.

East of Bibury you can either take the high road to **Coln St Aldwyns** 55, not neglecting to look back for a view of the many-gabled Bibury Court, built in

Map on pages 218–9

Cheltenham hosts both music and literature festivals.

BELOW: Arlington Row, Bibury.

1633, or you can take the valley footpath, following the banks of the gentle **River Coln**. This unspoiled river, fringed by meadowsweet and reedmace, makes Coln St Aldwyns, with its 16th-century manor house, barn and dovecote, a village of almost unreal beauty, like a living Constable painting.

The village is almost continuous with **Hatherop**, where the "castle", built in the 1850s in French Gothic style, is now a girls' school, and **Quenington**, where the little Norman church has two tympanums, one carved with the Harrowing of Hell, the other with the Coronation of the Virgin.

Three miles (5 km) east, **Eastleach Turville** and **Eastleach Martin** stand on opposite banks of the River Leach, linked by an ancient clapper bridge made of massive limestone slabs. In spring, visitors come from miles around to admire the riverbanks, smothered in wild daffodils. At **Southrop**, downstream, the church contains a unique and intriguing Norman font, carved with armoured figures representing the Virtues, trampling and stabbing beasts that represent the Vices.

At **Filkins**, off the A361 east of Southrop, the Cotswold Woollen Weavers make handwoven cloth in a converted barn, amid displays explaining the history of wool in the Cotswolds.

The **Cotswold Wildlife Park** ❻ (open daily 10am–6pm), 2 miles (3 km) north, is an open-air zoo where African and tropical animals graze incongruously in an English park around a neo-Gothic manor.

Quintessential England

BELOW: the traditional market town of Burford.

The market town of **Burford** ❼ to the north is traditionally English, with its broad High Street, lined with trees and wool merchants' houses, falling steeply to the River Windrush. The stately church, with its 180-ft (55-metre) spire,

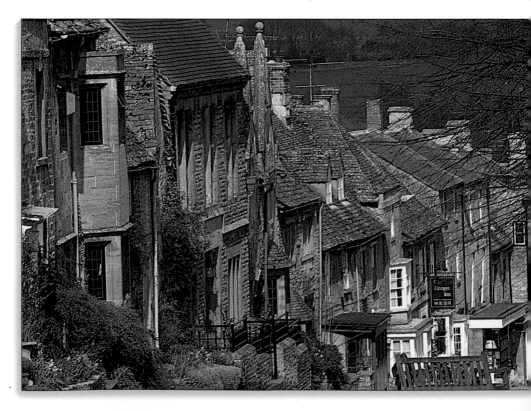

Map on pages 218–9

stands right by the river. The font has the words "Anthony Sedley prisoner 1649" scratched into its lead lining. Sedley was one of three Levellers, members of a breakaway religious sect who took part in a mutiny against Cromwell's army during the Civil War. The three men were trapped in the church, executed and buried in the churchyard.

Another monument to dissent is the curiously named hamlet of **Charterville Allotments** ❺❽, 5 miles (8 km) east along the A40. The hamlet was created by the wealthy socialist Feargus O'Connor around 1847 as a means of providing rural homes and smallholdings for poor families from industrial towns – the scheme failed when O'Connor went bankrupt soon afterwards.

Immediately north is the romantic ruined manor house of **Minster Lovell** ❺❾, standing among willow trees by the side of the River Windrush. The manor was built in 1432 by William, the 7th Lord Lovell. His grandson, Francis Lovell, was a prominent supporter of the Yorkist cause during the Wars of the Roses, and, according to local legend, he took refuge in the house after defeat in battle, hiding in a secret room where he starved to death. In 1728, workmen found a skeleton which they assumed to be his, and John Buchan vividly retold the tale in his novel *The Blanket of the Dark*.

The last stop before Oxford is **Witney** ❻⓿, famous since the 13th century for the production of soft woollen blankets. Blanket Hall, in the High Street, was built in 1721 for the weighing and measuring of blankets, and 18th-century mills and weavers' cottages ring the town.

Southeast, off the B4022, **Cogges Manor Farm Museum** ❻❶ (open Mar–Oct daily) recreates rural life at the turn of the century with cooking, washing and dairy demonstrations. ❑

Wild poppies are just one of the attractions along the Thames.

BELOW: leading a merry dance.

THE LOWER THAMES

*The lower part of the River Thames twists and turns southeast
from Oxford via ancient abbeys and beautiful villages
before eventually reaching London*

Map
on pages
218–9

Abingdon lics 8 m1iles (13 km) south of Oxford, and if you choose to walk there, along the western bank of the Thames, or take the river cruiser from Folly Bridge in Oxford, you will enjoy views of **Nuneham Park**. This huge, neo-Palladian mansion was built in the late 1700s in a natural amphitheatre landscaped by "Capability" Brown. Walpole called it "the most beautiful place in the world", but the poet Oliver Goldsmith thought differently. To create the park, the old village of Nuneham was cleared and a new estate village built to the north. Goldsmith's poem *Deserted Village* lamented the power of "the man of wealth and pride" to uproot his tenants and destroy their centuries-old way of life.

Ancient Abingdon

Abingdon ㊷, once the county town of Berkshire until the rapid growth of Reading, has a splendid Town Hall, befitting its former status. This magnificent Renaissance stone building was built in 1678 by Christopher Kempster, a master mason who had worked for Christopher Wren, and clearly shows Wren's influence. There is a museum upstairs in the former Assize Court, and the building is lit at night.

LEFT: West Hannay.
BELOW: Didcot
Railway Centre.

Abingdon claims to be the oldest inhabited town in England, but little now remains of its once-powerful 15th-century Benedictine Abbey, apart from the gateway attached to St Nicholas' Church. There is a famous Craft Fair in the abbey buildings each year in October.

From the Market Square, the graceful 150-ft (46-metre) spire of St Helen's Church draws the eye. The street leading to it is lined with characterful houses – a mixture of 16th-century timber framing and Georgian brick. St Helen's splendid churchyard is surrounded by almhouses; Christ's Hospital, founded in 1446, is fronted by a long timber cloister, while to the right Twitty's Almshouses (of 1707), and to the left Brick Alley Almshouses (of 1718) are both extraordinarily ornate, with chequered brick, balconies and roof-top belvederes.

St Helen's is remarkably wide and has no fewer than five aisles, representing 15th- and 16th-century additions to the 13th-century church. The roof of the inner north aisle is covered with a rare series of panels painted around 1390 with a Tree of Jesse.

Down to Didcot

Didcot ㊳, 5 miles (8 km) south of Abingdon, is visible from afar, since the six great cooling towers of the coal-fired power station, built in the 1960s, dominate the skyline. The railway station marks the point where the Great Western Railway (known to enthusiasts as

"God's Wonderful Railway") meets the line from Worcester and the Midlands. No-one with a passion for steam should miss the **Didcot Railway Centre**, with the engine sheds filled with lovingly restored locomotives (open Oct–Mar Sat and Sun 11am–5pm; April–Sept daily 11am–5pm).

Saxons and Normans

Five miles (8 km) northeast is the historic town of **Dorchester** ❻, with its beautiful abbey built on the spot where St Birinus, sent by Pope Honorius to convert the West Saxons, founded a church in 635. The former abbey Guest House contains a museum explaining the history of the town, and the abbey is packed with treasures: a rare Norman lead font, an east window of flowing tracery filled with 14th-century glass, and a Jesse window whose stonework is carved with figures of kings and prophets showing the lineage of Christ.

Ewelme ❻, 4 miles (7 km) southeast, is one of Oxfordshire's showplace villages. Rainwater filtered through the chalk emerges here, and the pure water used to be diverted to watercress beds dotted about the village. At the west end, the church, almshouses and school date from between 1430 and 1450, when they were endowed by the Duke of Suffolk and his wife Alice, granddaughter of the poet Geoffrey Chaucer. Alice, dressed as a nun but wearing a coronet and the Order of the Garter, lies under a magnificent tomb canopy. In St John's Chapel is the brass of her father, Thomas, Chaucer's son; he donated the splendid carved wooden font cover.

The history of **Wallingford** ❻, 3 miles (5 km) southwest, is summed up by its name. An important Roman town because of its position by a relatively safe ford across the Thames, it was walled by King Alfred in the 9th century, and

Jerome K. Jerome, author of that celebration of the pleasures of the Thames, "Three Men in a Boat", is buried in Ewelme churchyard.

BELOW: Dorchester.

further fortified by the Normans, who built the castle whose remains lie to the north of the present town. The defences remained strong enough up to the 17th century for this to be the last Royalist stronghold in the county to surrender to Cromwell; he ordered the destruction of the castle that had proved so useful to his enemies. The town has long since outgrown its walls, but the grid pattern of streets in the centre reflects its Saxon origins, and the graceful stone bridge, 300 ft (90 metres) long, with 17 arches and last rebuilt in 1809, still forms a major through route for traffic.

Commuter land

Below Wallingford the character of the riverside towns begins to change. The closer to London, the more you find large Victorian and Edwardian villas and railway stations for the commuters every few miles.

The last two towns, **Goring** and **Streatley** ⑰, are manicured villages facing each other across the Thames. Below Streatley, on the west bank of the river, is **Basildon House**, built in 1776 for Sir Francis Sykes who had made a fortune in India. The house is a severe neo-Palladian pile, but beautifully furnished and positioned to enjoy extensive views of the river and the wooded cliffs of the Chilterns beyond.

On the opposite bank, reached by narrow, tree-shaded country lanes from Goring, is the more ancient and more endearing **Mapledurham manor house** ⑱. Apart from the lovely Elizabethan house, with its great chimneys, oak staircases and portraits of the beautiful sisters Martha and Teresa Blount – celebrated by leading poets of the day – you can also visit the fully restored watermill in the grounds, the last survivor of the many mills that once harnessed the river's power.

Map on pages 218–9

In summer the Thames locks can get pretty crowded.

BELOW: once more with feeling at Mapledurham manor house.

DORCHESTER ABBEY

Dorchester's historical importance is out of all proportion to its relatively small size. The founding of the first church in 635 was the direct consequence of a royal marriage, and one of the first ceremonies to take place there was the baptism of a king.

The Christian King Oswald of Northumbria, so history relates, was keen to marry the daughter of Cynegils, King of the West Saxons. The main problem, however, was that King Cynegils was not himself a Christian. At this time, St Birinus was engaged in his evangelising work, and it was he, "the Apostle of Wessex", who converted Cynegils. The two kings gave Birinus the land on which to build the first church, probably a timber construction, before he went on to found what was to become Winchester Cathedral.

In its heyday, the Dorchester diocese stretched all the way from the Thames to the Humber, but the town's importance faded after the Norman Conquest and the new Norman bishop had his seat transferred to Lincoln. Even so, a community of Augustinians settled in Dorchester and during three centuries built the magnificent present-day abbey.

Much restored, the abbey has a reconstruction of the original shrine to St Birinus.

Reading **⑥⑨**, a sprawling town that has grown since the railway arrived, is best avoided – although it does has three excellent museums, devoted to archaeology (Town Museum), industry (Blake's Lock) and rural life (University).

Instead, thread through the country lanes north of the town via Sonning Common to **Greys Court**, a jumble of medieval, Tudor and Jacobean buildings with a maze in the garden, and a mighty wheel house, driven by donkey power, and used until 1914 to draw water from the 200-ft (60-metre) well.

Regattas

From here, you drop over the hill and down into **Henley-on-Thames ⑦⓪**, host since 1839 of the world-famous river regatta, held annually in the first week of July. Because the regatta is considered an important event in the London social season, the glittering balls and riverside parties – where eligible young ladies are introduced to the "right sort" of young men, and companies lavish entertainment on their clients – are every bit as important as the racing. Further insights can be gained by visiting the award-winning **River and Rowing Museum** in Mill Meadows (open summer Mon–Sat 10am–6.30pm, Sun 11am–6.30pm, winter till 5.30pm), which, as its name implies, casts a wider net than the world of rowing.

The town, too, is particularly "upper crust", with houses, especially those with riverside views, costing a fortune, and shops selling *haute couture* and delicatessen provisions suitable for long, lazy summer picnics; for chillier days, Henley also has several good pubs serving pints from the local Brakspear's brewery.

Ten miles (15 km) east, the picturesque village of **Cookham ⑦①** is protected from the suburban sprawl that spreads out from London by beautiful woodlands owned by the National Trust. The eccentric artist Stanley Spencer spent

BELOW: Henley-on-Thames, to which rowing crews flock each summer.

much of his life here, wheeling the perambulator in which he used to carry his canvases, easels and paints, and stopping to incorporate the local river scenes and buildings into his pictures. The town has a gallery devoted to his work, and his painting of the Last Supper hangs in the church.

Stately homes

On the opposite bank from Cookham is **Cliveden** 72, the huge classical house built by Lord Astor in 1851. As the home of Lady Astor, Britain's first female member of parliament, between the wars it was the glittering centre of the nation's social and political life. In the early 1960s, it was the scene of the first meeting of Christine Keeler and war minister John Profumo which led to a scandal that rocked the nation (because she was also having an affair with a Russian spy). The National Trust now owns the property and leases it as an hotel.

From Cliveden, we leave the Thames and head north through the uninviting commuter suburbs of Beaconsfield and High Wycombe. West of the long, straight road through Wycombe, where the Oxford and Aylesbury road divides, this sprawl suddenly ends, halted by the rising hills of the Chilterns and the estates of Sir Francis Dashwood.

The present Sir Francis still lives in **West Wycombe Park** 73, though the grounds are open to the public and used as the setting for spectacular theatricals, with firework displays, in summer. The earlier Sir Francis, who built the house in the mid-18th century, was a leading light of the Hell-Fire Club. This group of high-spirited young aristocrats mocked the religious piety of their day by holding Black Masses in honour of the Devil, and their motto was *Fay ce que voudras* ("Do as you please").

Map on pages 218–9

TIP

The spectacular gardens of Cliveden are the venue for a popular open-air theatre festival from the end of June to the beginning of July.

BELOW: Cliveden house, scene in the 1960s of the "Profumo Affair".

Map on pages 218–9

The eccentric Sir Francis also helped to relieve unemployment by hiring local men to dig a series of tunnels and caves into the soft chalk of the hillside above his home. The caves descend to an artificial river called the Styx and may have been used for Hell-Fire rituals. After visiting them, it is worth climbing the hill to see the parish church. The golden globe on top of the tower was used by Dashwood to entertain his friends (one of whom apparently called it the "Globe Tavern").

Higher still, and east of the church, is a strange hexagonal mausoleum, built both as an eye-catcher, crowning the hill's summit and visible from the road below, and as a memorial to members of the Dashwood family.

Just north of Wycombe, off the A4128, is another celebrated home, **Hughenden Manor** ⓴ (1–5pm Sat–Sun in Mar, Wed–Sun in Apr–Oct). This 18th-century house, bought in 1847 by Queen Victoria's favourite prime minister, Benjamin Disraeli, and converted to his tastes, is furnished with memorabilia and his possessions.

From Wycombe, the A40 – once very busy but now almost a rural lane, since the building of the M40 alongside – crosses the beech-covered heights of the Chilterns and then drops spectacularly over the edge at **Beacon Hill**, descending into the Vale of Aylesbury. The town of **Thame** ⓹ has a broad High Street, almost a mile (1.5 km) in length and lined with 18th-century brick houses.

Fowl versus fumes

Beyond, to the northwest, lies some of Oxfordshire's least-populated countryside. At **Brill** ⓺, with its hilltop windmill, you look down into the great bowl of Otmoor, a 4,000-acre (1,600-hectare) region of formerly waterlogged common land, much of it designated as a Site of Special Scientific Interest. In the 1980s, a public campaign to prevent the M40 motorway crossing the moor succeeded in having it diverted to the north, preserving this spot for the water birds who migrate in great numbers between their feeding grounds on the Wash and the River Severn.

At **Boarstall** ⓻, 2 miles (3 km) west, you can see a 17th-century duck decoy, originally for capturing the resident fowl for sale in local markets, and still used to catch ducks for ringing.

From here you can make a circular tour round the rim of the fens, visiting the "seven towns" of Otmoor. Best of them all is **Charlton** ⓼, with its landmark church, the "cathedral" of Otmoor. This contains a very rare pre-Reformation rood screen, decorated every May Day with a large cross of flowers which remains until September.

Charlton – meaning "free man's village" – was built by generations of moormen, who fought attempts to enclose the land so fiercely, destroying fences and hedges, that in 1829 the Oxford Militia was called in to arrest the leaders. They were taken to Oxford, only to be released by sympathetic townspeople with cries of "Otmoor for ever". Though enclosure did eventually take place, Otmoor still remains a marshy wilderness, and a complete contrast to the busy city of Oxford, just 5 miles (8 km) away. ❑

BELOW: quiet times by the river.
RIGHT: the Shell Fountain at Cliveden.

INSIGHT GUIDES

Travel Tips

New Insight Maps

Maps in Insight Guides are tailored to complement the text. But when you're on the road you sometimes need the big picture that only a large-scale map can provide. This new range of durable Insight Fleximaps has been designed to meet just that need.

Detailed, clear cartography
makes the comprehensive route and city maps easy to follow, highlights all the major tourist sites and provides valuable motoring information plus a full index.

Informative and easy to use
with additional text and photographs covering a destination's top 10 essential sites, plus useful addresses, facts about the destination and handy tips on getting around.

Laminated finish
allows you to mark your route on the map using a non-permanent marker pen, and wipe it off. It makes the maps more durable and easier to fold than traditional maps.

The first titles
cover many popular destinations. They include Algarve, Amsterdam, Bangkok, California, Cyprus, Dominican Republic, Florence, Hong Kong, Ireland, London, Mallorca, Paris, Prague, Rome, San Francisco, Sydney, Thailand, Tuscany, USA Southwest, Venice, and Vienna.

INSIGHT GUIDES

The world's largest collection of visual travel guides

CONTENTS

Getting Acquainted

The Place

Area Oxford occupies a gravel terrace between the rivers Thames (also known as the Isis) and the Cherwell, about 50 miles (80km) northwest of London.
Situation 51°46N, 1°15W
Population something over 90,000; when students are in residence it increases to more than 116,000.
Language English
Religion Protestant (Church of England): the monarch is the titular head of the church; the primate is the Archbishop of Canterbury.
Time Zone Oxford, like the rest of the UK, follows Greenwich Mean Time (GMT), 1 hour behind Continental European Time, 5 hours ahead of Eastern Seaboard Time. In late March the clocks go forward one hour for British Summer Time, and in late October they are moved back to GMT.
Currency Pounds (£) divided into 100 pence.
Weights and Measures Officially metric although imperial measurements are still widely used, notably for distances (miles) and beer in pubs (pints).
Electricity 240 volts is standard; square, three-pin plugs. Hotels will usually have dual 110/240 volt sockets for razors with two-pin plugs.
International Dialling Code 44-1865
Area code 01865

Climate

In addition to the general vagaries of English weather, Oxford is famous for its damp climate, enhanced by its position in the Thames Valley. Even if the sun is shining in the vicinity, there may well be a pall of mist hanging over the city itself, particularly during the winter months. Most of the summer is cool enough for a jacket. Expect rain at any time of the year.

For recorded weather information tel: 0891 505306.

Economy

For centuries, agriculture and the wool industry provided Oxford with an economic base as a thriving market town. However, it was only when William Morris started manufacturing cars in 1912 that Oxford became part of mainstream industrial Britain. Morris Motors was born, and Oxford, the city of learning, was transformed into a major industrial centre, increasing its population from 57,000 in 1920 to more than 80,000 in 1930. The present Rover Group, now owned by BMW, is still one of the city's major employers.

Printing and publishing on the other hand, are almost as old as the university itself. The first book was printed in Oxford in 1478 and the city is now the second most important publishing centre in the UK, its activities spearheaded by the Oxford University Press, but also including Aldens, Blackwells, Nuffield Press, Heinemann Educational Books, Holywell Press and over 100 others.

Town Twinning

Oxford is twinned with Leiden in Holland, Bonn in Germany and Leon in Nicaragua. Exchange visits are arranged on a regular basis and celebrations and annual events are organised by the Lord Mayor's office. Details are available at the Town Hall.

Geology

In no other part of Britain has geology so influenced the landscape and architecture. The underlying rock in the Oxford area is oolite limestone, formed under pressure millions of years ago from the crushed shells of primitive sea organisms. Its small spherical grains vary in colour and texture depending on their location and depth. Wind and rain has moulded the limestone into a rolling countryside and the rock favours the growth of beech trees.

The stone has delighted builders – from the creators of prehistoric burial mounds to the architects of Oxford's cathedrals of learning. When mellow, it alters dramatically in colour, often from one moment to the next, as a cloud formation shifts. Buildings made from this stone, wrote the novelist J.B. Priestley, can keep "the lost sunlight of centuries glimmering about them".

University Alumni

Oxford has been a centre of teaching since the 12th century, and its 30-odd colleges remain the big attraction for visitors. The highlights among the colleges are Christ Church, Magdalen, St John's, Corpus Christi, Merton, Keble and Trinity. Oxford's cultural development is inseparable from the men and women who have, over the centuries, attended the University, then gone on to change the course of history in the world at large.

Part of the fun of exploring Oxford lies in the realisation that so many of the world's most illustrious people have walked the same streets. Oxford graduates include 24 British prime ministers; 24 Nobel Prize winners; seven current holders of the Order of Merit (an honour awarded by of the Sovereign and limited to 24 holders at any one time); numerous writers, poets, founders of religions, scientists, artists, philosophers – some living, many dead.

Men of Religion

The poet John Donne (1572–1631), for example, attended Hart Hall; he later became Dean of St Paul's. John Wesley (1703–91) and his brother Charles (1707–88) were both at Christ Church. John became an English evangelist and founder of Methodism. John Henry Newman (1801–90), best remembered for his *Apologia pro Vita Sua*, in which he described the development of his religious thought, graduated from Trinity in 1816.

Philosophers

These include Thomas Hobbes (Magdalen Hall, 1603), who published *The Leviathan* in 1651; John Locke (Christ Church, c. 1654) and Jeremy Bentham (Queen's, 1760).

Writers

John Ruskin (1819–1900), who was at Christ Church until 1836, became a renowned art critic and author. Percy Bysshe Shelley (1792–1822), a master of language and of literary form, was sent down from Oxford for his pamphlet *The Necessity of Atheism*. Other literary luminaries include the lexicographer Dr Samuel Johnson (Pembroke 1728); Oscar Wilde (Magdalen 1874); Robert Browning (1812–89), who attended Balliol; and Lewis Carroll (Charles Dodgson), a mathematical don at Christ Church and author of *Alice in Wonderland* and *Through the Looking-Glass*. More recent names include J.R.R. Tolkien, W.H. Auden, Robert Graves, Graham Greene, Evelyn Waugh and T.S. Eliot.

Women Graduates

Well-known women graduates are mostly writers or politicians: Dorothy Sayers (Somerville, 1920), Indira Gandhi, Dame Iris Murdoch (both Somerville, 1938), and Benazir Bhutto (Lady Margaret Hall, 1973).

Prime Ministers

Hugh Walpole, generally regarded as the first "Prime Minister', was an Oxford man, and over 20 British prime ministers have followed in his footsteps. They are: Spencer Compton, Earl of Wilmington (PM 1742–43), Trinity; Henry Pelham (PM 1743–54), Hart Hall; George Grenville (PM 1763–65), Christ Church; William Pitt the Elder, Earl of Chatham (PM 1766–68), Trinity; Frederick, Lord North (PM 1770–82), Trinity; William Petty, Earl of Shelburne (PM 1782–83), Christ Church; William Henry Cavendish Bentinck, Duke of Portland (PM 1783 and 1807–09), Christ Church; Henry Addington, Viscount Sidmouth (PM 1801–04), Brasenose; William Wyndham, Lord Grenville (PM 1806–07), Christ Church; Robert Banks Jenkinson, Earl of Liverpool (PM 1812–27), Christ Church; George Canning (PM 1827), Christ Church; Sir Robert Peel (PM 1834–35 and 1841–46), Christ Church; Edward Stanley, Earl of Derby (PM 1852, 1858–59 and 1866–68), Christ Church; William Ewart Gladstone (PM 1868–74, 1880–85, 1886 and 1892–94), Christ Church; Robert Cecil, Marquess of Salisbury (PM 1885–86, 1886–92 and 1895–1902), Christ Church; Archibald Philip Primrose, Earl of Rosebery (PM 1894–95), Christ Church; Herbert Henry Asquith, Earl of Oxford and Asquith (PM 1908–16), Balliol; Clement Attlee, Earl Attlee (PM 1945–51), University; Sir Anthony Eden, Earl of Avon (PM 1955–57), Christ Church; Harold Macmillan, Earl of Stockton (PM 1957–63), Balliol; Sir Alec Douglas-Home, Lord Home of the Hirsel (PM 1963–64), Christ Church; Harold Wilson, Lord Wilson of Rievaulx (PM 1964–70 and 1974–76), Jesus; Edward Heath (PM 1970–74), Balliol; Margaret Thatcher (PM 1979–90), Somerville; and Tony Blair (PM 1997–present day) St John's.

Scientists

Roger Bacon first studied arts at Oxford in 1231, then devoted himself to experimental science, especially alchemy and optics. Founder of English philosophy, he became a Franciscan friar in 1257. Robert Boyle (in Oxford 1654–68) with Robert Hooke (1635–1708) laid the foundation for the modern sciences, chemistry and physics. The Astronomer Royal, Edmund Halley, (1656–1742) was at Queen's, 1673. He was the first to predict the return of a comet and his meteorological observations led to his publication of the first map of the winds of the globe (1686).

The Oxford scientists Howard Walter Florey and E.B. Chain shared the Nobel Prize with Alexander Fleming for the clinical development of penicillin. The most widely used antibiotic today, cephalosporin, was discovered in 1955 by Edward Abraham, working in a University laboratory.

Musicians

Famous musicians from Christ Church are Sir William Walton and Sir Adrian Boult, while Sir Thomas Beecham was at Wadham.

Young Students

Some students just couldn't wait to attend Oxford. Edward Gibbon (Magdalen) matriculated at 14 after staying up only a year and Jeremy Bentham (Queen's) when he was only 12. The latest child prodigy is Ruth Lawrence. Born in 1971, she came up when she was nine and matriculated with First-Class Honours in mathematics at 12.

Local Government

Oxford County Council is responsible for overall planning policies and large-scale services in the area, such as police, education, fire brigades, libraries and social services. Those services are financed by the council tax, payable by every householder, and by central government grants.

Oxford City is divided into 17 wards, which are represented by elected Councillors. The City Council is controlled by the party which wins a majority of the seats at the election. In the case of Oxford this has been Labour for many years.

Business Hours

Most of the shops in the city centre are open Monday to Saturday 9am–5.30pm, although many now open on Sunday 10am–4pm. There is late-night shopping every Thursday, when many shops remain open until 8.30pm.

Supermarkets on the outskirts of Oxford tend to be open 8.30am–8pm from Monday to Saturday and 10am–4pm on Sunday, although some are now beginning to open 24 hours from Monday to Saturday.

Offices usually operate 9am–5.30pm Monday–Friday with an hour for lunch.

British pubs are legally permitted to open between 11am and 11pm Monday–Saturday and from noon–10.30pm on Sunday. However, some may close for periods during the day.

Public Holidays

The public holidays are:
- New Year's Day (1 January)
- Easter Monday
- May Day (first Monday in May)
- Spring Bank Holiday (last Monday in May)
- Summer Bank Holiday (last Monday in August)
- Christmas Day (25 December)
- Boxing Day (26 December).

If 1 January, 25 or 26 December fall on a weekend the following Monday is a Bank Holiday.

Planning the Trip

Entry Regulations

Visas are not needed if you are an American, Commonwealth citizen or EU national (or come from most other European or South American countries).

Health certificates are not required unless you have arrived from Asia, Africa or South America.

Customs

Since the abolition of the duty-free system within the European Union, you may buy as many consumer goods as you like during your journey (if you are an EU visitor), provided it is for your own use. If you bring back more than the following guidance levels for consumer goods, customs may ask you to show the goods are for your own use: 800 cigarettes, 200 cigars, 1 kg of tobacco, 90 litres of wine, 10 litres of spirit and 100 litres of beer per person.

Duty-free goods are still available to travellers to and from countries outside the EU.

It is illegal to bring animals, certain drugs, firearms, obscene materials and anything likely to threaten health or the environment into the country without prior arrangement. Any amount of currency can be brought in. For further information, contact HM Customs and Excise, Eldon Court, 75 London Road, Reading RG1 5BS. For enquiries, call: 0118-964 4211.

Health & Insurance

If you become ill and are a national of the EU, you are entitled to free medical treatment for illnesses

arising while in the UK. Many other countries also have reciprocal arrangements for free treatment. However, most visitors have to pay for medical and dental treatment and should ensure they have adequate health insurance.

Money Matters

Some city centre banks offer bureau de change facilities on weekdays and Saturday mornings, as do some travel agents.

The majority of branches have automatic machines (ATM) where international credit or cashpoint cards can be used, with a personal identification number (PIN), to withdraw cash.

International credit cards are accepted in most shops, hotels and restaurants. However, there are exceptions in some shops.

What to Wear

In youthful, cosmopolitan Oxford, you can wear just about anything and not be considered out of place. Students wear very casual clothes – either jeans and sweaters of doubtful age and condition, or the fashions of the day. Older people tend to wear a range from everyday casual wear to smart outfits, depending on the situation. As weather is unpredictable at all times, it is advisable to bring along clothes for both rain and shine.

Even in summer, the weather is variable, so you will need some warm clothing and comfortable footwear for the notably uneven flagstones of some streets. Formal dress is encouraged in some hotels and restaurants and for evening entertainment, particularly in university circles.

Tourist Office

The Oxford Information Centre, (The Old School, Gloucester Green, Oxford OX1 2DA
Tel: 01865-7268710
Fax: 01865-240261)
Provides information on accommodation, local events and

attractions, guided walking tours and bus tours. A hotel and guest house booking service is also available. It is open Monday to Saturday 9.30am–5pm, Sunday (during the summer months) and public holidays 10am–1pm and 1.30–3.30pm. You can find all kinds of useful information on their website – www.oxfordcity.co.uk.

University Dress Code

During Encaenia, the main honorary degree ceremony in June, the Chancellor of the University leads a procession of dignitaries and dons along Broad Street. The magnificent scarlet and pink robes they wear are a reminder of the days up until the Reformation when all members of the university were in holy orders. This applied to students, too, and their successors today are still required to wear their black and white "subfusc" garments while sitting exams and receiving degrees.

Useful Websites

General
www.thisisoxfordshire.co.uk – from local news, movie listings, pubs and restaurants, to jobs in the area.
www.oxlink.co.uk – local infomation.
www.oxfordcity.co.uk – website of the tourist information centre.
www.oxford.gov.uk/tourism – tourist information.

Transport
www.oxfordbus.co.uk – Oxford Bus Company.

University
www.ox.ac.uk – information on the University of Oxford's colleges and their departments.

What's on
www.musicatoxford.demon.co.uk – all kinds of music all over Oxford.

www.oxfordplayhouse.demon.co.uk – the Playhouse theatre programme and events.
www.thezodiac.demon.co.uk – Oxford's premier live music and club venue.
www.picturehouse-cinemas.co.uk – Phoenix Picture House cinema.

Museums
www.ashmol.ox.ac.uk – Ashmolean Museum of Art & Archeology.
www.mhs.ox.ac.uk – Museum of the History of Science.
www.ashmol.ox.ac.uk/oum/ – Oxford Museum of Natural History.
www.prm.ox.ac.uk – Pitt Rivers Museum.
www.oxford.gov.uk – Oxford City Council.

Sport
www.oufc.co.uk – Oxford United FC.
www.oxfordshire.gov.uk – Oxfordshire Sports & Leisure Centres.

Getting There

AIR

London Heathrow Airport is situated to the west of London on the M25/M4, 45 miles (72 km) southeast of Oxford.

From Heathrow central bus terminus, the Oxford Bus Company operates the CityLink X70 coach service, which departs every half-hour during the day and every 2 hours overnight.

London Gatwick is situated to the south of London on the M23, 85 miles (136 km) southeast Oxford.

The bus from Gatwick (CityLink X80) runs every 2 hours (24-hour service).

Information on times and fares can be obtained on 01865-785400 or website www.oxfordbus.co.uk.

Birmingham International Airport is 65 miles (104 km) from Oxford; there are regular train connections, as well as six coach services a day operated by National Express (National Express bookings and enquiries tel: 08705-808080).

BY SEA/FERRY

Oxford is one of the UK's most inland towns. The nearest port offering a cross-Channel service is Portsmouth (80 miles/128 km). A National Express bus service links Oxford to the south coast every hour daily. The shortest route to the continent is to France from Dover to Calais, which takes about 90 minutes by ferry and half an hour by Hovercraft.
Brittany Ferries
Tel: 0990-360360
P&O European Ferries
Tel: 0990-980980
Hoverspeed
Tel: 0990-0240241
Stena Line
Tel: 0990-707070

BY TRAIN

There is a regular **Thames Trains** service between London Paddington station and Oxford. The journey takes about an hour, depending on the number of stops. Travellers can also use the fast **Great Western** services between London Paddington and Midlands destinations such as Worcester and Birmingham, which stop in Oxford. Oxford station is a 5-minute walk from the centre of the city.

Trains to London depart regularly about twice an hour during the peak period and less frequently during the day.

Cheap day returns from Oxford to London are available from 9am (the first available train departs 9.15am) and are much cheaper than the normal return.

A Travelcard includes the use of the London Underground. While any train can be boarded with a full-fare return ticket, with all other return tickets restrictions are applied to peak period departures (from Paddington between 4–7pm) on Great Western trains. Travellers should be given a leaflet advising on these restrictions when buying their ticket.

For fare enquiries and general

information, telephone National Rail Enquiry Service on 08457-484950.

BY BUS

Stagecoach (the Oxford Tube) and the **Oxford Bus Company** (CityLink), operate regular services between Oxford and London. With a fare about half that of a cheap day return by train, these services are very popular indeed.

From London, the Oxford Tube coach leaves from Grosvenor Gardens (to the left on leaving the main Victoria British Rail and Underground stations). All coaches stop on request at Marble Arch (10 minutes after departing Victoria), Notting Hill Gate (15 minutes) and the Kensington Hilton at Shepherd's Bush (20 minutes). The Tube runs every 10 minutes during rush hours, at 20-minute intervals for most of the day, and hourly between 12.15am and 5.10am.

CityLink X90 coaches leave from London's Victoria Coach Station every 20 minutes and stop at Grosvenor Gardens and Marble Arch.

Most journeys take about 1 hour 40 minutes but during peak periods you should allow more time due to traffic congestion in London. For travel information, tel: 01865-772250 (Oxford Tube) or 01865-785400, www.oxfordbus.co.uk (CityLink).

Both the above services arrive at and leave from Oxford's Gloucester Green Bus Station right in the heart of the city. Gloucester Green is also the bus station for **National Express** services, encompassing a nationwide coach network from Oxford. A timetable is available from National Express at the bus station. For enquiries and credit card bookings, tel: 08705-808080 or visit their website, www.nationalexpress.co.uk.

For a reservation fee you can book an assured reservation and travel at the journey time of your choice. This is particularly recommended for busy times and overnight journeys.

BY CAR

From both London and the Midlands, Oxford is well served by the M40 motorway, which passes within 8 miles (13km) of the city. The journey from central London takes about 80 minutes, except during rush hour when it can take considerably longer to get out of the city along the A40. Drivers coming from London should exit at Junction 8, while those coming from the Midlands should turn off at Junction 9.

If you are coming from Gatwick or Heathrow airports, join the M40 via the London orbital motorway, the M25. Oxford is accessible from Southampton and Portsmouth by the M3 and A34 and from Bristol by the M4 and A34.

Practical Tips

Media

NEWSPAPERS

The *Oxford Mail* is the city's leading evening newspaper. The *Oxford Times*, published on Friday, carries the week's news and the biggest coverage of property for sale. *The Star, the Courier* and the *Oxford Journal* are free papers delivered locally.

Oxford and County Newspapers
(Oxford Mail, Times and Star)
Newspaper House
Osney Mead, Oxford
Tel: 01865-425262
Fax: 01865-425557.
Oxford City Courier
Oxford Journal Newspaper
2 Ock Street, Abingdon
Tel: 01235-553444
Fax: 01235-523904.

Foreign Newspapers
Wendy News, 4 Broad Street, and W.H. Smith, 22 Cornmarket, usually have a reasonable selection of foreign newspapers.

TELEVISION

Oxford Channel, 270 Woodstock Road, tel: 01865-557000, fax: 01865-553355, website: www.oxfordchannel.com (tunes into channel 6). Oxford's own terrestrial television station, broadcasts 18 hours each day, featuring local news and programmes of local interest.
Central Television, Unit 9, Windrush Court, Abingdon, tel: 01235-554123. Broadcasts local news in the central area of England, covering the Midlands as well.

RADIO

BBC Thames Valley FM, 269 Banbury Road, Oxford OX2 7DW, tel: 0645-311111. (FM 95.2, MW 1485KHz/202m). Local news, talk programmes. When there are no local programmes, the channel reverts to BBC Radio 2.

Fox FM, Brush House, Pony Road, Cowley, Oxford, OX4 2XR, tel: 01865-871000. (Oxford FM 102.6, Banbury 97.4). An Oxfordshire commercial service with music and chat programmes. On air 24-hours a day.

Oxygen, Suite 41, The Westgate Centre, Oxford OX1 1PD, tel: 01865-724442. (FM 107.9). Oxford's very own student radio.

Postal Services

The main post office at 102/4 St Aldate's is open Monday to Friday 9am–5.30pm, Saturday 9am–6pm. A currency exchange service and a shop selling a wide range of stationery is also available there. The last collection for nationwide next-day delivery is at 7pm, or midnight for local mail.

Most post offices close at 5.30pm but those in shops may close for lunch and on Tuesday or Wednesday afternoons. For help or advice on all counter services call the Customer Help Line, tel: 0845-722 3344. For enquiries about parcels, try Parcel Force, tel: 0800-224466; for letters, call Royal Mail on 0345-740740.

Oxford postcodes start with OX1 in the city; OX2 – Summertown; OX3 – Headington; and OX4 – Cowley.

Telecommunications

Most of the modern phone boxes accept coins as well as Phonecards, sold by newsagents and post offices at £10, £5 and £2 denominations. Public telephones take £1, 50p, 20p and 10p coins (minimum charge 10p). Phone booths are located at Carfax, Queen's Street, St Aldate's post

Banks

Oxford is well supplied with banks. Barclays main branch at 54 Cornmarket Street is open Monday to Friday 9am–5pm, except Wednesday 9.30am–5pm, Saturday 9.30am–noon. LloydsTSB has its main branch at 1 High Street, open Friday 9am–5pm, except Wednesday 9.30am–5pm, Saturday 9am–12.30pm. Abbey National has its main branch at Carfax, open Monday to Friday 9am–5pm, except Wednesday 9.30am–5pm, Saturday 9am–4pm. National Westminster's main branch at 121 High Street is open Monday to Friday 9.30am–4.30pm, closed Saturday. The Royal Bank of Scotland, 32 St Giles, is open Monday to Friday 9.15am–4.45pm, except Wednesday 10am–4.45pm, closed Saturday. HSB, 65 Cornmarket Street, is open Monday to Friday 9.30am–5pm, Saturday 9.30am–3.30pm, and the Co-operative Bank, 12 New Road 9.30am–5pm, closed Saturday.

office, the railway station, Gloucester Green and in many pubs and restaurants.

Numbers starting with 0800 are free, 0345, 0645 and 0845 are charged at local rate and 0990 at national rate.

To call the Operator, local and national calls, tel: 100, international calls, tel: 155; Directory Enquiries, local and national calls, tel: 192, international, tel: 153.

Travelling with Children

Children are well catered for in Oxford, especially in recreation centres. During holiday periods, special programmes are designed by theatres, museums and sporting associations (*see also Children page 297*). The Tourist Office (*see page 276*) has full details.

The Early Learning Centre, 30 Queen Street and Blackwell's Too, 8 Broad Street, are two of the shops which offer nappy-changing facilities.

Oxford for Under-Eights, published by the New Parent Network, is available in bookshops, with useful tips for parents with young children in Oxford.

Gay Travellers

Oxford has an active gay scene. For details contact: Oxford Friend, Gay and Lesbian Helpline for counselling, advice and help, 111 Magdalen Road, tel: 01865-726893. Operates Tuesday, Wednesday and Friday 7–9pm. Oxford Lesbian and Gay Centre, Northgate Hall, St Michael's Street, tel: 01865-200249. Lesbian Line, tel: 01865-242333.

Travellers with Disabilities

The Oxford City Council has published a leaflet *Oxford on the Level*, which is a self-guided tour for

Embassies and Consulates

Most countries have diplomatic representation in London (a selection is given below). For others telephone Directory Enquiries (192).

Australia
Australia House,
Strand,
London WC2 4LA.
Tel: 0171-379 4334.

Canada
38, Grosuenor Street,
London WIX OAA
Tel: 0171-258 6600

New Zealand
Tel: 0171-930 8422.

United States
24 Grosvenor Square
London W1A 1AF.
Tel: 0171-499 9000.

people using a wheelchair. This leaflet, and a list of premises which are accessible to wheelchairs, is available at the Oxford Information Centre (*see page 276*). Free wheelchairs or scooters can be borrowed from Oxford Shopmobility, a scheme funded by the City Council. Booking is required, tel: 01865-744478. People using wheelchairs are welcome to join any of the guided tours.

Stagecoach runs modern easy-access buses on most of the city's bus routes.

The County Disability Information Centre, DIALability, can help you find out what's available in Oxfordshire for disabled people. Their information and advice line is 01865-791818.

Tipping

Most hotels and restaurants automatically add a 10–15 per cent service charge to your bill. Sometimes when service has been added, the final total on a credit card slip is still left blank, the implication being that a further tip is expected: don't pay it. You are not expected to tip in pubs, cinemas, theatres or lifts, but it is customary to give hairdressers, sightseeing guides, railway porters and taxi drivers an extra amount of around 10 per cent.

Useful Numbers

Emergency services (fire, police, ambulance) **999**.
Thames Valley Police, tel: 01865-266000 (burglaries, stolen bicycles and lost property).
Oxford Rape Crisis Line, tel: 01865-726295. Operates Monday and Thursday 6.30–9pm, Wednesday 3.30–6pm, Sunday 6–8.30pm. Answerphone at other times.
Samaritans, tel: 01865-722122 or 0345-909090. Assistance available 24-hours.
Citizens' Advice Bureau, 95–96 St Aldate's, tel: 01865-247578.

Religious Services

Public services are held at Christ Church Cathedral on Sunday at 8am, 10am and 6pm, and on weekdays at 7.35am and 6pm throughout the year. There are also services generally open to the public in the college chapels of Magdalen, New College, Mansfield (United Reformed) and Manchester (Unitarian) colleges during the University terms (Michaelmas: 1 October to 17 December; Hilary: 7 January to 25 March or the Saturday before Palm Sunday, whichever is earlier; and Trinity: 20 April or the Wednesday after Easter, whichever is later, until 6 July).

Anglican Churches
St Aldate's Church, St Aldate's: services Sunday 10.30am, 6.30pm; holy communion alternates between the morning and evening service during the week.
St Andrew's, Linton Road: services Sunday 8am, 9.30am, 11am, 6pm.
St Barnabas, Cardigan Street, Jericho: services Sunday 8am, 10.30am, 6.30pm.
St Mary-the-Virgin, High Street (University Church): services Sunday 8am, 10am (only during term-time), 11am (in winter), 6pm; weekdays 12.15pm; Tuesday 7.30am Taize service (only during term-time); Lutheran service every fortnight.
St Michael-at-the-Northgate, Ship Street (City Church): services Sunday 8am, 9.45am, 11am, 6.30pm; Wednesday 1.15pm; Friday 12.15pm.
St Ebbe's, Pennyfarthing Place: services Sunday 10am, 11.30am (winter only), 6.30pm.
St Giles', St Giles: services Sunday 8am, 6.30pm; weekdays 5.30pm.
St Mary Magdalen, Magdalen Street: services Sunday 8am, 5.30pm; weekdays 11.15am, 5.40pm, 6pm.
St Peter and St Paul's, Elms Parade, Botley: service Sunday 10am.

Roman Catholic
St Aloysius, 25 Woodstock Road: services Sunday 6.30am, 9.30am,

11am, 5.30pm, 6pm, 6.30pm; Monday to Friday 7.30am, 10am, 6pm; Saturday 10am.
Catholic Chaplaincy, Rose Place (off St Aldate's): services Sunday 9am, 11am, 5.45pm, 8.30pm; Monday to Friday 7.45am, 12.15pm; Saturday 12.15pm.
Blackfriars Priory, 64 St Giles: services Sunday 8am, 8.45am, 9.30am, 11.15am, Polish Mass 6.15pm; weekdays 7.45am, 1.05pm, 6.15pm.

Baptist
Baptist Church, Bonn Square, opposite the Westgate Centre: services Sunday 10.30am.
South Oxford Baptist Church, Wytham Street: services Sunday 10am, 6.30pm; Wednesday 7.30pm. There are also Asian Christian services held here.

Other Churches
First Church of Christ Scientist, 36 St Giles: services Sunday 11am (including Sunday school); Wednesday 7.30pm.
Orthodox Church of the Holy Trinity and the Annunciation, 1 Canterbury Road (used by Greek and Russian Orthodox communities): services Sunday 10.30am, 5.30pm.
Quaker Meetings, Friends' Meeting House, 43 St Giles: services Sunday 9.30am, 11am; weekdays 7.30am (Wednesday 12.15pm).
Salvation Army Citadel, Albion Square: services Sunday 11am, 6pm.
St Columba United Reformed Church, Alfred Street (off High Street): service Sunday 10.45am.
Wesley Memorial Church (Methodist) New Inn Hall Street: services Sunday 10.30am, 6.30pm.

Jewish
Oxford Synagogue, 21 Richmond Road. Open: Friday 7pm; Saturday 10am.

Muslim
Oxford Mosque, 10 Bath Street, (off St Clement's). Meetings five times a day. Teaching provided in reading *The Koran*.

Medical Treatment

In a medical emergency, either call an ambulance (999) or make your way to the nearest Accident and Emergency department (John Radcliffe Hospital, Headington). (See also *Planning the Trip – Health on page 276*.)

HOSPITALS

John Radcliffe Hospital (including accident and maternity units), Headley Way, Headington, Oxford. Tel: 01865-741166.
Churchill Hospital Old Road, Headington, Oxford. Tel: 01865-741841.
Radcliffe Infirmary (eye hospital), Walton Street, Oxford. Tel: 01865-311188.
Abingdon Hospital Tel: Abingdon 01235-522717.

DENTISTS

Oxfordshire Health Authority Dental Helpline
Tel: 01865-226532
They will give you information on dentists who are accepting new patients, emergency dental services as well as general information.
NHS Emergency Dental Clinics Tel: 01865-842609.

PHARMACIES

There are several pharmacies all over Oxford open during regular business hours. As well as selling over-the-counter medicines, they make up prescriptions. Open daily 9am–10pm is:
The Ten O'Clock Pharmacy
59 Woodstock Road
Tel: 01865-515226.

Security and Crime

Crime exists in Oxford as it does all over the world. Take special care in car parks. Don't leave any valuables in the car and secure it properly.

Getting Around

Orientation

Radical changes to the traffic system in 1999 have pedestrianised the busy city centre. As a result, access to motor vehicles is very limited. Cornmarket and High Street are closed to through traffic. Cornmarket is closed to all traffic (including buses) 10am–6pm, High Street 7.30am–6.30pm. The western end of Broad Street is closed all day and night, and Turl Street and Market Street are closed to all but delivery vehicles.

Buses in the city run along bus priority routes, closed to other traffic. Landscape designers have been commissioned to redesign the pedestrian precinct, but it will take until 2002 before work is finished. (*See also Driving on page 282*.)

Maps

The Ordnance Survey Landranger Map, scale 1:50,000, provides a good overview of Oxford and the surrounding area. Costing £5.25, it is an ideal aid to planning walks and drives in the vicinity of the city. Another invaluable map, covering the whole city, is the *Oxford A to Z*.

Taxis and Chauffeurs

The main taxi ranks are at Oxford railway station, St Giles, Broad Street, Gloucester Green and High Street. There are additional ranks at Carfax and Bonn Square on evenings only.

Due to the one-way traffic system there is no short route across the city to the railway station, so fares tend to be high. Some taxi meters start at £1.50, others might have a minimum charge of £2.
ABC Taxis, tel: 01865-770077, **001 Cars**, tel: 01865-240000, and **Oxford City Taxis**, tel: 01865-794000 all provide a 24-hour service.
Baldwins of Oxford, 51 Mead Way, tel: 01865-374767, fax: 01865-374656, provides a professional chauffeur service for business or pleasure.

Cycling

Cycling is popular in Oxford and there are well-marked routes for bicycles to avoid the main streets, as well as many bicycle lanes.

You can hire bicycles from several outlets. They are normally mountain bikes with a lock. Lights, basket and helmet are optional extras.
Cycle King, 128–130 Cowley Road, tel: 01865-728262.
Bike Zone, 6 Lincoln House, Market Street, tel: 01865-728877.
Warlands, 63 Botley Road, tel: 01865-241336.

Public Transport

Oxford and the surrounding area are served by local buses, mini-bus services and direct buses from car parks on the Park and Ride scheme into the centre. The local services are covered by the Oxford Bus Company (CityLine) and Stagecoach. In addition, Stagecoach operates numerous services to outlying towns. Both bus companies offer special day-return tickets, family tickets, as well as travel cards with unlimited travel in the city. You purchase your ticket from the driver.

By Boat

No visit to Oxford is complete without a trip on the water. For those who like to take it easy, Thames excursions by public cruiser are arranged by Salters Bros of Folly Bridge, tel: 01865-243421. In summer there is a regular Oxford–Iffley–Abingdon service

(2 hours), as well as 40-minute cruises on the Thames (both May to September).

For the more energetic, punts, canoes, rowing boats and private cruisers can be hired for use on the Thames, Cherwell or the Oxford Canal (*see box below*).

Punt and Boat Hire

PUNTS
Cherwell Boathouse, at the bottom of Bardwell Road, tel: 01865-515978. Punts, rowing boats and canoes. £8–£10 an hour, £40 deposit weekdays, £50 deposit weekends.
C. Howard & Son, Magdalen Bridge, tel: 01865-202643. Punts and rowing boats. £9 an hour weekdays, £10 an hour weekends, £25 deposit. Chauffered punts £18 per half hour.
W.T. Hubbucks, Folly Bridge, tel: 01865-244235. Punts, skiffs and canoes. £8–£10 an hour, £25 deposit.
BOATS
College Cruisers Narrowboat hire, Combe Road Wharf, Oxford, tel: 01865-554343.
Oxford Cruisers Ltd., Boat Hire Centre, Oxford Road, Eynsham, tel: 01865 881698.
Kingcraft, Abingdon Boat Centre, The Bridge, Abingdon, tel: 01235-521125.

Sightseeing

OPEN-TOP BUS

Open-top sightseeing tours are organised by **Guide Friday** and the **Oxford Classic Tour**. You can join the bus at several marked bus stops in the city. The complete tour lasts approximately one hour, but your ticket is valid all day and you can get off and on the buses at your leisure.
Guide Friday Tourism Centre, Oxford Railway Station, tel: 01865-790522, fax: 202154, e-mail: info@guidefriday.com, website www.guidefriday.com

Oxford Classic Tour, Didcot, Tel: 01235-819393, Fax: 01235-816464.

COACH TOURS

Cotswold Roaming organises half-day and full-day tours from Oxford to Blenheim Palace, the Cotswolds, Stratford and Warwick Castle, Bath, Stonehenge and Avebury. You can book at the Cotswold Roaming booking desk in the Tourist Information Centre (*see page 276*) or call 01865-250640.

WALKING TOURS

Walking tours led by qualified members of the **Oxford Guild of Guides** (Blue Badge guides) leave the Oxford Information Centre daily at 11am and 2pm, with additional tours at busy times. There are also walking tours from Carfax Tower on Friday, Saturday and Sunday at 1.45pm.

The Oxford Information Centre also organises special interest tours such as C.S. Lewis and Lewis Carroll tours, Inspector Morse Walking Tours, Spooky Ghost Tours, etc. For further information, call: 01865-726871, fax: 01865-240261.

Driving

Rules of the Road
In Britain you should drive on the left-hand side of the road and observe speed limits. It is strictly illegal to drink and drive, and penalties for drink driving are severe. Drivers and passengers, in both front and back seats, must wear seat belts where fitted. Failure to do so can result in a fine. For further information on driving in Britain consult a copy of the *Highway Code*, widely available in bookshops.

If you are bringing your own car into Britain you will need a valid driving licence or International Driving Permit, plus insurance coverage, vehicle registration and a nationality sticker.

Breakdown Services
The following motoring organisations operate 24-hour breakdown assistance. They have reciprocal arrangements with other national motoring clubs. All calls to these numbers are free.
AA 0800-887766.
RAC 0800-828282.
Green Flag 0800-400600.
Britannia Rescue 0800-591563.

Parking
Parking in central Oxford is very limited, and in residential areas you often need a resident's parking permit. There are car parks at Hythe Bridge Street, Oxford Station, Gloucester Green and St Clements (all pay and display), as well as a multi-storey car park at the Westgate Centre (pay on return to your car). There is further pay and display parking either side of St Giles, but during the day it is generally difficult to find a space.

Payment applies per hour 8.30am–6.30pm from Monday to Saturday, after which there is a fixed charge payment until 10pm. Sunday is a fixed charge payment of £1.50 however long you are there.

Visitors should note that traffic wardens in Oxford are extremely vigilant. In the evening (after 6.30pm) city centre parking is much easier.

Park and Ride
Major areas of the city centre have recently become traffic-free zones. If you want to avoid the problem of parking, take the reliable Park and Ride service offered by the Oxford Bus Company. You can park your car free of charge at the:
● Pear Tree (green circle) car park in the north, coming in on the A44 from Chipping Norton, the A34 or the A4260;
● Redbridge (red diamond) car park in the south on the A34 from Abingdon or the A4074 from Reading;
● Seacourt (blue square) in the west, convenient for A40 and A420 traffic;
● Thornhill (yellow triangle) in the east on the A40 from London.
You can then take a bus to the

centre. Don't forget to make a note of the colour symbol at your bus stop. Bus fares cost less than the city centre car parks.

A special freedom travel card allows you unlimited travel on the Cityline and Park&Ride network for a day. Services are frequent during the daytime, but, there are no services on Sunday evening on the Redbridge Pear Tree route, and none at all on Sunday on the Seacourt and Thornhill routes.

Petrol Stations

Most stations are self-service and are open 8am–8pm. 24-hour stations can be found at Oxpens Road in the city centre, Oxford Travel Lodge at the Pear Tree Roundabout on the A34 and at the Shotover Arms, Headington Roundabout, on the A40.

Car Rental

Conditions for car rental state that the driver must be over 21 (over 25 for some companies) and have held a full driving licence for more than a year. Most hire charges include insurance, unlimited mileage, road tax and a 24-hour breakdown service. Ask for special weekend deals. There are vans and minibuses available, too, and some of the companies offer one-way rentals. Payment is usually by cash, cheque or credit card.

Avis, 1 Abbey Road, Botley Road, tel: 01865 249000.

Budget, Unit 1, Oxford Business Centre, Osney Lane, tel: 01865 724884.

Euro Drive, Transport Way, off Watlington Road, Cowley, tel: 01865 715500.

Europcar, Littlemead Business Park, Ferry Hinksey Road, tel: 01865 246373.

Vauxhall Car & Van Rental, City Motors, Woodstock Roundabout, tel: 01865 559955.

Ford Rent-a-Car, Hartwell Ford, Seacourt Tower, West Way, tel: 01865 380348.

Where to Stay

Choosing a Hotel

Accommodation in Oxford is not cheap, and while there are plenty of bed and breakfast places, there is only a limited number of hotels.

Booking ahead is therefore essential, especially in summer, on weekends and during public holidays. For visitors arriving in the city without accommodation, the Oxford Information Centre offers a room booking service for a small fee (see page 276). Not all establishments take young children, so it is worth checking in advance.

Hotel Listings

IN THE CITY

Luxury ££££
Old Parsonage Hotel
1 Banbury Road
Tel: 01865-310210
Fax: 01865-311262
A fine and well-located hotel in the renovated old parsonage next to St Giles' church. Thirty luxuriously appointed en-suite bedrooms. The Parsonage Bar restaurant is open all day, also to non-residents. Excellent afternoon tea.

Randolph Hotel
Beaumont Street
Tel: 01865-247481
Fax: 01865-791678
Oxford's most famous hotel is situated in the city centre, opposite the Ashmolean Museum. There are two restaurants, two lounges, a coffee shop and bar. Extensive conference facilities.

Expensive £££
Bath Place Hotel
4–5 Bath Place
Tel: 01865-791812

Fax: 01865-791834
A family-run hotel situated in the heart of backstreet Oxford, occupying a group of restored 17th-century cottages. Excellent restaurant.

Cotswold Lodge Hotel
66a Banbury Road
Tel: 01865-512121
Fax: 01865-512490
Beautiful Victorian building, situated in a quiet conservation area, only a few minutes' walk from the city centre. Bar serving coffee and light meals, as well as a restaurant serving lunch and dinner. Conference facilities.

Eastgate Hotel
23 Merton Street
Tel: 01865-248244
Fax: 01865-791681
Traditional hotel in a central location, adjacent to the site of Oxford's old East Gate and opposite the Examination Schools. Restaurant and bar.

Linton Lodge Hotel
Linton Road, off Banbury Road
Tel: 01865-553461
Fax: 01865-310365
Restaurant, conference facilities, dinner-dances for 150 and private functions. TV, radio, telephone and en-suite in all rooms.

Price Guide

Prices are per double room.
Luxury ££££ – over £150
Expensive £££ – £95–£150
Moderate ££ – £70–£95
Budget £ – under £70

Moderate ££
The Galaxie Hotel
180 Banbury Road
Tel: 01865-515688
Fax: 01865-556824
Friendly, family-run hotel near the shopping and leisure facilities of the Summertown residential district.

Marlborough House Hotel
321 Woodstock Road
Tel: 01865-311321
Fax: 01865-515329
Small, luxurious hotel, situated in residential area about 1½ miles

(2.5km) from city centre. Continental breakfast in bedrooms, which are all en-suite and have their own kitchenettes.

The Old Black Horse Hotel
102 St Clements
Tel: 01865-244691
Fax: 01865-242771
Attractive hotel in a 17th-century building just across Magdalen Bridge. All rooms en-suite; restaurant and bar.

Palace Hotel
250 Iffley Road
Tel: 01865-727627
Fax: 01865-200478
Small hotel in a Victorian town house about a mile from the city centre. Parking available.

Parklands Hotel
100 Banbury Road
Tel: 01865-554374
Fax: 01865-559860
This privately-run hotel was originally an Oxford dons' residence built in the Victorian era. Mainly bed and breakfast accommodation but offering meals when required. Parking facilities.

Pine Castle Hotel
290–292 Iffley Road
Tel: 01865-24149
Fax: 01865-727230
Small, family-run hotel 1¼ miles (2km) from the city centre. Pleasant, personal service and licensed bar.

Victoria Hotel
180 Abingdon Road
Tel: 01865-724536
Fax: 01865-794909
Small, friendly hotel, within walking distance of the city.

Westgate Hotel
1 Botley Road
Tel: 01865-726721
Fax: 01865-722078
Very convenient for both the city (5 minutes' walk) and the coach and railway stations. Restaurant and bar.

Budget £

Cotswold House
363 Banbury Road
Tel/fax: 01865-310558
Highly commended bed-and-breakfast accommodation. Non-smoking.

Cumnor Hotel
76 Abingdon Road, Cumnor
Tel: 01865-863098
Fax: 01865-862217
Comfort and convenience in a village on the edge of the city. Individually furnished rooms and attractive garden.

Highfield West
188 Cumnor Hill, Cumnor
Tel: 01865-863007
Comfortable, well-appointed bed-and-breakfast accommodation in a residential area. Mostly en-suite facilities. Heated outdoor pool in summer.

Isis Guest House
45–53 Iffley Road
Tel: 01865-242466/248894
Fax: 01865-243492
Owned by the university's St Edmund Hall, this hotel is open for B&B in July, August and September. Private car park.

Price Guide

Prices are per double room.
Luxury ££££ – over £150
Expensive £££ – £95–£150
Moderate ££ – £70–£95
Budget £ – under £70

Norham Guest House
16 Norham Road
Tel: 01865-515352
Fax 01865-793162
Situated in a traditional Victorian building in a quiet part of North Oxford, close to University Parks and within 15 minutes' walk of the city centre. All rooms en-suite. Good restaurants nearby.

OUTSKIRTS OF OXFORD

Luxury ££££

Four Pillars Hotel
Henley Road
Sandford-on-Thames
Tel: 01865-334444,
Fax: 01865-334400
A luxury hotel 4 miles (7 km) from the city centre, incorporating buildings dating back to medieval times. Superb leisure centre and extensive conference facilities.

Expensive £££

The Westwood Country Hotel
Hinksey Hill Top
Tel: 01865-735408
Fax: 01865-736536
Comfortable hotel set in woodland and garden. Wheelchair users welcome.

Moderate ££

Foxcombe Lodge Hotel
Fox Lane
Boars Hill
Tel: 01865-326326
Fax: 01865-730628
Restaurant and conference facilities. All rooms with colour TV, radio, direct-dial telephone. Friendly.

Hawkwell House Hotel
Church Way
Iffley
Tel: 01865-749988
Fax: 01865-748525
Country house hotel set in own grounds. Weddings and conferences catered for.

The Tree Hotel
Church Way
Iffley Village
Tel: 01865-775974
Fax: 01865-747554
Comfortable hotel in attractive setting, just over a mile from centre.

IN THE COUNTRY

Luxury ££££

The Bear Hotel and Restaurant
Woodstock
Tel: 01993-811511.
Renowned for its luxurious accommodation and magnificent cuisine. An historic coaching inn with modern conference facilities.

The Oxford Belfry
Milton Common
near junction 7 off M40
Tel: 01844-279381
Fax: 01844-279624.
Sixty bedrooms en-suite, all with colour TV, radio, telephone. Specialises in conferences.

Expensive £££

Bay Tree Hotel
Sheep Street
Burford
Tel: 01993 822791

Fax: 01993 823008
Once the home of Sir Lawrence
Tanfield, Elizabeth I's Lord Chief
Baron of the Exchequer, this 16th-
century house has 23 en-suite
rooms, some oak-panelled and with
four-poster beds. There's also a
walled garden and terraced lawns.

The Bell at Charlbury
Charlbury
Tel: 01608 810278
A quiet hotel, where gliding, fishing
and horse riding can be arranged.

The Feathers Hotel
Market Street
Woodstock
Tel: 01993 812291
Fax: 01993 813158
Famous restaurant but impersonal
service. Rooms en-suite, with TV.

Lords of the Manor Hotel
Upper Slaughter
Gloucestershire
Tel: 01451 820243
Fax: 01451 820696
Much extended 17th-century rectory
in idyllic parkland, with the trout-
filled River Eye meandering through.

Lower Slaughter Manor
Lower Slaughter
Gloucestershire
Tel: 01451 820456
Fax: 01451 822150
This 17th-century manor, on the edge
of one of the Cotswolds' prettiest
villages, offers tennis courts, a
croquet lawn and putting green, as
well as an indoor pool and sauna.

The Swan Hotel
Bibury
Gloucestershire
Tel: 01285 740695
Fax: 01285 740473
Situated in one of the prettiest
villages in the Cotswolds. Excellent
food in the award-winning restaurant.

Weston Manor
Weston on the Green
Tel: 01869 350621
Fax: 01869 350901
A 16th-century manor house set in
beautiful gardens. Excellent cuisine
in the Baronial Hall.

Moderate ££

Bibury Court
Bibury
Gloucestershire
Tel: 01285 740337

Fax: 01285 740660
This glorious Jacobean house fulfils
everyone's idea of the perfect
Cotswold manor. Rarely does such
a sense of history come for such a
reasonable price.

Calcot Manor
Tetbury
Gloucestershire
Tel: 01666 890391
Fax: 01666 890394
Calcot Manor, with its 17th-century
farm buildings, has been converted
into a complex combining one of the
area's most popular restaurants,
the Gumstool Inn, and a separate
hotel with a range of rooms: choose
between four-posters and antiques,
or family rooms with children's bunk
beds and playroom.

Budget £

Andrews Hotel
High Street
Burford
Tel: 01993 823151
Fax: 01993 823240
Good-value accommodation in an
area more generally noted for high
prices. The hotel is set in a mellow
Tudor building full of beams and
maze-like corridors. Relaxing.

The Coach and Horses Inn
Watlington Road
Chislehampton
Tel: 01865-890255
Fax: 01865-891995
On B480, 7 miles (11 km) from
Oxford and 5 miles (8 km) from
junction 7 on the M40, adjacent to
farmland in rural Oxfordshire.
Excellent accommodation for the
tourist or business person.

The King's Arms Hotel
Horton-cum-Studley
Tel: 01865-351235
Fax: 351721
Country hotel offering rural peace,
yet close to Oxford. Restaurant and
lounge bar. Four poster bedroom is
more expensive (££).

The Maytime Inn
Asthall, between Burford and Witney
Tel: 01993 822068
Fax: 01993 822635
Comfortable accommodation, all on
the ground floor, with private
bathroom, shower, TV, radio and
tea-/coffee-making facilities. Good

restaurant, with extensive seasonal
menu and vegetarian dishes at very
reasonable prices.

Tavern House
Willesley, Tetbury
Gloucestershire,
Tel: 01666 880444
Fax: 01666 880254
Up-market B&B in former coaching
inn near the beautiful Westonbirt
Arboretum.

IN AND AROUND STRATFORD-UPON-AVON

Luxury ££££

Alveston Manor
Clopton Bridge
Stratford-upon-Avon
Tel: 01789 204581
This large, half-timbered hotel is a
landmark on the far bank of the
River Avon from the Royal
Shakespeare Theatre. Part of it
dates from the 16th century and it
is traditionally held to be the site of
the first performance of *A
Midsummer Night's Dream*.

Charlecote Pheasant
Charlecote
Warwickshire
Tel: 01789 470222
Close to Charlecote Park, with its
herds of deer and Shakespearean
associations, is this luxury country
hotel with accommodation in fine
old farm buildings as well as in
purpose-built contemporary blocks.
Swimming pool.

Shakespeare Hotel
Chapel Street
Stratford-upon-Avon
Tel: 01789 294771
One of the finest buildings in the
historic centre of Stratford, the half-
timbered Shakespeare dates from
the 17th century and could hardly
be more atmospheric, though the
recently refurbished bedrooms are
far from lacking in contemporary
comforts. A Forte Heritage hotel.

Expensive £££

Stratford House
18 Sheep Street
Stratford-upon-Avon
Tel: 01789 268288
This small, private hotel in a

delightfully furnished Georgian house is conveniently located close to the River Avon and the Royal Shakespeare Theatre.

Welcombe Hotel
Warwick Road
Stratford-upon-Avon
Tel: 01789 295252
This grandiose, 19th-century, Jacobean-style mansion is set in its own spacious parkland and offers every amenity including its own golf course and gourmet restaurant, named after a former owner, the historian Sir George Trevelyan.

White Swan
Rother Street
Stratford-upon-Avon
Tel: 01789 297022
A key example of Stratford's heritage of half-timbered buildings, the Swan dates from the 16th century and features a wall-painting of that era in its bar. Rooms are mostly in later extensions.

Camping

The Camping & Caravanning Club, (behind Touchwood Sports), 426 Abingdon Road, Oxford, tel: 01865-244088. Cotswold View Caravan and Camping Site, Enstone Road, Charlbury, tel: 01608 810314, fax: 01608 811891.

Youth Hostels

Oxford's Youth Hostel is nearly 2 miles (3 km) west of the city at 32 Jack Straw's Lane, Headington, Oxford
Tel: 01865-762997
Fax: 01865-769402.
Accommodation for members only. Adults £9.75, children £6.55. Non-members may join on arrival (£10 a year for adults).

Oxford Backpacker's Hostel
9a Hythe Brige Street
Tel/fax: 01865-721761,
www.hostels.co.uk
Ideally situated hostel only 2 minutes' walk from train or bus station. From £11 a night.

Where to Eat

How to Choose

As far as dining out is concerned, the cosmopolitan flavour of Oxford is reflected in the wide choice of cuisine offered by the numerous restaurants in the city and beyond.

A key figure in putting this provincial English city on the international culinary map has been the renowned French chef Raymond Blanc, with his award-winning Le Manoir Aux Quat'Saisons in Great Milton, and Le Petit Blanc restaurant in Walton Street.

Restaurant Listings

Caribbean
Hi-Lo Jamaican Eating House
70 Cowley Road
Tel: 01865-725984
Some love it, some hate it. You're treated to the best reggae record collection this side of Kingston. The Jamaican rum drinks are magical, and the food, which takes hours to arrive, is tasty and unusual. **££**

Chinese
The Liaison Chinese Restaurant
29 Castle Street
Tel: 01865-242944
Beautiful interior and marvellous food with a diversity of set menus. **£**

Mongolian Wok Bar
67–69 George Street
Tel: 01865-792919
You can create your own meal from a wide range of ingredients, which will be cooked by the chef in a wok, Mongolian style. **£**

Opium Den
79 George Street
Tel: 01865-248680
Authentic Chinese cuisine. **£**

Paddyfield Restaurant
39–40 Hythe Bridge Street
Tel: 01865-248835
Hong Kong-style Chinese food, specialising in lunchtime dim sum, a favourite among the local Chinese. **£**

English and Continental
Bistro 20
20 Magdalen Street, under the Randolph Hotel
Tel: 01865-246555
Bistro-style restaurant serving excellent Italian and French dishes. Convenient place to dine before a night out at the theatre. **£**

Browns
5–11 Woodstock Road
Tel: 01865-511995
This well-established restaurant offers breakfast, light lunches and three-course meals in a relaxed atmosphere. Open 11am–11.30pm. Advance booking only Monday to Friday, so expect queues at busy times. Children welcome. **££**

Cherwell Boathouse
Bardwell Road
Tel: 01865-552746
Imaginative creations based on seasonal local produce in a beautiful location on the Cherwell River. Complete the day out with a punt on the river. **££**

Gee's Brasserie
61a Banbury Road
Tel: 01865-553540
Well-established restaurant in the Raymond Blanc tradition, in a beautiful Victorian conservatory. Excellent seafood specialities and attentive service. **££**

The Nosebag
6–8 St Michael's Street
Tel: 01865-721033
A split-level restaurant with an oak-beamed ceiling and warm decor that has a special charm of its own. Serves a wide range of healthy food, all home-made, including famous cakes. There is a tearoom downstairs. **£**

Rosamund the Fair
Castlemill Wharf
Cardigan Street
Jericho
Tel: 01865-553370
Enjoy a four-course meal on a 3-

hour cruise on Oxford's canal and the River Thames. But wrap up warm if you decide to do it in winter. **££**

French
Café Français
146 London Road, Headington
Tel: 01865-762587
Nice bistro in Oxford suburb. **££**
Michel's Brasserie
10 Little Clarendon Street
Tel: 01865-552142
Regional French cuisine served 7 days a week. Vegetarian food too. **££**
Le Petit Blanc
71–72 Walton Street
Tel: 01865- 510999
Raymond Blanc's latest venture in Oxford. Light but traditional French dishes in an airy atmosphere, in young and lively Jericho – somewhere to eat well all day, including breakfast time. Decor by Terence Conran. **££**
Pierre Victoire
9 Little Clarendon Street
Tel: 01865-316616
Quality, good-value French food from menus that change every day. **££**

Gourmet Eating

Bath Place Hotel
4–5 Bath Place
Tel: 01865 791812
Award-winning restaurant in the hotel, serving "modern European" dishes. Set lunch and dinner menu which changes daily. Open to non-residents. **£££**
Le Manoir Aux Quat'Saisons
Great Milton
Tel: 01844 278881
Raymond Blanc ensures a unique but financially debilitating dining experience in his 14th-century manor house set in garden and parkland, 8 miles (13 km) southeast of Oxford. Reservations essential. **£££**
Restaurant Elizabeth
84 St Aldate's
Tel: 01865 242230
This small, select restaurant with mainly French cuisine is probably the best in town, with prices to match. Reservations essential. **£££**

Greek
The Greek Taverna
272 Banbury Road, Summertown
Tel: 01865-316983
No plate-throwing but pleasant, animated chatter and exquisite Greek-Cypriot cuisine. **££**

Indian
Aziz Indian Cuisine
230 Cowley Road
Tel: 01865-794945
Established Bangladeshi restaurant, well known among the local community as well as discerning regular visitors. **£**
Chutney's Indian Brasserie
36 St Michael's Street
Tel: 01865-724241
Trendy Indian restaurant. Popular among students. In central location. **£**
Jamals Tandoori
108 Walton Street
Tel: 01865-310102
Many curry connoisseurs consider this to be one of the best in Oxford. Book in advance. **£**
The Polash
25 Park End
Tel: 01865-250244
Tandoori restaurant, specialising in the cuisine of Madras, with high-quality Indian cuisine. Opposite the railway station. **£**
The Saffron
204–206 Banbury Road
Tel: 01865-512211
Modern, café-style restaurant serving a mixture of French and Indian dishes. **££**
Shimla Pinks
16 Turl Street
Tel: 01865-245564
Award-winning Indian cuisine in tasteful modern decor. Specialities are Moghul dishes from northern India. **££**

Italian
Ask
George Street
Tel: 01865-726850
Italian food from pizza to pasta in modern setting. **£**
Caffé Uno
41–47 George Street
Tel: 01865-246652
New Italian café and restaurant with the usual dishes. **£**

Luna Caprese Restaurant
4 North Parade
Tel: 01865-554812
Well-established restaurant serving classical Italian cuisine. Enthusiastic proprietor. **££**
Pizza Express
Golden Cross Walk, Cornmarket
Tel: 01865-790442
The Golden Cross provides a pleasant setting for this branch of the justly popular pizzeria chain. **£**
Pizzeria Mama Mia
8 South Parade, Summertown
Tel: 01865-514141
Pleasant and long-established Italian restaurant, popular among families and serving probably the best pizzas in Oxford. **£**

Price Guide

Prices are for two people and include a drink.

Expensive £££ – over £60
Moderate ££ – £30–60
Inexpensive £ – under £30.

Japanese
Edamamé
15 Holywell Street
Tel: 01865-246916
Japanese home cooking as you would experience it in a private house. Open Tues–Thurs 11.30am–2.30pm, Friday and Saturday 11.30am–2pm and 4.30–8.30pm, Sunday noon–4.30pm, closed Mon. **££**

Lebanese
Al-Shami
25 Walton Crescent
Tel: 01865-310066
Very popular Lebanese restaurant serving Middle Eastern specialities. Quiet lunches, busy evenings with two sittings. **££**

Malay-Indonesian
The Bandung
124 Walton Street
Tel: 01865-511668
Excellent service and romantic ambience. A very reasonable set menu on Tuesday, Wednesday, Thursday and Sunday night. **£**

Thai

Chiang Mai Kitchen
130a High Street
Tel: 01865-202233
Top-quality Thai cuisine at very
reasonable prices in one of the
finest 17th-century houses in the
city, Kemp Hall. Special lunchtime
menu. **££**

Price Guide

Prices are for two people and
include a drink.

Expensive £££ – over £60
Moderate ££ – £30–60
Inexpensive £ – under £30.

Cafés and Sandwich Bars

Ashmolean Café
Ashmolean Museum,
Beaumont Street
Tel: 01865-278000
The café is situated on the lower
ground floor of the museum,
accessible from the museum or
from the outside. Try the excellent
pastries. **£**

Café Coco
23 Cowley Road
Tel: 01865-200232
Great atmosphere and friendly
staff. Excellent coffee and
interesting Mediterranean-style
dishes. **£**

Café M.O.M.A.
Museum of Modern Art,
30 Pembroke Street
Tel: 01865-813814
Serves light lunches and vegetarian
food, in a pleasant environment.
A very welcoming place for
children. **£**

Convocation Coffee House
University Church of St Mary the
Virgin, High Street
Tel: 01865-794334
An annexe to the church built in
1320 specifically to house the
University governing body. Home-
cooked meals, tasty salads,
pastries and cakes. **£**

Freud's
Walton Street
Tel: 01865-311171

Atmospheric café in a converted
neo-classical church. Good
wholesome food. Live music most
weekends. **£**

Heroes Sandwich Bar
8 Ship Street
Tel: 01865-723459
Really good sandwiches, so lunch
early or late to avoid the inevitable
queues. **£**

Mortons
Sandwich Shop, 22 Broad Street
and in the Covered Market
Tel: 01865-200860
Excellent variety of sandwiches with
all kinds of fillings. **£**

Prêt-à-Manger
2 Cornmarket Street
Tel: 01865-792513.
Extremely good and healthy
sandwiches and snacks, cappucino
and freshly squeezed orange juice. **£**

The Nosebag
(*See page 286.*)

Queen's Lane Coffee House
40 High Street
Tel: 01865-240082
Next to Queen's College. There has
been a coffee house here since
1654. What it lacks in style is made
up for by the chocolate brownies
and student atmosphere. **£**

Rosie Lee Café
51 High Street
Tel: 01865-244429
The place for delicious cream teas.
Conveniently situated near the
Bodleian. **£**

St Aldate's Church Coffee House
94 St Aldate's (opposite Christ
Church College on the corner of
Pembroke Street)
Tel: 01865-245952
A peaceful oasis in the heart of the
city providing the best in home
cooking from coffee and cakes to a
three-course meal. Monday to
Saturday 10am–5pm. **£**

St Giles' Café
St Giles
Large plates of chips, sausages
and beans are guaranteed to fill you
up for the rest of the day. Oxford's
truest English-style café. **£**

The Grand Café
84 High Street
Tel: 01865-204463
Art Deco-style café on the site of
the grocery shop where Frank

Cooper's Oxford Marmalade was
once produced and sold (*see page
128*). **£**

The Oxford Sandwich Company
In the Covered Market
Tel: 01865-250558
A great sandwich provider, but avoid
lunchtime when the queues are
long. **£**

Kebab Vans

Between late evening and the
early hours of the morning, vans
selling inexpensive kebabs are
dotted all over the centre of
Oxford – much to some
residents' dismay and late night
clubbing students' delight. A
large doner kebab costs about
£4 – a price fixed by all the van
owners, so there's no point in
shopping around.

The vans have been approved
by Oxford City Council, whose
Health Inspectors keep an eye on
the hygiene, but the myth
persists that kebab-eaters live
dangerously. Try St Giles, where
several vans are located.

Restaurants in the Country

The Ark
Frilford, near Abingdon (A338 to
Wantage Road)
Tel: 01865-391911
Conservatory restaurant with a
country menu. The Corinthian Room
specialises in game, such as
venison and guinea fowl. **££**

The Bear Inn
North Morton,
Didcot
Tel: 01235-813236
Revamped free-house pub with a
wood-burning fireplace. Steak, duck
and salmon regularly on the menu. **£**

Crown of Crucis
Ampney Crucis,
Cirencester,
Gloucestershire
Tel: 01285 851806
Reliably good food at reasonable
prices, including a special
children's menu. Try homemade
sausages, a ploughman's or the

excellent vegetarian pancakes for lunch, or more substantial balti dishes and pies in the evening. **£**

Old Woolhouse
Market Place, Northleach
Tel: 01451 860366
Authentic French cuisine in the heart of the Cotswolds, with excellent game (in particular hare and venison) a speciality in season, plus fresh fish and hearty meat dishes. Dinner only. Closed Sunday and Monday. Set menu. **£££**

Tiffany's Restaurant
Market Place, Deddington
Tel: 01869 338813.
English country cooking with French provincial flair and imaginative vegetarian dishes. **££**

Wickens
Market Place, Northleach
Tel: 01451 860421
The best local ingredients are used in dishes of eclectic origin – so cassoulet, for example, is made with locally produced lamb, pork and sausages in cider – not quite the approved Gascon version, but a delicious English adaptation all the same. Closed Sunday and Monday. Set menu. **££**

In and Around Stratford-upon-Avon

Billesley Manor
Billesely (off A46, 3 miles west of Stratford-upon-Avon)
Tel: 01789 279955
The Stuart Restaurant of this 16th-century manor house hotel, run by

the Moat House group, serves reliable food in its large panelled dining room. **£££**

Liason
1 Shakespeare Street
Stratford-upon-Avon
Tel: 01789 293400
An attractive and spacious modern restaurant set in what was once a Methodist chapel and later a motor museum. Sophisticated cooking both à la carte or from a sensibly short fixed-price menu. Bouillabaisse with a chive and champagne sabayon is highly recommended. Good selection of not over-expensive wines. **£££**

The Opposition
13 Sheep Street
Stratford-upon-Avon
Tel: 01789 269980
This understandably popular bistro has straightforward, tasty food at affordable prices, and its prompt service makes it a good bet for theatre-goers. **££**

Pubs In the City

There are an enormous number of pubs in Oxford. Some of them go back a long time, others are fairly recent establishments. Many serve real ale and excellent bar food. Further attractions might include fruit machines, video machines, darts, pool, table football, bar billiards, pinball, piano, cribbage and dominoes, and live music – mostly jazz.

The Bear
Alfred Street
Tel: 01865-721783
Usually full of Christ Church students, The Bear is one of Oxford's oldest pubs (there has been a pub on its site since 1242) and has genuine charm. Enclosed in its tiny, panelled rooms, with their smoke-kippered ceilings, are over 7,000 ties displayed in cabinets on the walls and rafters. There is excellent pub grub, and in summer you can eat outside in the adjoining yard.

Eagle and Child
49 St Giles
Tel: 01865-310154
J.R.R. Tolkien, C.S. Lewis and others visited this pub every morning between 1939 and 1962 to discuss and read their work. Mixed clientele, very popular, with a new covered extension at the rear.

The Grapes
7 George Street
Tel: 01865-793380
A narrow, one-bar Victorian pub with mahogany panelling and old prints on the walls. Conveniently situated opposite the Apollo Theatre, it tends to get very busy both before and after performances. Bar food, hot and cold meals.

The Head of the River
Folly Bridge
Tel: 01865-721600
Converted from a former wharf house and boatyard into a massive drinking complex with a huge paved courtyard, bars on three levels, a

Breweries

Beer has been brewed in Oxford ever since the first monasteries and abbeys sprang up by the Thames and its many streams. The first brewery was established by the monks of Osney Abbey in Tidmarsh Lane, utilising the pure well water found deep beneath the river. The colleges tended to brew their own, and there was stiff competition to produce the strongest and tastiest ale.
In the 1800s there were as many as 14 breweries located by the

Castle Mill Stream and the canal. Today, there are none left to carry on the long tradition; the last brewery – Morrells– closed its gates in 1999. There are still many long-established breweries in Oxfordshire, but their markets are contracting as a result of drink/driving campaigns and the popularity of lagers, low-alcohol beers and wines. Hook Norton Brewery has 34 tied houses and a free trade business in the Midlands, while the Henley

Brewery, W.H. Brakspear and Sons, founded in 1779, supplies many traditional pubs tucked away in the Oxfordshire countryside. Morland & Co. of Abingdon can claim to be one of the oldest surviving breweries in England. In 1711 John Morland started brewing in the village of West Ilsley on the Berkshire Downs. Although Whitbread has a large shareholding in Morland, the company has remained independent.

spacious restaurant and salad bar and, at the back, a sandwich place. Busy during the summer.

Horse and Jockey
69 Woodstock Road
Tel: 01865-552719
A superbly restored pub close to the Radcliffe Infirmary. Outside dining in summer. Cold food as well as hot pots, casseroles, grills and real ales. Two centuries ago it was full of jockeys who raced in nearby Port Meadow. Big screen for satellite TV sports broadcasts.

King's Arms
Holywell Street
Tel: 01865-242369
A pub with a certain amount of class, popular with both students and locals. There is a broad range of real ales and a good lunchtime buffet.

Lamb and Flag
12 St Giles
Tel: 01865-515787
A 500-year-old pub with original beams over the fire. A good place for a cosy chat in the back bar or a blast on the six video machines.

O'Neills Irish Bar
37 George Street
Tel: 01865-812931
New Irish theme pub decorated with relics from Ireland. Popular among young clientele. Serves genuine Guinness along with Irish bitters and lagers.

The Royal Oak
42–44 Woodstock Road
Tel: 01865-310947
Due to its position directly opposite the Radcliffe Infirmary, most of the customers are either medics or nurses. Numerous interesting small rooms. Well-stocked games room.

The Turf Tavern
4 Bath Place, Holywell Street
Tel: 01865-243235
Reached by narrow winding passages, the Turf is a famous Oxford hostelry with origins in the 13th century. There is a good selection of real ales, country wines, cider and mulled wine and excellent buffet meals. Visitors can stay outside even in winter, keeping warm by the braziers.

The Welsh Pony
48 George St
Tel: 01865-725087

A mixture between a European café and an English tavern. The majority of the clientele are travellers waiting for a bus at the nearby bus station.

The Wheatsheaf
Wheatsheaf Yard,
129 High Street
Tel: 01865-243276
A 300-year-old character pub reached down a medieval passage off the south side of the High Street. Gill and Co, England's oldest ironmongers, is down the same alley.

Wig and Pen
9–13 George Street
Tel: 01865-246906
One of Oxford's newest pubs is especially popular with the younger residents of Oxford.

Yates Wine Lodge
51–53 George Street
Tel: 01865-723790
A large new pub on several floors. Serves reasonably priced food until 7pm. There is entertainment every night, ranging from live bands, quiz nights and karaoke.

OUTSIDE THE CENTRE

The Boat Inn
Thrupp, Kidlington
Tel: 01865-374279
A watering hole for houseboat owners whose colourful homes line the canal alongside.

The Golden Ball
2 College Lane,
Littlemore
Tel: 01865-779370
This old stone-built, cottage-style pub with its low ceilings and oak beams has recently been refurbished, and serves a wide range of hot and cold bar food. Morris dancers perform outside in the summer.

The Isis Tavern
Riverside, Iffley Lock, Iffley
Tel: 01865-247006
The only way to reach this beautifully located pub beside the river is by foot, boat or bike from Iffley Lock. Huge garden. Plenty of rowing memorabilia inside and an old-English nine-pin bowling alley.

The Perch
At the end of Binsey Lane,
Binsey Village
Tel: 01865-240386
Lives off its name. Moderate food, but an excellent garden and playground for the kids.

The Plough Inn
The Green,
Wolvercote
Tel: 01865-556969
Well-appointed pub in a pleasant setting adjacent to the Oxford Canal and near Port Meadow. Excellent bar food and restaurant meals. There is a public playground nearby.

The Trout
195 Godstow Road,
Wolvercote
Tel: 01865-302071
In a magic setting next to the weir with peacocks strolling about in the gardens. The food is reasonable, but could be better given the surroundings. Interesting literary and historical associations lend their charm – from Fair Rosamond, Henry II's mistress, whose ring (now in the Ashmolean) was found on the island opposite, to Alice in Wonderland and Inspector Morse.

The Victoria Arms
Mill Lane, Old Marston
Tel: 01865-241382
Punt on the Cherwell past the Parks and Parson's Pleasure, then under the Marston Ferry Road Bridge before finally pulling in for a well-deserved drink at the "Vicky". Good range of beers and lagers, friendly staff and a restaurant.

White Hart Inn
Wytham
Tel: 01865-244372
Wonderful selection of home-cooked dishes and varied salad bar. Cotswold stone, beams and cosy corners on different levels. Garden open all year round. Lovely for lunch.

Pubs in the Country

The Barley Mow
Long Wittenham,
near Dorchester
Tel: 01865-407847
A riverside pub with attractive gardens and a pleasant view from the restaurant. Uncomfortably

In and Around Stratford-upon-Avon

Dirty Duck
Waterside, Stratford-upon-Avon
Tel: 01789 297312
The classic actors' pub, always full of theatrical hangers-on and extremely popular.

Slug and Lettuce
38 Guild Street
Stratford-upon-Avon
Tel: 01789 299700
This is a highly successful and consequently popular pub, an

crowded in winter in bars designed centuries ago for short people. Good food and ambience.

The Bell Inn
Main Road,
Long Hanborough
Tel: 01993 881324
A traditional village pub renowned for its jovial country inn atmosphere and excellent food at reasonable prices.

The Clanfield Tavern
Bampton Road,
Clanfield
Tel: 01367 810223
Delightful 16th-century listed building situated in a pretty Cotswold village. À la carte restaurant every day for lunch and dinner.

The King's Head and Bell
10 East St Helen's Street,
Abingdon
Tel: 01235-520157
Said to have been used by Charles I for council meetings during the Civil War and by Handel while he composed his Water Music. Delicious home-cooked food is served in the bar and the bistro restaurant. There is a charming old courtyard where you can enjoy a drink. Popular with residents and visitors.

The Trout
by St John's Bridge,
Lechlade
Tel: 01367 522313
Fishing, by rights granted by Royal Charter, is one of the many attractions at this superb ancient pub. Several beamed bars with cosy log fires in winter; a garden lawn

excellent venue for a pre-theatre meal, though it gets very crowded with the smart young set later on.

The Castle
Edge Hill
Tel: 01295 670255
Sanderson Miller's 18th century mock castle makes a characterful pub, with a drawbridge leading to turreted WCs. There's a children's playhouse in the garden and fine views.

set with tables stretching to the edge of the Weir Trout Pool for summer barbecues; a pretty candlelit restaurant with excellent food; welcoming and friendly staff.

Village Pub
Barnsley
Tel: 01285 740421
Opposite Rosemary Verey's well-known garden, this friendly local offers generous salads, ploughman's lunches and home-made puddings, plus daily specials that might include locally cured ham or gammon, locally smoked trout and at least one vegetarian dish. £

The White Hart
Fyfield (off the A420, 8 miles (13 km) from Oxford)
Tel: 01865-390585
A 15th-century Chantry House with an original beamed ceiling and gallery. It is a free house with a wide range of real ales. The restaurant specialises in Old English game dishes and bar food catering to all tastes – from frogs' legs to chicken and chips.

Culture

Ticket Sales

A free booklet, *This Month in Oxford*, is published monthly with a listing of all the major events. Full details of other events can be found in the *Oxford Times* every Thursday, and also listed on their website: (www.thisisoxfordshire.co.uk).

Those interested in Oxford's music scene should get *Nightshift*, a comprehensive monthly guide to what's on.

Tickets can be purchased from the box offices of the different venues.

Theatre & Opera

Apollo Theatre
George Street, Oxford
Tel: 0870 606 3502;
groups, tel: 01865-723834
There is a varied programme for all ages of opera and ballet, plays, musicals, pop and classical concerts, comedy and shows for young theatre-goers.

Burton-Taylor Theatre
Behind the Oxford Playhouse,
Gloucester Street
Tel: 01865-793797
Built in 1973 after a generous donation to the University by Richard Burton and Elizabeth Taylor, and recently refurbished with a new foyer and dressing rooms. Specialises in student and fringe productions with new plays and Edinburgh Festival comedies all year round.

Newman Rooms
Rose Place, St Aldate's
Tel: 01865-722651
The venue for a variety of plays and musicals at reasonable prices.

Old Fire Station
George Street

Tel: 01865-794490
Contains a fully-equipped (if small) studio theatre and rehearsal space in a complex of bars, restaurants and galleries. Student productions often staged here.
Pegasus Theatre
Magdalen Road, off Iffley Road
Tel: 01865-722851
Fax: 01865-204976
E-mail: pegasust@dircon.co.uk
Youth theatre and dance activities.
Oxford Playhouse
11–12 Beaumont Street
Tel: 01865-798600,
www.oxfordplayhouse.demon.co.uk
A recently renovated premises with a diverse range of productions, including a traditional Christmas pantomime and experimental theatre and dance.

Classical Music

Holywell Music Room
Holywell Street
Tickets available at the Playhouse box office, tel: 01865-798600
The oldest music room in Europe; many famous musicians, including Haydn, have played here since it opened in 1748. Evening and Sunday lunchtime coffee concerts are very popular.
Jacqueline du Pré Music Building
St Hilda's College
Recorded information, tel: 01865-276821, fax: 01865-286174
Tickets are also available at the Playhouse box office, tel: 01865-798600
This hall was created in the memory of the great cellist Jacqueline du Pré and is one of the best modern music venues in the city. A variety of musical styles are performed, as well as music examinations taken.
Sheldonian Theatre
Broad Street
Tickets available at the Playhouse box office, tel: 01865-798600
Designed and built by Christopher Wren in the style of a Roman theatre, the famous Sheldonian is used for concerts, university ceremonies and other events. Beware, however, that the seats are mainly wooden with no back rests.

Cinemas

Two mainstream MGM cinemas show recently released films (programme information, tel: 01865 251998): MGM Cinema, George Street, with three screens, credit card booking, tel: 0541 550501. MGM Cinema, Magdalen Street, credit card booking, tel: 0541 550509.

The Phoenix Picture House, Walton Street (tel: 01865 512526 for box office and 01865 554909 or www.picturehouse-cinemas.co.uk for programme information), shows some mainstream movies, but concentrates on modern cult films, classics and a variety of international productions.

Art Galleries

Apart from the permanent and changing exhibitions in Oxford's museums, there are several private art galleries, and the art colleges at the University hold regular exhibitions. The best time to explore the art scene is in May and June, when local artists open up their studios to the public during art weeks. Here are a few venues exhibiting art:
Freud Café, Walton Street, regular exhibitions on the walls of the café.
Jericho Café, Walton Street, regular exhibitions on the walls of the café.
Oxford Gallery, 23 High Street, changing exhibitions showing contemporary applied art.
Wiseman Gallery, South Parade, commercial gallery showing contemporary art.

From May to September local artists display their work along the railings of University Parks, Parks Road (Sunday 2–6pm).

Oxford Colleges

Most colleges are open to visitors in the afternoon only, from 1 or 2 to 4 or 5pm. Christ Church, Magdalen, New and Trinity colleges normally open in the morning also, while Brasenose opens 10–11.30am.

Queen's College is only open to visitors on a tour booked at the Oxford Information Centre with the Oxford Guild of Guides. Visitors wishing to see Pembroke and University colleges are requested to enquire at their respective porter's lodges.

Visitors should note that published times cannot be relied upon. Colleges have the habit of closing often for weeks on end, particularly during exam times, but also as a result of building works, conferences or simply at the whim of the all-powerful porter. For further information, call the individual colleges (*see Places section*).

Language Schools

Many people visit Oxford to learn English and there is a wide choice of language schools. Here is just a small selection:

● **Anglo World**
108 Banbury Road,
Oxford OX2 6JU
Tel: 01865 515808
Fax: 01865 310068.
● **Lake School of English**
14b Park End Street,
Oxford OX1 1HW
Tel: 01865 724312.
● **Oxford Brookes Language Services**
Gipsy Lane Campus,
Oxford OX3 0PB
Tel: 01865 483692
Fax: 01865 483690.
● **Oxford Language Training**
9 Blue Boar Street,
Oxford OX1 4EZ
Tel: 01865 205077.
● **Regent Oxford**
90 Banbury Road, Oxford OX2 6JT
Tel: 01865 515566.
● **Swan School of English**
111 Banbury Road,
Oxford OX2 6JX
Tel: 01865 553201
Fax: 01865 552923.
● **The Eckersley School of English**
14 Friars Entry, Oxford OX1 2BZ
Tel: 01865 721268

Nightlife

Nightclubs & Discos

All nightclubs and discos in Oxford are geared to young people. Anyone nudging 30 will probably wish they were somewhere else.

Downtown Manhattan
George Street (Apollo Theatre)
Tel: 01865-721101
Full, hot and sweaty. Student nights are Monday (The Playpen) and Wednesday (The Mudd Club).

5th Avenue
35 Westgate
Tel: 01865-245136
Popular venue for the younger crowd in the city centre (open Tues–Sat). Holds 400 people.

The Coven II
Oxpens Road
Tel: 01865-242770
The place to go on a Saturday night to meet Oxford non-student youth. Impressive, with lights, lasers, smoke and a video screen. Closed Sun.

Live Music

The Zodiac
190 Cowley Road
Tel: 01865-420042
www.thezodiac.demon.co.uk
For Oxford's live music and club venue. There is a bar on the ground-floor and a dance hall upstairs.

The Old Fire Station
George Street
Tel: 01865-794494
Live music on Fri and Sat.

The Jericho
Firkin pub, 56 Walton Street
Tel: 01865-799794
Gigs on Tuesdays, Saturdays and the occasional Thursday.

The Point
The Plain, Cowley Road
Tel: 01865-798794
Gigs most nights of the week.

Festivals

Diary of Regular Events

The Oxford Information Centre (*see page 276*) will be able to give visitors precise dates and times of events.

Degree Days: days on which degrees are conferred by the University are listed in the University diary.

February

Torpids: Traditional college rowing races on the Isis. Usually held in the 6th week of Hilary Term. One of the great rowing events in the University calendar. In February or early March a competition is held to introduce freshmen (first-year undergraduates) to the University rowing course between Iffley Lock and Folly Bridge.

May

May Morning (1 May): At 6am, the Magdalen College choir sings from Magdalen Tower. Morris dancing in Radcliffe Square and Broad Street. A not-to-be-missed event. Take up position half-way across Magdalen Bridge at about 5.30am, and after the chorus wander around town having a boozy breakfast and watching the revellers making merry in all manner of fancy or formal dress.

Lord Mayor's Parade: On Spring Bank Holiday Monday, a parade of decorated floats starts at St Giles and finishes at South Parks.

Eights Week: Held in late May or early June, this is a series of inter-collegiate rowing races. College crews move up and down a league table depending on each day's racing. The race is in a single line

and each crew attempts to "bump" or touch the boat in front. Once this has been achieved the race is won or lost.

Beating the Bounds (Ascension Day): Starts at the Church of St Michael at the Northgate at 10.30am.

Artweek: Artists and craftspeople of all ages open their workshops and homes so that the public can meet them and discover their methods and motivations. From end of May to beginning of June.

Whitsun: The Headington Quarry Morris Dancers occupy a unique position in Oxford's history and in the story of Morris dancing. A chance meeting between the folk song collector Cecil Sharp and the Headington Quarry Morris Dancers, led by their musician William Kimber, on Boxing Day 1899, led eventually to the national revival of interest in Morris dancing. William Kimber was to lead the Headington Morris to world fame. He inherited his skills from his father, who in turn had learned his Morris from an earlier generation of Quarry dancers. The tradition continues to this day.

June

Encaenia: The ceremony takes place at noon on the first Wednesday in the week following full Trinity term. Honorary degrees are conferred by the University at the Sheldonian Theatre.

July

Sheriff's Races: Held on Wolvercote Common. Amateur horse races, side shows and stalls.

August

Oxford Regatta: Details from the City of Oxford Rowing Club, tel: 01865-242576.

September

St Giles' Fair: Held on the first Monday and Tuesday in September. A once-famous annual enjoyment for town, gown and surrounding countryfolk. It can still be fun, but some see it as an expensive, tacky fair with a dubious safety record and knee-deep litter.

October

Oxford Round Table Firework Display: Britain's firework displays traditionally take place on Guy Fawkes' Night (5 November). This one is held in late October in South Parks, and is a worthwhile spectacle.

November

Christ Church Regatta: Generally held the 7th week of Michaelmas term. All enquiries to the Boat Captain, Christ Church, St Aldate's, Oxford.
New College: End November. Advent Carol Service.

December

Lord Mayor's Carols: Held in the Town Hall. Date announced in autumn.
Christmas Music: At Christmas the chapel choirs of Christ Church, Magdalen and New College combine their regular liturgical duties with carol concerts that sometimes feature major orchestras and famous soloists. Advance tickets available.
Christ Church: 23 December. Nine Lessons and Carols. Tickets from the Chapter Secretary no later than 16 November. Enclose a stamped, addressed envelope.
Magdalen College: Mid-December. Carols by Candlelight (tickets in advance from the College Office).
New College: Early December. Carol Service (tickets in advance from the Precentor).
The Headington Quarry Morris Dancers' Mummers Play and Sword Dance: Boxing Day.

Shopping

Shopping Hours

Most of the shops in the city centre are open Monday to Saturday 9am–5.30pm, although some (increasing all the time) open on Sunday as well 10am–4pm. There is late-night shopping every Thursday, when many shops remain open until 8.30pm.

Shopping Areas

Oxford offers an intriguing mixture of traditional and modern shops, catering for every taste and pocket. There are two modern indoor shopping arcades in the centre, which house a variety of shops, and there are the usual chain shops, as well as trendy fashion boutiques. The main shopping area is compact and easy to explore on foot.

To the north of Oxford's central crossroads, known as Carfax, is **Cornmarket**, closed to all traffic (including buses) 10am–6pm. Along Cornmarket are many of the high street chains you can also find in many other large towns, including Boots, Gap, Laura Ashley, W.H. Smith, Miss Selfridge, HMV, Virgin Megastore as well as many other shops.

The courtyard of the Golden Cross Inn on Cornmarket now leads, via an attractive arcade of shops, to the **Covered Market**. This yard contains all kind of shops selling a wide variety of gifts and goods from souvenirs, model cars and jewellery to healthfoods and herbal remedies. At Nos. 2 and 3 Golden Cross is Collectors of Oxford – one of the most atmospheric shops in town – selling Town v. Gown chess sets; tiny boxes with enamelled miniature views of the

1877 Boat Race; playing cards backed with 18th-century caricatures of University personalities, and a wide range of other nostalgia products.

The **Clarendon Centre**, which you can enter either from Cornmarket, Queen Street or New Inn Hall Street, is a modern arcade with shoe shops, fashion boutiques, sport shops, electrical goods and computer Shops. Gap, at the Cornmarket entrance, has a Gap Kids on the first floor.

Broad Street, running east from the northern end of Cornmarket, is Oxford's book street, with no fewer than six bookshops, including Blackwell's. At No. 17 is the first ever Oxfam shop. Professional and amateur artists will be interested in the two excellent art and craft shops, The Brush & Compass at No. 14 and Broad Canvas at No. 20.

West from Carfax runs **Queen Street**, also a pedestrian area but open to buses. It includes a large Marks & Spencer store, Bhs, Next, Gap and an Early Learning Centre, as well as many smaller shops. At the end of Queen Street is the fully enclosed **Westgate Centre** with numerous stores including Sainsbury's, Alders, a Disney Store and C&A. The fine public Central Library, with a large local history section and a periodicals reading room, is at the entrance to the Westgate Centre. The Westgate is also easily accessible from the multi-storey car park to which it is linked. Opposite the library is New Inn Hall Street with Argos, Culpeper and Kings Fabrics.

The **High Street** joins Carfax from the east and curves down to Magdalen Bridge. The college buildings which line it are interspersed with small traditional businesses, including antique and print dealers, as well as trendy modern shops. Near the Oxford University Press Bookshop, Shepherd & Woodward at Nos. 109–114 sells traditional menswear (including Barbour jackets), while Sanders of Oxford at No. 104 sells rare prints and maps. In Wheatsheaf Yard behind No. 128

is Gill & Co, Britain's oldest ironmongers. Established in 1530, they stock over 7,000 lines. Art collectors will be attracted by Oxford Gallery at No. 23, whereas film enthusiasts can search in Vin Mag Co. at No. 50 for a postcard or poster of their favourite star.

There are several modern designer fashion boutiques. Particularly interesting is Sahara at 46 High Street, which donates 50% of the profit from their sales to endangered forest conservation projects and to the support of indigenous people's rights. Other interesting fashion boutiques are Narda Fashion Studio at No. 67–68 and Agnès Design Fashion at No. 56. And should you need a new pen, Pens Plus at No. 70 is the right place to go. They buy, sell and repair old pens.

High Street is connected to Broad Street by **Turl Street**, where there are a number of traditional shops, including Walters & Co. at No. 10, selling high-class menswear, and Past Times at No. 4 selling historical gifts, including traditional games. Ducker & Son at No. 6 sells high-quality handmade shoes.

The fourth arm of Carfax is **St Aldate's**, which leads south. At 107 St Aldate's is Touchwoods, a sports and outdoor gear shop. A little further down is the main Post Office at No. 102, with a philatelic counter and the post shop, selling a selection of stationery. At No. 83, opposite Christ Church, is Alice's Shop, the little 15th-century "Sheep Shop" said in Lewis Carroll's *Through the Looking Glass* to be "full of all manner of curious things". The real-life Alice, daughter of the Dean of Christ Church, to whom Lewis Carroll told his tales, used to buy her Barley Sugar sweets here. Carroll wove the shop into his story, transforming the old lady who kept it into a sheep who sat at the counter knitting with a multitude of needles. It now sells the largest selection of "Alice" memorabilia in the country, together with Oxford gifts and souvenirs, Oxford University T-shirts and sweatshirts

in the University colours.

George Street, with a variety of shops and restaurants, links Cornmarket to **Gloucester Green** where the city's open markets are held. The Gallery, surrounding the square, houses a wide range of shops. Among them is Once a Tree at 99 The Gallery, where you can buy all kind of wooden objects from toys to furniture. In Rowan at No. 102 you can find unusual fashions, accessories, wool, jewellery, cards, gifts and some very lovely buttons.

Beyond Gloucester Green, **Walton Street**, at the heart of trendy Jericho, has some interesting shops, particularly of the

Bookshops

Oxford is the home of bookshops and Broad Street is where most of the bookshops are located, almost monopolised by the name of Blackwell. Blackwell's have always operated a policy of allowing shoppers to browse quite freely, and this is nowhere more enjoyable than at the main Blackwell's Bookshop at No. 50, where there is a newly opened café on the first floor.

The main competition to Blackwell's is provided by Waterstones on the corner of Cornmarket and Broad Street. W.H. Smith, another rival, is at No. 22 Cornmarket and in Templar's Square, Cowley.

Those interested in second-hand and rare books might want to browse at Thorntons at No. 11 Broad Street, at Arcadia Booksellers at 4 St Michael's Street, Classics Bookshop at 3 Turl Street or Waterfields Booksellers at 52 High Street.

Everything published by Oxford University Press can be bought at their outlet at No. 116 High Street, while St Andrew's Christian Book Shop at No. 57c St Clement's sells religious books. Books on the mind, body, spirit and health can be found at The Inner Bookshop, 111 Magdalen Rd, Cowley.

crafts and design variety. Exotic tastes are also catered for in Little Clarendon Street, which cuts through to St Giles. Here, Tumi Latin American Craft Centre sells jewellery, ceramics and clothing as well as a good choice of Latin American music. Ideal gifts for children can be found at Animal Animal just opposite.

Markets

The **Covered Market**, built in 1774 to provide a permanent home for the many stallholders who had earlier cluttered the city streets, is located between High Street and Market Street. There are several entrances. It is a gourmet's paradise for fresh and cooked meat, game, fish, cheese, fruit, vegetables and flowers, bread and cakes. But there are also boutiques, a hat shop, leather goods and upmarket delicatessens. and some good, reasonably-priced cafés. Next to Nothing, in the 4th avenue, has a fantastic selection of hand-knitted sweaters, and their chidren's shop, just opposite, has cuddly toys and selected children's fashions.

The city's **open market** is held every Wednesday on Gloucester Green, next to the bus station. Stalls sell food and a wide range of other goods. On Thursday mornings there is an antique and crafts market at the same place.

Sport

Participant Sports

GOLF

Oxford and its surrounding area is well supplied with golf courses. The new course at Hinksey Heights to the west of the city has the additional attraction of stunning views of Oxford's dreaming spires.

Hinksey Heights Golf
South Hinksey (just off the A34 west of Oxford)
Tel: 01865-327775.
North Oxford Golf Club
Banbury Road
Tel: 01865-554415.
Southfield Golf Club
Southfield, Hill Top Road, Oxford
Tel: 01865-242158.
Frilford Heath Golf Club
Frilford Heath, near Abingdon,
(7 miles/11 km from Oxford on A338)
Tel: 01865-390864.
Drayton Park Golf Course,
Steventon Road, Drayton, Abingdon
Tel: 01235-550607.
Burford Golf Club
Swindon Road,
Burford (19 miles/30 km from Oxford, 1 mile off A361)
Tel: 01993 822583.
Chesterton Country Golf Club,
Chesterton,
near Bicester, Oxon (10 miles from Oxford, off the A421)
Tel: 01869 241204.
Haddon Hill Golf Course and Range
Wallingford Road, Didcot
Tel: 01235-510410.

ICE SKATING

The Oxford Ice Rink
Oxpens Road
Tel: 01865-248076

Near the railway station, with a car and coach park next to the rink. Facilities include a 185- by 52-ft (56- by 16-metre) rink, fully licensed bar and fast food cafeteria, professional instructors, ice shows and special events, and a fully stocked skate shop.
Public session times are: Monday, Wednesday and Friday 11am–4pm, Tuesday, Thursday, Saturday and Sunday 10am–noon. Afternoon: Tuesday, Thursday, Saturday and Sunday 2–4pm, Evening: Monday, Tuesday, Thursday 5.45–7.15pm and 8–10.30pm, Friday 6–7.30pm and 8–10.30pm, Saturday 8–10.30pm and Sunday 9–10.30pm. Disco Session: Thursday, Friday and Saturday 8–10.30pm. During school holidays Monday to Friday 11am–4pm.

SQUASH

Ferry Sports Centre
Diamond Place, Summertown
Tel: 01865-310978 or 510330
Open: Monday to Friday 8am–9pm; Saturday 8am–9.30pm; Sunday 9am–6pm. Book a court in advance.

Leisure Centres and Health Clubs

Blackbird Leys Leisure Centre
Blackbird Leys
Tel: 01865 771565
Sports hall with badminton and tennis courts, pitches for basketball, volleyball, football, and netball, a snooker room, a fitness room and a café for lunch. The licensed bar is open Tuesday, Wednesday and Thursday from 7pm. All kinds of fitness classes and coaching sessions are on offer. A crèche for children of parents who are using the centre is available Tuesday, Thursday and Friday 9.30am–12.15pm. Booking in advance is essential. Open: Monday to Friday 8am–11pm, Saturday 9am–8pm, Sunday 9am–9pm.
Temple Cowley Pools
Temple Road, Cowley
Tel: 01865 749449

SWIMMING

Temple Cowley Pools
Temple Road, Cowley
Tel: 01865-749449
Three pools: the Main Pool, 82 ft (25 metres) long and ranging from 3–6 ft (1–1.8 metres) deep, a learner pool for children and a separate diving pool. There are self-contained sauna and steam rooms. Opening times can vary, with certain times allocated to particular swimmers, for example women only, the over-50s, or swimmers with disabilities – so telephone first or pick up a leaflet. All sessions can be booked in advance. Opening hours Monday to Friday 6.10–10pm, Saturday and Sunday 8am–7pm.
Ferry Sports Centre
Ferry Pools, Diamond Place, Summertown
Tel: 01865-510330
Two pools, including a learner pool. The pool is reserved at certain times, so opening times for general swimming can vary. General opening hours: Monday to Friday 6.30–10pm, Saturday 9am–9.30pm and Sunday 9am–6pm.

The fitness room offers a wide range of modern single station exercise machines and cardio-vascular equipment. Before using the equipment an induction and basic health check is required. For information about fitness classes, tel: 01865 749449. Open: Monday to Friday 6.10–10pm, Saturday and Sunday 8am–7pm.
High Health Club
6 High Street
Tel: 01865 251261
For weight control and fitness. Exercise studio, dance studio, jacuzzi, sauna, sunbeds.
Arena Fitness
109 Oxford Road, Cowley
Tel: 01865 779115
Fully equipped gymnasium, computerised fitness assessment, saunas, aerobic classes. The place to see and be seen.

Hinksey Pools
Lake Street or Abingdon Road
Tel: 01865-247737
Mixed swimming in a range of newly
renovated open-air pools. Open:
end May to beginning September.

Spectator Sports

ATHLETICS

Regular meetings are held at the
Iffley Road running ground and at
the city owned track at Horspath
Road Sports Ground.

CRICKET

Oxford University plays first-class
games against county sides in the
University Parks, Parks Road.
Tel: 01865-554050.

FOOTBALL

Oxford United play at the Manor
Ground, London Road, Headington.
Tel: 01865-761503.

GREYHOUND RACING

Tuesday, Thursday and Saturday
6–11pm (first race at 7.30pm) and
Friday noon–2.30pm at the Oxford
Stadium, Sandy Lane, Littlemore.
Tel: 01865-778222.

ICE HOCKEY

Oxford City's ice hockey team, the
Fox Blades, plays in the British Ice
Hockey League. Home matches are
from September to April on Sundays
at 6pm at the Oxford Ice Rink,
Oxpens Road.
Tel: 01865-248076.

RUGBY

Oxford University Rugby Club plays
at Iffley Road, tel: 01865-432000,
and the Oxford Rugby Football Club
plays at the Southern Bypass.
Tel: 01865-243984.

Children

Museums

In Oxford itself, children will be
particularly fascinated by the **Pitt
Rivers Museum** (see page 177)
where they can ask the attendant to
show them the giant toad or even
the witch in a bottle.

As well as the dinosaurs, the
University Museum (see page 176)
also has the portrait of the same
Dodo that features in *Alice's
Adventures in Wonderland*.

Young visitors to the **Ashmolean
Museum** (see page 159) will be
enthralled by its large collection of
Egyptian mummies as well as
Powhattan's Mantle (Powhattan
being the father of Pocahontas).

Displays in the **Museum of
Oxford** (see page 149) include
some interesting finds from
prehistoric times, as well as a large
placard with a simplified version of
the Legend of St Frideswide, the
city's patron saint.

The Oxford Story (see page 111)
provides an unusual ride back in
time to show the history of Oxford
and its University; a special
commentary for children is available.

Outdoor Activities

For kids who prefer to be outdoors,
there are plenty of attractions within
easy reach of the city.

Shotover Country Park, beyond
Headington (see page 209), is a
delight for all those who like playing
hide and seek and climbing trees;
there is also a "natural" sandpit.

At **Port Meadow** (see page 204),
children will enjoy patting the
horses and also feeding the ducks,
geese and swans at the bridge over
the Thames.

To the north of the city, beyond
the ring road, **Cutteslowe Park** has
an aviary as well as a fine
playground; on occasional Sundays
hobby enthusiasts take children for
rides around their miniature train
circuit.

Indoor Activities

Ideal for a rainy day is a visit to **Wiz
Kids**, 2nd floor, Threeway House,
Gloucester Green, tel: 01865-
791331 (open daily 10am–6pm).
This is an indoor playground, where
younger kids under the age of eight
can let off steam while mum and
dad have a rest and a cup of tea in
the cafeteria.

Another place worth seeking out
is **Curiosity**, 2nd floor, Old Fire
Station, 40 George Street,
tel: 01865-247004 (open during
school holidays daily 10am–4pm,
during term-time pre-booking
necessary), a hands-on science
exhibition with more than 30 exhibits
ranging from a giant kaleidoscope
to a build-it-yourself bridge.

Activities in Oxford's Environs

The environs of Oxford also have
much to offer children.

Cotswold Wildlife Park near
Burford (open daily 10am–6pm or
dusk if earlier) is a half-hour drive
from the city. Even before seeing
the animals, children will probably
demand a session in the adventure
playground as well as a ride on the
narrow gauge railway.

A similar railway trundles through
Blenheim Park (see page 221)
which also has an adventure
playground.

At **Cogges Manor Farm Museum**
in Witney (see page 263) children
will be fascinated by the hand-
milking and butter-making, as well
as crafts demonstrations held in
the barn.

Young steam buffs should be
taken to the **Didcot Railway Centre**
in Didcot (see page 265).
Telephone beforehand to enquire
when the steam trains will be put
through their paces.

Further Reading

General

Hugh Casson's Oxford, by Sir Hugh Casson (Phaidon Press). An illustrated guide to Oxford with watercolour drawings and pen and ink sketches by the author.

Oxford in Verse, edited by Glyn Pursglove and Alistair Ricketts (Perpetua Press). An anthology of poetry on the city of dreaming spires.

Oxford, by Jan Morris (Oxford Paperbacks). A brilliant account of the character, history, mores, buildings and much more.

The Oxford Book of Oxford, by Jan Morris (Oxford Paperbacks). An entertaining lively anthology, tracing Oxford's history back to its origins.

The Story of Alice, by Mavis Batey (Macmillan). By using diaries, newspapers and university records, this book tells the story behind the story of Lewis Caroll's Alice.

Oxford: an Architectural Guide, by Geoffrey Tyack (Oxford University Press). A detailed description of buildings and features characteristic of Oxford's architecture.

Fiction

Inspector Morse Mysteries, by Colin Dexter (Macmillan and Pan). A series of crime novels set in Oxford, which achieved world-wide fame in their television adaption.

Zuleika Dobson, by Max Beerbohm (Modern Library). First published in 1911, this is a satirical story of the devastating effect of a beautiful adventuress on Oxford students.

Brideshead Revisited, by Evelyn Waugh (Penguin Classics). First published in 1945. Young aristocrats in Oxford living a life of eternal summers.

Alice's Adventures in Wonderland, by Lewis Caroll (Puffin Classics). First published in 1865. The famous fantastical adventures of Alice.

Through the Looking-Glass, by Lewis Caroll (Puffin Classics). First published in 1872. The sequel to *Alice's Adventures in Wonderland*. Both Alice books were inspired by Oxford, its people and its sights.

Oxford Guides

Our Canal in Oxford, by Mark Davies and Catherine Robinson (Towpath Press). A guided walking tour along the towpath from Wolvercote to the city centre, with lots of interesting historical details.

An Encyclopedia of Oxford Pubs, Inns and Taverns, by Derek Honey (Oakwood Press). A concise reference book of Oxford's pubs in alphabetical order.

Pubwalks in Oxfordshire, by Nick Channer (Countryside Books). Thirty circular walks around Oxfordshire inns.

Oxford for Under-Eights, edited by Vicki Cullen and Dave Dalton (New Parent Network). Extremely useful information for parents with young children in Oxford.

Other Insight Guides

The British Isles are fully covered by Apa Publications' three series of guidebooks, whose 440 titles embrace the world: **Insight Guides**, which provide a full cultural background and top-quality photography; **Insight Compact Guides**, which combine portability with encyclopedia-like attention to detail and are ideal for on-the-spot reference; and **Insight Pocket Guides**, which highlight recommendations from a local host and include a full-size fold-out map.

COMPACT GUIDES

This series comprehensively covers the whole of the United Kingdom – from the South Downs to the North York Moors, from Cornwall to the Scottish Highlands – in 24 highly portable and attractively affordable guidebooks. They are the ideal reference books to carry with you while travelling around the country. Titles include:

Compact Guide: Oxford provides instantly accessible data on the city's many attractions.

Compact Guide: The Cotswolds describes the delightful villages and towns in the charming Cotswolds, to the west of Oxford.

Compact Guide: Shakespeare Country covers Warwick Castle and Shakespeare's town of Stratford-upon-Avon to the northwest of Oxford.

Compact Guide: London is the ultimate on-the-spot reference to Britain's activity-packed capital.

INSIGHT GUIDES

Insight Guide: Great Britain captures the essence of England, Scotland and Wales in 400 pages of incisive and entertaining text and memorable photography.

Insight Guide: England, the newest addition to the British Isles series, concentrates on the wealth of attractions packed into this relatively small country.

Insight Guide: Scotland, in more than 350 pages, provides comprehensive insights into the Highlands, Lowlands and islands – and the Scots.

Insight Guide: Wales is a full guide to this creative and very distinctive part of the United Kingdom.

Insight Guide: London, a companion volume to this Oxford guide, is a fact-filled and provocative guide to Britain's eternally popular capital city.

POCKET GUIDES

Pocket Guide: Southeast England contains carefully timed itineraries and restaurant recommendations designed to help visitors with limited time to get the most out of their trip. Its full-size fold-out map is cross-referenced to the routes suggested in the text.

ART & PHOTO CREDITS

Chris Andrews/Oxford Picture Library 2/3 10/11, 68, 103, 104, 106, 144, 132, 133, 134, 135, 143, 148, 117, 158, 165, 169, 175, 187, 203, 211, 212/213, 214/215, 216, 221, 228, 229, 254/255, 263, 268
Bodleian Library 20, 21, 22, 23, 37, 33, 34/35
Marcus Brooke 155
John Davidson 6/7, 8/9, 105, 249
Chris Donaghue 1, 4/5, 14, 65, 66, 70, 77, 80/81, 82/83, 88, 91T, 91, 101, 103T, 119L, 121, 142, 170/171, 183, 184, 185, 196
Alain Le Garsmeur 24, 30, 37, 38R, 92, 222, 224, 225, 240, 241, 244, 245, 246, 248, 251, 256, 258, 262, 265, 267
Glyn Genin/Apa back cover bottom & top right, front flap top & bottom, back flap top & bottom, 4BL, 5, 63, 93, 93T, 94, 95, 98, 98T, 100, 107, 116, 116T, 118, 119T, 120T, 122, 125, 125T, 128T, 129, 131T, 132T, 140T, 144, 145, 151, 152T, 153L, 153R, 154, 154T, 159, 161, 162, 163, 178, 189T, 197, 201, 220L, 221T, 237, 238, 238T, 252T, 253, 259, 260, 261, 261T, 263T, 267T, 269, 271, 272
Tony Halliday/Apa spine top, back cover centre, back cover centre right, 2, 4BR, 61, 62, 89, 90, 94T, 97L, 105T, 106T, 110, 111, 119L,

119R, 112T, 114, 115, 117, 120, 121,123, 127T, 129T, 130, 135T, 138, 142T, 146/147, 149, 150T,156, 157, 166, 166T, 167, 167T, 173, 175T, 176, 179, 180, 181, 182, 188, 189, 190L, 190R, 201T, 202L, 202R, 203T, 204, 206, 207, 209, 210, 230, 230T, 231, 231T, 232, 233, 233T, 234, 235, 236, 236T, 239, 242, 242T, 243, 247, 249T, 250, 250T, 251T
Hans Höfer 99, 257, 270
Andrew Holt 264, 266
Ray Hutton 53, 54/55, 57
Sally Jenkins 139, 199
Lyle Lawson back cover main left, 58/59, 78/79, 84, 97R, 124L, 124R, 127, 194/195, 205
Lincoln College 118
Norman McBeath 12/13, 69, 96L, 172, 200
Robert Mort 67
Oxford & County Newspapers 48, 49, 50, 51, 56, 191
Oxford County Libraries 36, 42, 43, 44, 45, 46, 47
The Oxford University Museum 177
Angus Palmer/Oxford Picture Library 128, 168
Henry Taunt Collection 40
Topham Picturepoint 64
Bill Wassman/Apa spine centre, 26, 131, 220R, 223, 226/227, 252
Crispin Zeeman 115T

Picture Spreads

Pages 108–109
Top row, left to right: Topham Picturepoint, Sally Fear/Impact, Topham Picturepoint, Topham Picturepoint. *Centre row, left to right*: Angus Palmer/Oxford Picture Library, Topham Picturepoint. *Bottom row, left to right*: Tony Halliday/Apa, Topham Picturepoint, Chris Andrews/Oxford Picture Library, Topham Picturepoint.

Pages 136–137
Top row, left to right: all Chris Andrews/Oxford Picture Library *except far right*: Crispin Zeeman. *Centre row, left to right*: Chris AndrewsOxford Picture Library, Mark Davies. *Bottom row, left to right*: Tony Halliday/Apa, Homer Sykes/Impact.

Pages 192–193
All photography by: Mark Davies *except centre right*: Oxfordshire County Council Photographic Archive *and bottom right*: Glyn Genin/Apa

Map Production Maria Donnelly/Apa Publications
© 2000 Apa Publications GmbH & Co. Verlag KG (Singapore branch)

INSIGHT GUIDE
OXFORD

Cartographic Editor **Zoë Goodwin**
Production **Stuart A Everitt**
Design Consultants
Carlotta Junger, Graham Mitchener
Picture Research **Hilary Genin, Natasha Babaian**

Index

Numbers in italics refer to photographs

☀ INSIGHT GUIDES

The world's largest collection of visual travel guides

Insight Guides – the Classic Series
that puts you in the picture

Alaska	China	Hong Kong	Morocco	Singapore
Alsace	Cologne	Hungary	Moscow	South Africa
Amazon Wildlife	Continental Europe		Munich	South America
American Southwest	Corsica	Iceland		South Tyrol
Amsterdam	Costa Rica	India	Namibia	Southeast Asia
Argentina	Crete	India's Western	Native America	Wildlife
Asia, East	Crossing America	Himalayas	Nepal	Spain
Asia, South	Cuba	India, South	Netherlands	Spain, Northern
Asia, Southeast	Cyprus	Indian Wildlife	New England	Spain, Southern
Athens	Czech & Slovak	Indonesia	New Orleans	Sri Lanka
Atlanta	Republic	Ireland	New York City	Sweden
Australia		Israel	New York State	Switzerland
Austria	Delhi, Jaipur & Agra	Istanbul	New Zealand	Sydney
	Denmark	Italy	Nile	Syria & Lebanon
Bahamas	Dominican Republic	Italy, Northern	Normandy	
Bali	Dresden		Norway	Taiwan
Baltic States	Dublin	Jamaica		Tenerife
Bangkok	Düsseldorf	Japan	Old South	Texas
Barbados		Java	Oman & The UAE	Thailand
Barcelona	East African Wildlife	Jerusalem	Oxford	Tokyo
Bay of Naples	Eastern Europe	Jordan		Trinidad & Tobago
Beijing	Ecuador		Pacific Northwest	Tunisia
Belgium	Edinburgh	Kathmandu	Pakistan	Turkey
Belize	Egypt	Kenya	Paris	Turkish Coast
Berlin	England	Korea	Peru	Tuscany
Bermuda			Philadelphia	
Boston	Finland	Laos & Cambodia	Philippines	Umbria
Brazil	Florence	Lisbon	Poland	USA: Eastern States
Brittany	Florida	Loire Valley	Portugal	USA: Western States
Brussels	France	London	Prague	US National Parks:
Budapest	Frankfurt	Los Angeles	Provence	East
Buenos Aires	French Riviera		Puerto Rico	US National Parks:
Burgundy		Madeira		West
Burma (Myanmar)	Gambia & Senegal	Madrid	Rajasthan	
	Germany	Malaysia	Rhine	Vancouver
Cairo	Glasgow	Mallorca & Ibiza	Rio de Janeiro	Venezuela
Calcutta	Gran Canaria	Malta	Rockies	Venice
California	Great Barrier Reef	Marine Life ot the	Rome	Vienna
California, Northern	Great Britain	South China Sea	Russia	Vietnam
California, Southern	Greece	Mauritius &		
Canada	Greek Islands	Seychelles	St. Petersburg	Wales
Caribbean	Guatemala, Belize &	Melbourne	San Francisco	Washington DC
Catalonia	Yucatán	Mexico City	Sardinia	Waterways of Europe
Channel Islands		Mexico	Scotland	Wild West
Chicago	Hamburg	Miami	Seattle	
Chile	Hawaii	Montreal	Sicily	Yemen

Complementing the above titles are 120 easy-to-carry Insight Compact Guides, 120 Insight Pocket Guides with full-size pull-out maps and more than 60 laminated easy-fold Insight Maps